Yoga inVision 6

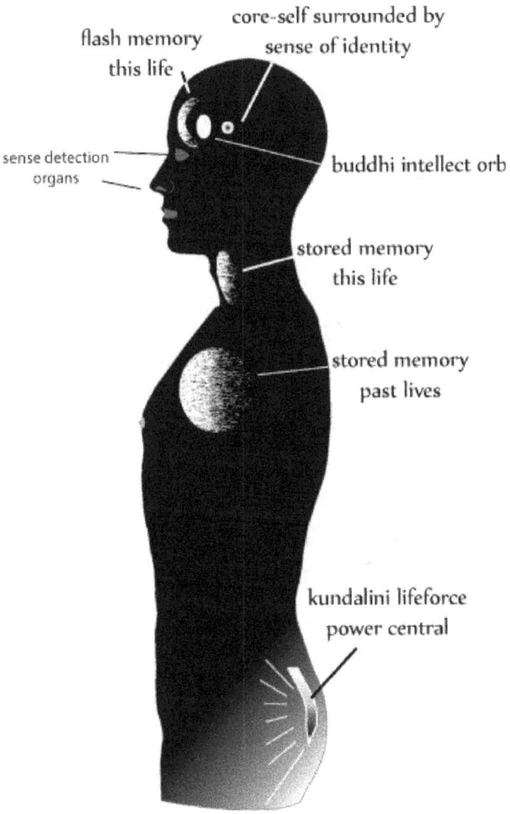

Michael Beloved

Shiva Art: Sir Paul Castagna
Illustrations: Author
Correspondence:
Michael Beloved
19311 SW 30th Street
Miramar FL 33029
USA
Email: axisnexus@gmail.com
michaelbelovedbooks@gmail.com

Paperback ISBN: 9781942887188
eBook ISBN: 9781942887195
LCCN: 2018915245

Table of Contents

INTRODUCTION

This is the sixth of the Yoga inVision series. It relates experiences and practices done from August to October 2010. These give beginners ideas of the physical, psychological and spiritual experiences one may have when doing asana postures, pranayama breath-infusion and *pratyahar* sensual energy withdrawal. Beyond that is higher yoga, which Patañjali named the *samyama* procedures. He defined *samyama* as a combination of dharana deliberate focus, *dhyana* spontaneous focus and *samadhi* continuous spontaneous focus. During practice these progress one into the other. If one is expert at *pratyahar* sensual energy withdrawal, one may graduate to dharana which is deliberate focus of the attention to a higher concentration force or person. As soon as one masters dharana one may slip into *dhyana* which is an effortless focus on a higher concentration force or person. Once you practice *dhyana*, *samadhi* happens as the continuous effortless focus on a higher concentration force or person.

Many persons who take to spiritual life feel that they can construct a path as they advance. This idea denotes failure. After all, if the supernatural and spiritual environment, is not already there, no one will create it now. It is either there or it is not. For instance, if one moves to a different country, then of course one will fail if the country intended does not exist. It has to be there prior. Similarly what you aim for as spiritual life, must be there already, or one will find that one's idea is incorrect. This is why I speak of a concentration force or person. I could have said concentration person or divine person, or God. I did not because I do not know how one's spiritual path will develop.

One may leave an island in the safest boat and still the vessel may sink. One should keep one's mind open and be willing to work with providence. In spiritual development, there is providence too. What one desires to have one may not achieve. What one wishes to see may never appear.

These Yoga inVision journals show how sporadic my course of yoga was. This is after years of practice. It gives some idea of what to expect. Once you get through the lower yoga practice, you will see advancement in a more stable way but it may be incremental, accruing little by little, with bright flashes here and there.

Part 1

September 16, 2008

Drowsiness / Meditation

Drowsiness can be used for observing the movements and shifts of consciousness, as well as to gage the coreSelf's relationship with the intellect and the sense of objectivity.

That is a productive meditation, where one studies how consciousness recedes from this world and becomes indistinct or non-detectable during deep sleep, as well as when one slips into dreamscape and into lucid astral projections.

Drowsiness may be induced or one may observe it when it is involuntary. The easier of the two is to practice when drowsiness comes of its own accord.

If you notice that the mind phases out now and again into drowsiness, recline the body comfortably. Allow the mind to continue the movement towards more and more drowsiness. Observe how it shifts. It is important to release one's interest from the effort to stop or retard the drowsiness. Place the interest into observing what takes place as the drowsiness advances. If you fall asleep while doing this, check the mind for the record of observations just as you awaken. Check the memory record. Review it in slow motion.

- Is the connection with the memory severed first?
- Or is the connection with the intellect broken first.
- Did the drowsiness spread from the front of the head, the back of it, the right or left side, below it in the neck, from the top of it?
- Where does the drowsy energy originate.
- How does it spread?
- Does it penetrate like an arrow which pierces?
- Does it spread like a dye which gradually colors a liquid?
- In drowsiness are you drawn away from another function or object in the mind space?
- What do you adhere to when you resist drowsiness?

Time control

On some days it seems that there is a force, a providence, which does not allow someone to achieve anything. On other days, the same individual hardly notices that he or she is conveyed through accomplishments.

Time, the medium in which we exist, has rhythms and patterns, lulls and accelerations.

The idea of controlling time is like that of controlling the weather. Who can do it?

coreSelf and psychological equipment

In the *Bhagavad Gita* there is a declaration about the comparative value of the self and its psychological equipment:

इन्द्रियाणि पराण्याहुर्
इन्द्रियेभ्यः परं मनः ।
मनसस्तु परा बुद्धिर्
यो बुद्धेः परतस्तु सः ॥३.४२॥
indriyāṇi parāṇyāhur
indriyebhyaḥ paraṁ manaḥ
manasastu parā buddhir
yo buddheḥ paratastu saḥ (3.42)

indriyāṇi — the senses; parāṇyāhur = parāṇi — are energetic; āhur (āhuḥ) — the ancient psychologists say; indriyebhyaḥ — the senses; paraṁ — more energetic; manaḥ — the mind; manasas — in contrast to the mind; tu — but; parā — more sensitive; buddhir = buddhiḥ — the intelligence; yo = yaḥ — which; buddheḥ — in reference to the intelligence; paratas — most sensitive; tu — but; saḥ — he, the spirit

The ancient psychologists say that the senses are energetic, but in comparison to the senses, the mind is more energetic. In contrast to the mind, the intelligence is even more sensitive. But in reference, the spirit is most elevated. (Bhagavad Gita 3.42)

एवं बुद्धेः परं बुद्ध्वा
संस्तभ्यात्मानमात्मना ।
जहि शत्रुं महाबाहो
कामरूपं दुरासदम् ॥३.४३॥
evaṁ buddheḥ paraṁ buddhvā
saṁstabhyātmānamātmanā
jahi śatruṁ mahābāho
kāmarūpaṁ durāsadam (3.43)

evaṁ — thus; buddheḥ — than the intelligence; paraṁ — higher; buddhvā — having understood; saṁstabhyātmānamātmanā = saṁstabhya — keeping together + ātmānam — the personal energies+ ātmanā — by the spirit; jahi — uproot; śatruṁ — enemy; mahābāho — O powerful man; kāmarūpaṁ — form of passionate desire; durāsadam — difficult to grasp

Thus having understood what is higher than intelligence, keeping the personal energies under control of the spirit, uproot, O powerful man, the enemy, the form of passionate desire which is difficult to grasp. (Bhagavad Gita 3.43)

Krishna discussed material nature, comparing it to an ashvattha tree. He advised Arjun to cut down the tree using the axe of non-attachment:

श्रीभगवानुवाच
ऊर्ध्वमूलमधःशाखम्
अश्वत्थं प्राहुरव्ययम् ।
छन्दांसि यस्य पर्णानि
यस्तं वेद स वेदवित् ॥१५.१॥

śrībhagavānuvāca
ūrdhvamūlamadhaḥśākham
aśvatthaṁ prāhuravyayam
chandāṁsi yasya parṇāni
yastaṁ veda sa vedavit (15.1)

śrī bhagavān — The Blessed Lord; uvāca — said; ūrdhvamūtam = urdhva — upward + mūlam — root; adhaḥśākham = adhaḥ — below + śākham — branch; aśvatthaṁ — ashvattha tree; prāhuḥ — the yogī sages say; avyayam — imperishable; chandāṁsi -Vedic hymns; yasya — or what which; parṇāni — leaves; yaḥ — who; taṁ — this; veda — knows; sa = saḥ— he; vedavit —knower of the Vedas

The Blessed Lord said: The yogi sages say that there is an imperishable Ashvattha tree which has a root going upwards and a trunk downwards, the leaves of which are the Vedic hymns. He who knows this is a knower of the Vedas. (Bhagavad Gita 15.1)

अधश्चोर्ध्वं प्रसृतास्तस्य शाखा
गुणप्रवृद्धा विषयप्रवालाः ।
अधश्च मूलान्यनुसंततानि
कर्मानुबन्धीनि मनुष्यलोके ॥१५.२॥

adhaścordhvaṁ prasṛtāstasya śākhā
guṇapravṛddhā viṣayapravālāḥ
adhaśca mūlānyanusaṁtatāni
karmānubandhīni manuṣyaloke (15.2)

Adhaścordhvaṁ = adhaḥ — downward + ca — and + urdhvam — upward; prasṛtāh — widely spreading; tasya — of it; śākhā — branches; guṇa — mundane influence; pravṛddhā — nourished; viṣayapravālāḥ = viṣaya — attractive objects + pravālāḥ — sprouts; adhaśca = adhaḥ — below + ca — and; mūlāni — roots;— stretched out; karmānubandhīni = karmā — action + anubandhīni — promoting; manuṣyaloke = manuṣya — of human being + loke — in the world

Branches spread from it, upwards and downwards. It is nourished by the mundane influences and the attractive objects are its sprouts. The roots are spread below, promoting action in the world of human beings. (Bhagavad Gita 15.2)

न रूपमस्येह तथोपलभ्यते
नान्तो न चादिर्न च संप्रतिष्ठा ।
अश्वत्थमेनं सुविरूढमूलम्
असङ्गशस्त्रेण दृढेन छित्त्वा ॥१५.३

na rūpamasyeha tathopalabhyate
nānto na cādirna ca saṁpratiṣṭhā
aśvatthamenaṁ suvirūḍhamūlam
asaṅgaśastreṇa dṛḍhena chittvā(15.3)

na — not; rūpam — form; asyeha - asya — of it + iha — in this dimension; tathopalabhyate = tathā — thus + upalabhyate — it is perceived; nānto = nāntah = na — not + antaḥ — end; na — nor; cādiḥ = ca — and + ādiḥ — end; na — nor; ca — and; saṁpratiṣṭhā — foundation; aśvatthaṁ — ashvattha tree; enam — this; suvirūḍhamūtam = suvirūḍha — well-developed + mūlam — root; asaṅgaśastreṇa = asaṅga — non-attachment + śastreṇa — with the axe; dṛḍhena — with the strong; chittvā — cutting down

Its form is not perceived in this dimension, nor its end, nor beginning nor foundation. With the strong ax of non-attachment, cut down this Ashvattha tree with its well-developed roots. (Bhagavad Gita 15.3)

ततः पदं तत्परिमार्गितव्यं
यस्मिन्गता न निवर्तन्ति भूयः ।
तमेव चाद्यं पुरुषं प्रपद्ये
यतः प्रवृत्तिः प्रसृता पुराणी.॥१५.४॥

tataḥ padaṁ tatparimārgitavyaṁ
yasmingatā na nivartanti bhūyaḥ
tameva cādyaṁ puruṣaṁ prapadye
yataḥ pravṛttiḥ prasṛtā purāṇī(15.4)

tataḥ — then; padaṁ— please; tat— that; parimārgitavyaṁ — to be sought; yasmin — to which; gatā — some; na — not; nivartanti — they return; bhūyaḥ — again; tam — that; eva — indeed; cādyaṁ = ca — and + ādyaṁ — primal;

puruṣaṁ — person; prapadye — I take shelter; yataḥ — from whom; pravṛttiḥ — creation; prasṛtā — emerged; purāṇī — in primeval limes

Then that place is to be sought, to which having gone, the spirits do not return to this world again. One should think: I take shelter with that Primal Person, from Whom the creation emerged in primeval times. (Bhagavad Gita 15.4)

Reproduction Rights

Many frustrations come from the reproduction rights of ancestors who are in need of embryos. There is a pressure from the astral world. It is transferred into our minds and bodies. It drives us to act in a way which promotes the interest of the departed souls who need embryos. In that sense, the dead are more powerful than the living. The dead are not dead. Though invisible they influence the living. They inject emotions and ideas.

For the most part the ancestral influence is manifested as sexual interest. It is present as our ambitions for convenience and opulent lifestyle.

- Should one beget children?
- Suppose the age of the body hampers reproduction!
- Suppose one is impotent!
- Then what?
- Why does the desire for begetting linger in the mind even of those who are impotent?

Winter evacuation

As the winter season approaches the lifeForce will respond by slowing certain activities, particularly digestion and excretion. If one is observant, if one tracks evacuation, one may notice that it takes longer for releasing of waste from the body. This is because with less heat, the lifeForce has less energy to expend for prompt evacuations. It will move the foodstuff at a slower speed through the intestinal track.

For that matter it may increase evacuation times by hours or even by days. If for instance, the average evacuation time was 18 to 32 hours, it may increase to 24 to 48 hours. If was two days, it may increase to three days, all because the air is colder.

What can be done about it?

If one has the choice be in a warm building. Avoid eating cold foods. If one has cold food and one has facility to warm it, do so. Whatever one eats which is cold will have to be heated by the body before it can be digested. That takes energy which could be used for more efficient digestion and evacuation.

Eat early on, before one goes outdoors into the cold. Do not wait until one is cold to seek food for inner warmth and energy. Do not starve the system for heat and food.

If the passage of waste slows to a haul and the body becomes constipated, one should act to change that. For instance one may do a finger clean out to stimulate removal of stool from the anal pouch or squat and apply evacuation pressure.

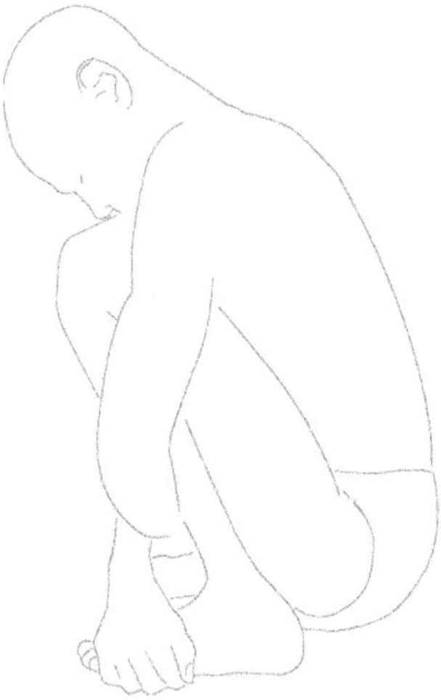

The body may have a habit of hoarding stool in the anal pouch or colon. In that case one may use the middle finger to remove waste from the pouch and stimulate movement in the colon.

Realize that even though the lifeForce maintains the body, it is in one's interest and it contributes to health, if one assists the process. One can help the lifeForce or one may hamper the maintenance.

Regarding enemas

The main interest is the evacuation of stool from the colon. When the system shuts down entirely enemas are recommended only as a last resort. In yoga the concern is there. To take care of that, we do stomach flexes daily. These churn the intestines, up and down, to the left and to the right.

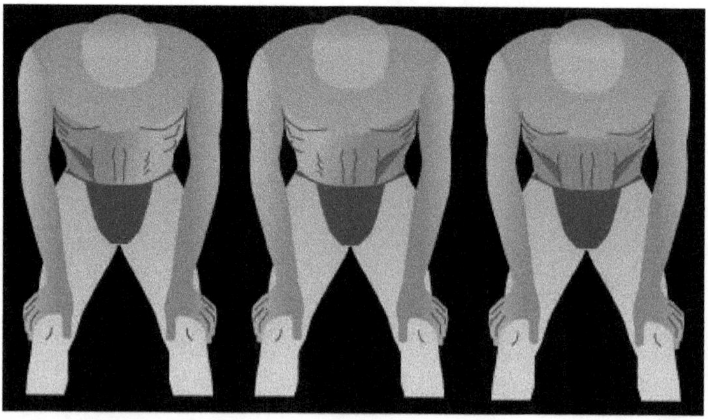

A yogi should be attentive to the food intake and its resulting stool formation. He should note what food produces what waste. He should act to improve evacuation by using food which facilitates prompt digestion and excretion. He should note the effects of using dry foods like chips and fried rice. He should note the effect of peppered foods. He should note the effect of dairy products and other food. In a gist, he should not be careless in diet. He should eat to facilitate yoga.

When dried foods are eaten does the body produce a harder dryer stool?

Does the anal region burn during evacuation after ingesting peppery foods?

Is there diarrhea when using dairy products?

One may show concern for the large intestines by changing food. Usually, if the stool which lingers in the rectum is removed either by natural evacuation or by finger clean out, any stool which lingers in the large intestines will move into the anal pouch. Thus usually there is no need for enemas.

One type of enema is where a liquid is flowed into the rectum. This is an ancient method. It used to be done while the patient reclined with a rubber bag of distilled water or some liquid, elevated above the patient. The liquid oozes into the rectum.

What happens in that case?

The liquid oozes into the anal pouch, which is a small bag with two openings. The lower opening is the anus. The higher is a circular muscle which operates as a valve to release stool from the larger intestines. If that valve functions correctly, it opens as soon as stool in the larger intestines touches it. If it functions incorrectly, it will remain closed even when stool in the larger intestines bear upon it.

When doing finger clean out, one can factually realize this, because in some instance, that valve opens and stool descends suddenly from the larger intestines into the anal pouch.

An enema should soften or cause liquefaction of dried stool which is in the anal pouch. It hardly does anything in the large intestines, because usually that valve is contracted in its relaxed position.

Enemas do nothing to help with sluggish muscular action of the system. This is why it is not preferred in yoga. Instead we are advised to do the stomach flexes, and to eat a diet which facilitates prompt digestion and evacuation. We are concerned with the large intestines, but we want a solution besides enemas.

Dried stool is caused by one or by a combination of two or more of the things listed below:

- Too little liquid in diet
- A body which is genetically designed to squeeze all liquid from foods no matter what
- Taking dried foods
- A sluggish digestive and excretive system
- A system which is habituated to generating gas in the intestines
- A system which is genetically disposed to constipation or dried stool.
- Defective muscular action

Genetics are a big part of this. Be informed of the kind of stool produced by various species. A goat, even if it eats the same type of grass and has the same water facilities as a cow, will produce manure in round dry pellets. The cow will produce a slushy wet dung from the same diet.

If I have a body which is genetically patterned after a goat's, my system will have the tendency for dried stool. If someone else's is genetically patterned from a cow's, it will produce wet slushy stool.

In a child's body I had the opportunity to observe the stool of elder relatives. This is because some primitive flush toilets did not always flush the stool passed into a commode. I remember that some relatives passed dry stool. Some passed airy dried stool which floated and resisted the suction of the toilet. Some dried stool formed into round compacts like giant goat turds. Some passed dried stool like that of a dog.

Why the variation? These people ate from the same pot and had the same basic lifestyle. Obviously there is much to the genetic variations of the bodies.

Some elderly relatives took constipation medicines like Ex Lax, Epsom salts and castor oil. In old age when they found that they could not pass stool for periods of many days many resorted to enemas. In a child's body I observed this.

Perception / Memory

There are many small steps in the process of meditation, many small realizations, which if overlooked or not noticed, cause one not to make advancement. It is essential that one should be willing to notice the smallest change in the activities of consciousness.

Make notations mentally and in writing. Mention these to others who practice. Discuss this. That is how one increases the motivation to practice and develops a progression habit.

Let us consider perception and memory. Are these one and the same actions in mental or emotional consciousness?

Perception means to become aware of another object. This other object may be physical, mental or emotional, or it may be an object which exhibits combined physical, mental and emotional attributes. Is this the same as memory?

Memory is information which was stored somewhere in the psyche and which may assist one in identifying and relating to an object. It may mislead one as well. A toddler walked over to a space heater. He was attracted to its red glow. He touched the coils, and was burnt.

A year after the incidence, when it was forgotten by him, he saw another heater. He became attracted. At first with no memory of the first encounter, he smiled and walked towards the object, but then he felt some hesitation. He stopped and without remembering the previous incidence, an instinct from within the mind, turned his body away from the heater.

In that example there were three distinct factors,

- perception of an object
- recorded and stored memory of an unfavorable incidence with the object
- developed instinct which controlled future responses to the object

This may be observed in meditation and in day to day mental observation of what happens in the psyche. This observation would give one the ability to understand higher yoga, to read *Yoga Sutras of Patañjali* and *Bhagavad Gita* with more clarity and relevance.

Proper practice

We should go to the *Yoga Sutras* where Patañjali defines meditation as the stoppage of five routine operations in the psyche. If in meditation one experiences a stoppage of the mind's routine functions that would be a proper practice. A higher state is any experience one gets while the mind ceases those routines.

In chapter three of *Yoga Sutras*, there is an in-depth explanation of the types of experiences one should get when the mind ceases its conventions.

Lower meditation has two parts to it, the effort of a particular practice and the attainment of the effort. Just as in social life, one keeps a job which is an effort and one receives wages which are the result of the employment, so in the beginning and intermediary stages of yoga, one becomes concerned with certain efforts and their results.

This varies from person to person. Each one is at a different stage and requires a particular effort to achieve a particular type of psyche control.

Some people feel that yoga should be standardized and that a teacher should give standard classes to everyone. However that idea is undermined by the varied nature of the individuals. Suppose I hold a general class. I instruct everyone to sit quietly and meditate on chanting Om, or to meditate on silence, or to meditate on the center of the eyebrows, then this would be a general instruction.

However if one questions each student one may find that the experiences vary. Overall, general instructions for meditation are not effective unless the teacher deals with each person after the session and focuses on the requirements of each. Beginners need a diagnostic consideration and resulting prescription.

Whatever advice one gets should be practiced. When one gets results from the effort, one may apply more advice. The problem is that if one is not in an ashram or hermitage where one practises daily, one may not follow the advice given. Instead of realizing the benefit of the practice, or its ineffectiveness, one's mind may encourage one to criticize the teacher.

Here is an example of how to follow an advisory. Let us say for instance, that a yoga teacher advised one to focus on the imaginary point in the center of the eyebrows for fifteen minutes.

You try to comply but you cannot complete this daily. The social life causes you to neglect this. What should you do?

Here again we find that there has to be a digression. The first challenge would be to discipline oneself. One asked for an advice. One got a valid instruction but one found that one could not comply.

What next?

That all depends on one's nature. Some students return to the teacher for a new instruction. Others take action either to stop the effort or find a way of improving the condition for practice.

Which alternatives should one take?

Would one streamline the social life?

Would one check the mind's behavior and develop a method for self-discipline?

When these things are seriously considered, there would be progress towards a proper practice.

Subtle Perception

When we say that someone is psychic what we really mean is that the person sees higher frequencies such as ultraviolet and infrared. Just as X-rays can penetrate bones, so can certain energies in the subtle body. In kundalini yoga, one shifts focus into the subtle body. One perceives frequencies which the physical eyes cannot detect.

The subtle body is made of higher frequencies. Sometimes in practice one experiences yogis or superior beings who are manifested in visions. They have bodies which are made of light. In this case, I mean physical light, such as sunlight, or light which would eradiate from molten metal, or light which would radiate from radioactive materials.

The subtle body can exhibit perceptive capabilities which are similar to those used in modern science with X-ray machines, MRI equipment, radar and the like.

Scientific instruments and the subtle body itself, deal with mundane energies which have shape and form. Neither a yogi, nor a scientist can change those energies or the world in which those energies exist. Both can only discover what already exist but which is normally unseen.

In the course of pranayama breath infusion practice when the locks are applied and the eyes are closed, the colors perceived with the sensing equipment of the subtle body, are perceptions of the world in which the subtle body is manifested. That body exists with a subtle atmosphere surrounding it just as the physical body moves about in air.

The application of locks causes the charged kundalini system to be energized. That results in a higher energy charge in the subtle body, which in turn causes subtle perception, as the sensing energies shift focus to frequencies which are higher than what a human being normally perceives.

The closing of the eyes combined with the inner focus on the charged energy, causes the psyche to curtail its interest in the physical level. This results in even more subtle perceptions.

Transition to the spiritual plane

During breath infusion, a yogi should trace the sensations which are aroused in the psyche. This causes familiarity of the subtle body, resulting in more focus into and use of that form. Currently the obsession is the physical form. We use it to procure the fulfillments which only the physical system can provide. The next step is to get the fulfillments which can only be acquired with the subtle body. Just as initially an infant is obsessed with food, then later with getting attention and with playing, and then later with competing with others and with acquiring status, then later with sexual contact, family formation and societal influence, then later with health of an aging body, so after shedding the need for a physical form, one should confront the issue of the subtle body.

Mastery of pranayama breath infusion includes learning to trace sensations which arise during practice and which are particular to the subtle body. One should continue tracing the sensations until one can sort feelings of the subtle body and nerve sensation of the physical one.

After this is sorted by the yogi, where he is clear about nerve energy and subtle energy, there is the movement of focus from the subtle body into using the highest level of the same subtle body to perceive into the supernatural atmosphere.

Yoga has to do with migration from the physical plane and from the lower astral levels to the higher ones, and then to levels beyond that. Read *Bhagavad Gita*.

परस्तस्मात्तु भावोऽन्यो
ऽव्यक्तोऽव्यक्तात्सनातनः ।
यः स सर्वेषु भूतेषु
नश्यत्सु न विनश्यति ॥८.२०॥

parastasmāttu bhāvo'nyo
'vyakto'vyaktātsanātanaḥ
yaḥ sa sarveṣu bhūteṣu
naśyatsu na vinaśyati (8.20)

paraḥ — high; tasmāt — than this; tu — but; bhāvo = bhāvaḥ — existence; 'nyo = anyaḥ — another; 'vyakto = avyaktaḥ — invisible; 'vyaktāt = avyaktāt — than the unmanifest state of the dissolvable creation; sanātanaḥ — primeval; yaḥ = which; sa = saḥ — it; sarveṣu — in all; bhūteṣu — in creation; naśyatsu — in the disintegration; na — not; vinaśyati — is disintegrated

But higher than this, there is another invisible existence, which is higher than the primeval unmanifested states of this dissolvable creation. When all these creatures are disintegrated, that is not affected. (Bhagavad Gita 8.20)

The focus of yoga is migration from lower levels to higher ones, until one reaches a place which lacks what is undesirable. It is related in the *Mahabharata* that Yogi Mudgal rejected access to the Swarga heavenly paradise, because that place was flawed due to its inconvenience of not sustaining the presence of anyone whose resulting pious activities became exhausted. He continued austerities to reach the place which was mentioned by Krishna.

At first just realizing the subtle body is the big achievement for a yogi. He should learn how to use that body and teach himself to rely on it without respect to the physical form. This non-reliance frees him from having to transmigrate as physical bodies. After that he should figure the influence of the subtle body. Once he can tag that, he may get beyond it.

Once that is achieved, he can begin using it to locate and explore the higher subtle levels and the causal plane. Once that is done he can migrate to the spiritual levels proper.

Collective consequences

The word *karma* became popular and is used in English, as well as in Hindi to mean consequences of one's actions which come to one in this or in some other life. Webster's dictionary gave the meaning as the total effect of one's conduct.

However that word meaning was altered. *Karma* in Sanskrit means the action which will bear consequences. The consequences are termed *phalam*, which means the fruit or result. Still since it was grafted into English the word karma now means what *phalam* means in Sanskrit.

There is such a thing also as collective consequence of collective actions. The collective consequence affects everyone in an environment. Suppose ten people board a ship for a journey across deep water. During the journey, the ship develops a leak. The boat sinks. They are not rescued. They die by drowning. Who is to blame?

Is it the mechanic who checked the boat during its last service check? Is it the captain who took the craft for granted and never bothered to check her bottoms? Is it the passenger who was blighted with bad luck on Fridays, the day which the ship set to sea?

Is it nature, because of its constant wear, tear and destruction of whatever human beings manufacture?

Who is the blame?

Collective consequence mean that something happens which affects a group, putting them in a helpless predicament where they are subjected to forces which are beyond control.

Collective consequence is compounded. It over-rides individually-due situations. In fact the individual is lucky if at all he/she is allowed to receive good consequences or is unlucky if he/she must endure bad consequences.

On that boat, there was a man who intended to journey to Egypt to receive a large sum of money. Due to the mishap, he was deprived of the fortune. But there was another man who was being escorted under arrest to Egypt where he was to face charges for murder. In a sense the boat's mishap was his fortune, as it saved him from the trauma of the trial and the resulting lifetime imprisonment or execution. Collective fate may override individual fortune or misfortune.

Even though we take it for granted, we are lucky or unlucky to be alive, depending on how material existence is viewed. Modern humans were on this planet for a short period when compared to the duration of existence of the planet. Species like bacteria, even insects like cockroaches, even reptiles like crocodiles, were on this planet transmigrating for a much longer period.

The over-riding collective consequential energy takes precedence over the individual compensations. The individual destiny functions only if the collective accommodation is provided.

How long will human beings exist on this planet? When will we be added to the list of vanished species? At the time of the last human, where will the displaced human spirits go? What will happen to their collective and individual consequences?

Will that energy be transferred into another creation? Will it be suspended as psychic force, forever waiting for an opportunity to surface, the way some departed ancestors now wait for rebirth?

Willpower / desire

Willpower is for the most part a contrived force. Desire arises sensually on the basis of emotional moods. Desire influences the formation of will. That in turn can influence the shape of desire. More often than not, the desire force controls what we do. The willpower tags behind and makes minute adjustments when it is temporarily freed from being a captive of desire.

How to strengthen willpower?

A good place to start is to properly estimate the desire force. When desire is strong, willpower gives way to desire or it is suspended until the desire force achieves its aim. This implies that the willpower may not override the desire force. A proper estimation of the potency of the desire force is the first step in creating an effective method in strengthening willpower.

Consider this example.

Tim began doing yoga about two years ago. He got this idea that it would be beneficial to become a vegetarian. He tried to stop eating flesh but for one year he was unable to do so. After speaking to a friend he got a hint that perhaps it would help if he changed his bike route to work. The route passed through a restaurant district which had meat dishes which Tim liked.

Taking the hint, Tim changed the route. By this, he developed the will to override the desire for flesh meals. Why was Tim unable to give up the habit for one year? It seems that the memory of the restaurants, the sight of the buildings, the smell of the food when he passed that area, the sight of the cars of the customers, all served to strengthen his desire for flesh foods and to weaken his willpower effort at becoming vegetarian.

Once he changed route, his willpower strengthened and the desire force weakened. Two years after Tim does not feel attracted to those restaurants. He resumed the old route without fear of being attracted to a flesh meal.

Desire, when it is strong, derives its strength from other sources besides the desire itself. If one can identify these sources, and break contact with them, the willpower will increase. With that increase and with consistent practice in the new habit, one may develop sufficient willpower to fully overcome the desire.

Naad / coreSelf

What should be done if after doing breath exercises, and sitting to meditate, the naad sound seems to be barely audible?

Once one did breath infusion and charged the system before meditating, one's first objective should be to make note of the energy charge in the system, to record mentally where the charge is located, the intensity of it, the flow or redirection of it and the general condition of the mental and emotional energy which resulted from that charge. None of this should go unnoticed. Once this is noted, one should locate and become absorbed in naad sound.

With the naad sound one should note its intensity, the ability to synchronize one's attention with it, its location, its penetration force, or its seemingly detached distant force. Unless it has surrounded the coreSelf already one should make an effort to enter it.

In some experiences naad will surround the coreSelf and saturate the entire subtle head, if not the entire psyche including the head. At other times it will seem to be something that comes from faraway. These observations should be made.

After being situated in naad vibration for some time, a yogin should evaluate its status when the system is not charged by breath infusion. Is there a difference in naad when the system is charged as compared to when it is not energized?

Where does naad originate? What does it represent? What is the benefit of listening to or being saturated with naad? These questions should be pondered and researched in meditation.

coreSelf location

If after breath infusion, one feels sensations throughout the body, even after one sits to meditate, if those sensations are like innumerable needle points, particularly in the hands, one should use the experience to achieve two objectives:

- Locate the coreSelf
- Locate the extent of the throw of consciousness outwards from the core

A detailed study of the make-up of the psyche should be done by each yogi. Just as biologists and people of the medical profession take great pains to dissect bodies and catalog the various parts and their operations, so a yogi should in time become concerned of the psyche components.

We know that the physical body has various parts. Even though it functions as a unit, we know that certain parts have more importance than others. If someone pinches the arm, one will feel it but if someone were to push a steel pin through the skull into the brain, the pain or the sensation felt would be much more acute. This means that some parts of the body are not equal in the utility of consciousness.

Let us take the example of the sex organs. If an adult participates in a sexual act, he or she readily understands that the sensations through the genitals are more intense than the sensations which pass through other parts of the body.

When one sits to meditate after a session of breath infusion, when the breathing charged the physical and subtle bodies, the first focus should be to observe the charged energy. Map it to describe which part of the body it saturates and in what intensity. As soon as one make that observation, one should turn to the matter of the observer himself or herself. Where is the observer situated in the field of consciousness?

A newsman takes photographs on a busy corner of a city street. Much happens there every day as people whiz by on their concerns. One day his supervisor questions him by phone, "Where are you located?

He replied, "I am at the intersection"

The supervisor responded, "Where exactly are you at that intersection? Tell me where the tripod is? Tell me if you stand by it or behind it? Tell me the distance between the camera and the fatal accident?"

How would you answer?

Would you say, "I cannot be specific. I only know that I am at the corner. For that matter I am where I am. How can I know where I am?"

If one cannot be specific it means that one is merged into everything on the corner. That is due to a lack of objectivity.

The first thing one should do after one finds oneself behind the camera in the psyche is to observe what occurs. The newsman reported that he recognized a female celebrity on the opposite corner. To her left, he recognized a wealthy stock broker. To her right there was a well-known coffee shop. Besides that there was the constant roar of cars and taxis.

Observe, what is around you in the psyche.

Once this is done, the yogi should focus on himself. He should try a few things, like turning the camera so that its lens is focused on himself. Can he do this?

Is the camera attached to his face so that he cannot remove it?

Does it move with his face if he walks away?

Is the camera attached to his face like goggles?

Where is the coreSelf?

What is the mechanism of perception through which the sensations are felt?

Is the coreSelf in the big toe?

Is it in the shoulder?

Meditation practice

Resting, meditating and sleeping are related but they are separate activities. Sometimes one of these activities involuntarily moves into or converts into the other.

Patañjali listed sleeping as one of the vrittis, one of the automatic activities of the mind which affect the objective of yoga negatively. He defined meditation as a condition of consciousness in which sleep and four other states of mind are no longer present.

Meditation should be conducted at least twice per day, early in the morning and then in the evening. It is best done immediately after doing breath infusion exercises, but if one is unable to do the exercises, one should practise meditation anyway.

The first step in meditation is to continue the practice done in the previous session. In meditation one should have a sense of progression, where one knows that one progressed from one state and is moving into a more advanced condition. If one sits to meditate, one should check on the progress from the previous day.

About two years ago I did on a thigh muscle stretch which is part of the practice in kundalini yoga. In two years, I mastered it. If I was more attentive I may have done it in two months.

If one listens to naad sound for instance, one will be at one state on Tuesday. On Wednesday when one resumes practice, one should connect to what one learned, observed and did on the previous day.

Meditation must be a daily activity. It should not be missed. If one misses the progress will not be consolidated. Faith will be weak. One will give up the practice.

If meditation is troublesome, if for instance on the last session one could not stop the mind from presenting ideas and images on and on and on, then one should sit with oneself or with someone who is advanced, and draft a scheme of mental actions to discipline the mind. One should plan for the mind just as one would plan to curb a criminal. Draft a plan. Discuss it with others who have similar concerns.

Meditation is an aggressive activity. One should put oneself out. One must be motivated to do it. If there is no motivation, more than likely, one will not meditate. One must endeavor for it. One should maintain it by renewed efforts. One should habituate the self to it.

Bowel movement / exercises

Evacuation is based on eating habits. As one eats, so one evacuates. Thus if one observes how food is processed one will in time adjust the diet, regarding the type of food, the quantity of it, the time of taking it, its liquidity and/or dryness. This is how one may control evacuation.

The control of evacuation is for the most part control of food intake. If one controls what and when food goes into the body, one will have most of the evacuation process under control.

One may notice that exercises promote evacuation or cause it to be accelerated. If you find that exercises causes you to evacuate, then try this. Go to the facilities. Try to evacuate each time before one does exercises. It does not matter if you actually evacuate just get in the habit of patiently going to the facilities and make the effort. It is alright if nothing happens. Then regardless of whether the system responds or not, do the exercises. Keep doing this, because even though there may be no result for months of trying, still one puts the system into a habit. Over time it may respond.

If one feels to evacuate during the exercise session, do so, but return to the exercises soon after, say about ten minutes after, and do at least a half session. That half session means that if one usually does a thirty minute session one will do an extra fifteen minutes after evacuation. But as I suggested wait ten minutes before you begin that fifteen minute session. That ten minutes will be sufficient time for the lifeForce to readjust itself and for the rectum to resume its regular posture and to relax from the evacuation maneuvers.

During evacuation the lifeForce applies itself to the base chakra and its offshoot channels in the subtle body,. It takes about ten minutes for it to retract this interest. There was a time during my practice, when the same thing happened where evacuations would come on during or after exercises. I noticed that it took about ten minutes for the lifeForce to retract itself from the bowel operations. This is why I suggested that ten minute delay period. Will one be endangered if one does not wait for ten minutes? No, one will not be endangered but one will not get the full benefit of the exercises because the lifeForce will not devote itself entirely to the session as it will be concerned with retracting the rectum and its valves. It will be relaxing the pushing operations which are required for the expulsion of liquid and solid waste.

When one does stomach flexes, if there is waste in or near the rectum, there should be an urge to evacuate. One should promptly honor the urge.

In hatha yoga, yogis do stomach flexes when the rectum is empty of waste and the stomach is empty of food. We do not do flexes just for prompt evacuation. The actual reason is to tone the stomach and intestines for good health and efficient operation.

Pornography / yogi

Some three months ago, a friend called. He explained that he developed a habit of looking at pornography. I said to him, "You endeavored for this. Is it worth it?"

He replied, "It does not take endeavor. Pornography is free to view on Internet."

I explained that though it was free, it was not in his interest.

Recently in the astral world some persons mentioned the same topic. These are persons who practice yoga and religious disciplines, but who are attracted to pornography. Subsequently I checked the Internet to see how easy it was to view pornographic videos. I found out that it was easy. Some sites are free of charge. Some charge a small fee. Some are expensive. I want to make a few points to yogis and aspirating ascetics on this issue.

First of all Yogeshwarananda explained that when the genital organs serve for expelling urine its use is beneficial. Without the expulsion of urine the body would become diseased. The brain would malfunction. The body would die. To know about this one should research what happens when the kidneys malfunction. If the kidneys malfunction and the toxic chemicals are not removed from the blood stream, the brain is poisoned, the body soon dies.

The kidneys alone cannot do the job. The kidneys merely filter chemicals. After they are removed they need to be expelled from the body. For this they are transported to the bladder. The genitals have the tubing system for expelling liquid chemicals. This is a valuable service. Yogesh expressed his appreciation for this service. He appraised the genitals for that necessary service.

In the case of females, the tubing for expulsion of urine is not the same as the tubing for expulsion of sexual hormones. In the case of the males, both systems use the same tubing. It is not a big issue however. In the case of the males, their sexual pleasure is mostly felt in the head and skin of the genital organ, while for females that pleasure comes through the cells of the vaginal passage and the protrusion which is called the clitoris

Biologist surmised that the clitoris is a rudimentary representation of a male organ. This is natural because when nature manufactures these bodies it starts out with the potential for male and female. It develops genetically in one or the other. Even in the case of a male, the body begins as female with an opening in the genital region. That opening is sealed during fetal development. Evidence of this mark of female anatomy is present in every male. The scrotum or sack which hold the testes, has a seal line around the center of it. It was originally an opening as in females but then nature sealed it to manufacture the bag of skin which contains the testes.

Why is pornography not in the interest of a yogi? Simply this:

The genital organs apart from their most valuable and necessary usefulness in expelling liquid chemicals from the body, is most sacred as an avenue into this world. We could not take these bodies unless we take help from the genital organs of parents.

If the attraction to the organs in pornography has to do with the pleasure which may be derived from the organs, we should also know that even the pleasure is sacred. Without it, we could not get these bodies. Nature uses that pleasure as a speedway to create the embryos. It is that pleasure energy which activates and propels semen from the father's body into the mother's. It is the same pleasure energy which encourages the mother to accept the responsibility for the wellbeing of the infant which develops in, and is expelled from her body at a later date.

If the female organ does not function properly at the time of delivery, the child is eventually expelled as still born, which means that the person must find another birth opportunity, either through the same woman or another. It must again take help from genital organs.

Pornography as sexual violence or recreation is not concerned with this. It is concerned mainly with criminal or consensual sexual pleasure and the activities through which a human being can exploit that. But that exploitation does not help someone to get an infant form. Most of the persons who are involved in pornographic videos are not interested in producing children. In fact the whole posture is avoidance of pregnancies and continued exploitation of the pleasure aspects of the genitals. In other words, many who are involved in pornography are unwillingly to give anyone an embryo body, what to speak of raising such a body through infancy.

If this is remembered while viewing pornography I feel that eventually one will abandon the habit. When all is said and done, when one leaves the body, the only thing that may count, is how one may get the next embryo. Who will be the mother or father? Even if one finds the most attractive woman in a pornographic video or the best male there, none of these persons would volunteer to be part of a pregnancy. None wants the responsibility of having to raise an infant. In that sense, it does not add up that we should patronize their activities.

The next time one views pornographic content, ask oneself if it would be possible for that man or woman to agree to give a body as a child if one lost the present form and needed to be in the world again.

What would be one's lot if one entered the body of the man involved and one was merged into his sexual pleasure and was passed out in his semen, only to be dead semen, without becoming the embryo of the woman involved? What frustration would that be?

What attitude would one have after one eventually got a body through another woman who was not sexually attracted, was not as good looking, and was not involved in pornography?

Time control

On some days it seems that there is a force, a providence, which does not allow a particular individual to achieve what is desired. On other days, the same individual hardly notices that he or she is conveyed for many accomplishments.

Time as the medium in which we exist, has a weather pattern, its own sunny or gloomy days, its own calm or hurricane.

Controlling time is like controlling the weather. Who can do it?

September 16, 2008

Reproduction rights

Many frustrations come from the reproduction rights of ancestors who are in need of new bodies. From the astral world there is a pressure which is transferred into our minds and bodies and which drive us to act in a way which promotes the interest of the departed souls who need embryos. In that sense, the dead are more powerful than the living. The dead are not dead. By psychic link to our emotions and ideas they are influential in this world.

If one carefully studies chapter one of *Bhagavad Gita*, one may conclude that Arjuna was under the influence of ancestors. His opponents headed by Duryodhan were under a similar force from another group of ancestors.

For the most part this force is manifested in our bodies as sex interest. It is present as our ambitions in life, and our selected or preferred lifestyle.

Should I beget more children?

Suppose the age of my body hampers reproduction? Suppose I am impotent?

Why does the desire for begetting linger in someone's mind, even though the person is impotent?

What should one do with sex desire? Does one have to endure its pressure no matter what?

Part 2

Meditation posture and duration

The posture for meditation should be an easy sitting or reclining posture. When doing asana postures, one should assume whatever pose one is instructed or inclined to do but when meditating one should be in an easy pose which does not tax the mind.

The popular posture is the lotus pose or its easy variation which is the easy pose. Either of these may be unsuitable for meditation if either is difficult to assume. If there is pain in the posture and if the mind is intolerant of the pain, that painful posture should not be assumed. If sitting on a couch or reclining on a bed puts the mind at ease where it does not ponder bodily pains, then one should use whatever posture best allows one to do a mental focus for meditation.

Ideally, meditation should be for at least twenty minutes. It can be longer. It may even be shorter, say for five minutes. The perplexity is the focus of meditation. What is to be done in the mind during the period of time allotted?

The procedure in *inSelf Yoga™* is to do breath infusion before meditation. The yogi should do a thorough session of breath infusion as kapalabhati/bhastrika pranayama. That is rapid breathing in various postures with intentions to pull the carbon dioxide out of the cells of the body and to replace that with fresh air (oxygen).

When this is done the subtle body will jump to a higher frequency which will cause meditation to be on a higher plane.

Evacuation process

We are concerned with stool in the colon, but enemas are not recommended except when there is an emergency and the system shuts down entirely, and perhaps one gets that advice from a physician. In yoga the concern is there. We do stomach flexes daily. These churn the intestines, up and down, to the left and right.

One should be attentive to the food intake and its resulting waste formation. A yogi should note the waste production of particular foods. He should improve evacuation efficiency by using foods which facilitate prompt digestion and excretion. He should note the effects of taking dry foods like chips or fried rice. He should note the effect of spicy peppered foods like hot Indian curries. He should note the effect of dairy products and other food. In a gist, he should not be careless in dietary intake. Eat in a way which facilitates the practice.

Does the body produce harder dryer waste when dried foods are taken?

After ingesting peppery foods does the rectum burn during evacuation?

Usually, if the stool which linger in the rectum is removed either by voluntary expulsion or by finger clean out, any waste which linger in the colon will descend into the rectum.

Learning

Which direction should be taken in meditation?

This question comes up repeatedly if one does not have a sense of direction. Sense of direction is felt when one can say to oneself that one was at a certain point one year ago and one progressed in the intervening time. Once one has a sense of direction, it is sufficient for motivating practice.

A sense of wanting to learn, a sense of caring for the self, all this must be in place for progress. If one does not feel this, there is a way, which is to associate with a progressive person.

Correspond with someone who makes progress. Make oneself accountable to someone who teaches and who can review the practice. If one is not accountable to oneself nor to anyone else, it is unlikely that one will practice.

I publish books on meditation. I do that because I feel accountable to yoga gurus. I also have a sense of responsibility to anyone who may learn from the publications. If the books are not available, such persons may be deprived of the information. Someone said recently that few human beings read my literature. Still even if one person was deprived, I feel that I would be accountable for that person's lack of progress.

It is a matter of relationship. I have yoga gurus. I could not face them if I do not practice. That is how much I care for them. If one is not in a steady practice, if one is accountable to no one, why should one endeavor?

One should review the relationships with various teachers to see how much one holds oneself to their expectations. One may consider how to relate to anyone who may benefit from one's progression. Is there anyone who may benefit? If so why is one not motivated to assist? These are the questions one needs to settle with oneself regarding practice.

Each of us went to school in youth. In most countries school is the law. Did we like school? Can any of us say for sure that he desired to attend school initially? Most of us probably do not remember the attitude on the first day when a parent or sibling took one to school. Many children who attend school for the first time, do not like it. They cry and behave in an antisocial way. Still because it is the law, parents take toddlers to school. Even if the mother or father does not think that the infant should attend school at 5 years of age, still it is done because of government laws and social pressures in the community.

Now we are adults. No one can force us to learn, nor to assume a discipline. Now it is on us. We make the decisions. It is not easy. We can gage the energy which the parent or guardian exerted to make the child attend school.

For the past year, I escorted myself to school each day, just as my senior did when I was an infant. I do not have to do this, I could neglect it. I can be lazy and indifferent about it, but I must do this because of a sense of wanting to progress in my relationship with the yoga gurus and with my sense of responsibility for anyone, even a single person who may benefit from the information. If you have no sense of direction in meditation, you should affix yourself to an authority and get a purpose from that person to practice.

I went to Trinidad sometime around 1965. My father tried to get me into school but the Trinidad government was such that foreigners were not allowed in the public schools. Eventually my father found a private school which was managed by a former Principal by the name of Morain. He had about eight students.

After he checked my lessons, he said to me, "Do not come every day. Do every exercise in the books. Come once a week or once every two weeks to question me about things you do not understand."

That was it. I studied for University of London Exams in a little house my father had at the back of the property he rented. I used to see Mr. Morain about once every two weeks.

I was accountable to my father. I was accountable to Mr. Morain. He gave an instruction. I complied.

In meditation it is the same. Report to someone. Get instruction. Follow it. Report again to be reviewed. Ask questions regarding what you were instructed to do. This is the same learning process, just as we faced in schools as youths.

I am in school to learn computer programs. My teachers are present in the form of tutorial books. I take it seriously. It is just as if the teachers were present like teachers in schools. That is how one progresses and learns. Someone is the teacher. Somebody, oneself or myself, is the student.

If one sees oneself as an adult, if one feels no one should instruct one, then no one can be trusted to guide one. If one feels that one should not be accountable to anyone how will one learn?

Thus even if one does not want to be handled as a student by anyone, still that is temporary for again one will have to transmigrate and again one will be an infant but one's attitude will carry over. One will be a miserable infant when again one is subjected to studentship as a necessary part of one's upbringing.

When I see an infant, I put myself into his position, to estimate my situation when and if again I would be an infant. I will again be evicted from a woman's body, and again be tended as a baby, and again be corrected as a toddler, and again be taken to school, and again learn an alphabet. Thus, it is not in my interest to avoid accountability and to make demands of what and when I should learn from teachers.

How we learn

It is beneficial to learn all the way through life, even after leaving school and even after there is absolutely no need for education, even if one is successful acquiring a livelihood.

Reason?

One must transmigrate very soon. Going to another place will entail learning again. More than likely one will take rebirth in this earthly place. As an infant one will be confronted with learning, with being schooled, and with being corrected. Every step of the way in the new life, just as in this one, one will learn something or the other. The faster one learns the quicker one will be approved by others.

Bad behavior has to do with not learning what is best for oneself and others. Anti-social behavior has to do with not learning. Many faults are due to not learning. Since learning is such a useful tool, it is wise to continue it. Be willing to learn.

Learning is the realm of the kundalini energy. How does it learn? Its usual method is one of orientation to a skill. Education as it is generally defined today is a classroom activity, but that is not how kundalini usually learns. Kundalini learns by orientation.

Academics, classroom learning, is a very efficient way of teaching but it is usually focused on knowledge about manufacture of items, which concern making a livelihood. Kundalini is more concerned with social interaction.

Kundalini likes to learn in a tribal environment such as in a family setting. Our learning habits are mostly govern by, sponsored by and initiated by kundalini. We can better understand ourselves and the way we learn by studying the kundalini habits.

This gets to the issue of caring for oneself. Does one care for the self? Is the self worthy of self-concern?

Brow chakra / subtle perception

There are different means of subtle perception. Some methods are documented in my books about meditation. It is a good idea to read and re-

read those books to find subjects of interest which did not attract one's attention on the previous reading.

Sometimes one reads a book. Then one puts it down. Then if one again goes through it, one finds information which one did not observe in the previous reading. This happens when reading the *Bhagavad Gita*.

These are some means of subtle perception:

- Third eye vision into the psyche
- Third eye vision outside the psyche
- Third eye vision into cross dimensions
- Intellect vision without interlocking of third eye
- Intellect vision with interlocking of the third eye
- pranaVision without visual visibility
- coreSelf as vision
- spiritual body vision

Any of these perceptions may be experienced while doing meditation. These may happen spontaneously during yoga practice

First there is the coreSelf in the central head, right behind the center of the eyebrows about three to four inches back in the brain. Immediately around the coreSelf, there is the sense of identity, which is generally called the ego, the expression of *I am*. Around that but usually focused more towards the front, is the imagination orb or intellect which is experienced as the analytical function of the mind. Beyond that there is the edge of the mind. On that edge there are the senses. One of the senses is the third eye chakra.

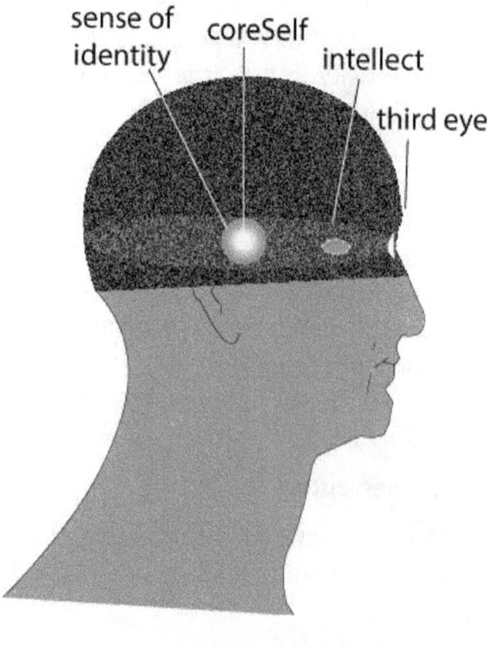

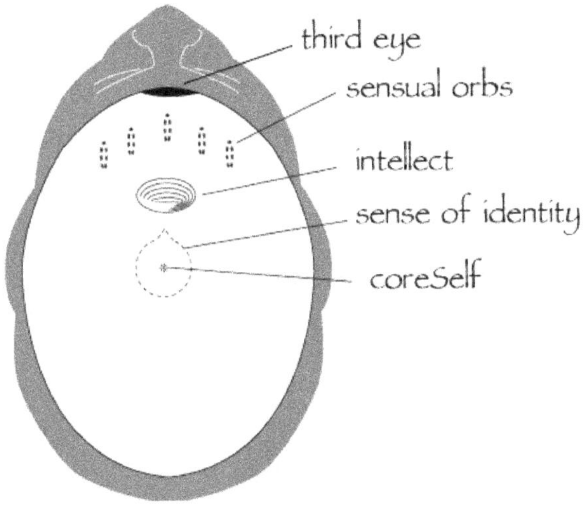

The coreSelf itself may function as an all-seeing eye. It allows one to see in all directions either into one dimension or into multiple dimensions simultaneously. Even for great yogins this experience is rare. The yogi does not control this, nor invoke it. It occurs that one finds oneself without limbs or senses but with multiple eyes seeing in all directions.

The sense of identity is an all-surround energy but it is usually focused to the face side of the head. It becomes pin-pointed or focused into a beam of energy, when there is reason for such sharp focus. This is experienced as a visual means of perception. Sometimes in meditation it suddenly transforms into being a seeing eye. This eye appears to be one seeing-eye, not all around but with a wide angle like a wide angle lens of a camera. Its perception is usually into very high levels of existence.

If a beginner experiences these visual means of perception, he or she may not know how they occur. But if one describes the experience, a more advanced yogi may explain which means of perception was activated.

Beyond the sense of identity, there is the analytical organ which is known in Sanskrit as *buddhi*, a word which is translated as intellect in English. The normal use of this organ is thinking, planning, reasoning and visualizing. If this organ is controlled by the advice of Patañjali it would bring the meditator into transcendental experiences.

Patañjali condemned the routine use of the analytical organ as denying yoga practice. His advice is that this organ should be silenced. If the thinking operations of this organ are regularly suspended in meditation, the organ changes suddenly into supernatural vision. One sees within it various scenes from either this or from other astral dimensions. These are rare events, even for advanced yogis. The reason why this type of vision is usually off-limits is given in a hint of Patañjali where he said in his second statement that yoga means the curtailment of the regular operations of the mind. He hints that so long as the mind continues its regular operations, one will never get the higher experiences which advance yogis describe.

Suppose I manufacture aircraft. According to the law of gravity, an airplane of a certain weight cannot lift unless it accelerates to a certain speed. This is also seen in the lives of bird. Wild birds are usually very skinny under the feathers, such that a large bird, when killed by a hunter yields only a little meat. Most of the bird is feathers, which is a light material.

If one keeps a wild bird in a cage and feeds it sumptuously, the bird will have to run for a while before it becomes airborne. There are restrictions. If one wants to experience like the great yogins, one has to acquire certain criteria.

If I manufacture an aircraft, and attached a powerful engine to it but leave some seals in the engine in a leaky condition, the aircraft may never develop sufficient speed to cause it to become airborne. I can correct the situation by taking the engine apart and assembling it carefully, making sure that there is no leak. Then the complete power of the engine will be applied to the aircraft. It will quickly become airborne. Unless we curtail the conventional operations of the mind, there will be reductions in psychic power. We will never experience the subtle perceptions. We should create conditions for the development of subtle perception.

Self as energies in a subtle casing

Initially meditation consist of an experience of the psyche as energies which are enclosed or felt within what we identify as the physical body. Essentially, and by the grace of nature, we came to understand ourselves as individuals through feelings. Six ladies stood on a street corner. There was an accident where a school girl was struck by a car. Only one of the witnessing ladies cried. She was the girl's mother.

Why did the others not lament?

By the grace of nature we identify ourselves and others on the basis of feelings. The other ladies did not experience remorse.

Let us consider that perhaps one of those indifferent ladies, was the mother of the girl in a former life, then why did that former mother not cry? Why is it that only the current mother was affected?

This indicates that feelings towards others is regulated by nature on the basis of current relationships. Nature may not react on the basis of a past life.

In meditation we must begin where we are. That is where nature endowed us with feelings. One begins by feeling that one is a material body which is affected and which affects other bodies.

I experience myself as a form of energy within the physical body.

Let me write that in another way:

I experience myself as a form of energy which has a membrane or limiting edge which is the skin of the physical body.

Let me rephrase that:

I experience myself as a subtle body which is energy which is housed in a physical body which has a skin for membrane.

Let me restate that:

I experience myself as a sensing energy without visual perception, but confined to the space which my physical body inhabits.

Let me restate that:

I experience myself but it seems that I do not have senses. I am energy, which perceives physically when it is linked into a body.

These statements give some idea of how I would use the same experience to make progress in meditation. At first in mediation one will experience the self as random energies which are housed in the physical form. As one becomes detached from anxieties and commits the self to meditation, other sensual experiences will occur. The secret, the big secret, is to commit oneself to meditation as a daily practice. Are you committed? If you are not, you will hardly get the experiences to know the capacity of consciousness. Be committed!

Just as an infant grows and reaches sexual maturity, a similar type of growing occurs if you meditate sincerely. You cannot make it happen but it happens. The committed state puts you in a psychological position which causes more psychic integration.

Questions are:

- Are you committed to meditation?
- Are you willing to let it develop in its own time?

Objectivity / Psychic perception

For the most part, one cannot command the psyche to give astral vision. That may develop of its own accord. The effort at meditation is an attempt to encourage the psyche to do this, or to produce the conditions in the psyche which would cause this.

Everything is based on natural conditions. When those conditions are absent there is no manifestation. Willpower works if the environment responds. How did we become these material bodies? Physical existence is a wonderful experience. How are we seeing visually?

If for instance, one found oneself in a cave lizard's body and if another lizard from outdoors entered and described its visual perception, one would be appalled at the description. One may wonder why one does not have that vision.

Some cave lizards have no eyes. Besides these there are lizards with eyes. It depends on the life form assumed. The entities in the caves use a body which is designed for sensing without sunlight. Those which evolved outdoors use a body which is designed to utilize light. The difference is the life form, not the coreSelf in the body.

In the subtle world some are blind because some subtle bodies do not have a means of visual perception. Meditation may cause the development of such perception.

Physically, once you find the self in a species which has vision, one can control the vision to some extent. Control of the vision comes about only after one is awarded it by nature. Similarly one cannot command the psyche to give such vision, but if it develops in the psyche, one may regulate it.

In infancy I saw through the astral senses. Later when I did yoga and meditation, I tried to control and regulate the psychic perception.

Even physically a toddler must learn how to control and regulate visual perception, otherwise the child miscalculates and falls repeatedly. The same applies to the development of third eye vision and other sorts of supernatural perception. But such control can only be executed after the development of the perception. The beginner should aspire for the development, not for the control.

Third eye perception and such clairvoyance is there in a developed highly charge subtle body. The yogi cannot cause it. What he or she can do, is to encourage the psyche to shift into that vision.

This is done by adjustment in lifestyle, association, diet, self-conception, meditation, posture and breath infusion.

Sexual attraction

Sexual attraction must be the oldest type of attraction between males and females on this planet. Yet it comes on afresh day after day and baffles us. Every major religion has stories about the emergence of sexual activity in the very beginning of creation, thus indicating that all the great religious leaders pondered its mystery.

What is it? Why are we so enamored of it, even now, after so many millions of years of evolutionary development?

Can anyone recall, the first sexual attraction?

How strong was it?

Was it strong enough to cause you to move across a street to get near to the person whom you were attracted to?

Was it strong enough to get you to be untruthful to parents about where you went and what you intended?

Was it strong enough to get you to skip school?

Was it strong enough to cause you to mistrust your parents?

Was it like a magnet drawing you to do things you had no attraction to before puberty?

Christianity and Islam originate from the Jewish religion, which gave the legend of Adam and Eve. Apparently, God created Adam by combining God's breath with the clay of the earth. After Adam came alive, God felt that Adam needed a companion. The legend says that God put Adam to sleep. God took one rib from Adam's body and created a woman named Eve. Soon after God instruct them not to eat from the tree of good and evil.

As the story goes, Eve met a serpent who lived in the tree. He advised her to eat of the fruits which God prohibited. She then convinced Adam that they should at least taste the fruits. He complied. The result was their banishment from an easy-go-lucky-life in the garden. They were cursed to eat only after endeavoring for food.

Many preachers feel that this is an analogy about sex desire. They interpret that Adam was told by God not to have sexual intercourse with Eve. Once they indulged, life became a challenge.

What is the idea behind this story? Even if it is a myth, a legend or a representation of something that really happened, what conclusion, may we derive from it?

In India, there are various creations myths or legends. One that directly applies to sex is one about Brahma, the creator-god. He was supposed to create the planets and species, but initially he was a bit confused about the order of everything. At one time, when he thought of reproducing human beings, a woman magically appeared from his body. He was attracted to the woman and moved towards her with sexual overtones.

The woman felt that he was her father. She moved away from him, appealing the way a daughter would to a father. In one creation of Brahma when this happened he restrained himself and then created some sons, one of whom assumed the position of husband of the woman who was first created.

However in another creation, Brahma became sexually linked with the first woman. And yet, in another creation Brahma created two other persons, a son and daughter who became unified sexually and created the human race. These two became known as Manu and Satarupa (pronounced Muh-nu and Shuh tuh roo pah). Every major religion submitted ideas about the origins of sexual intercourse.

There is a story in Upanishads about Yama and Yami. (Yuh-muh and Yuh-mee). This brother and sister were powerful celestial beings on this planet. Once Yami, the sister, said to the brother, "I have this idea that we should have sexual intercourse. It is our duty to beget a family. If we do not beget we will frustrate the natural urges for generation of children."

Yama replied, "Are you crazy? It was never approved for brother and sister to be sexually linked? I advise you to locate a male who is not related to you."

Yami did not like the idea because her mind was already set on Yama. She argued but Yama did not agree. They were estranged. Social restrictions of sex were there in ancient times, just as it faces us today.

Providence

We can observe how providence is interwoven into our lives. It can make or break anyone. When you ride a wave of history, it is very much like a small insect riding a piece of floating straw on the swell of a tidal wave which approaches a cliff at the shoreline. Sooner or later the wave will collapse. Its glory will terminate. For this we can surely trust providence. Only a foolish person who repeatedly ignores the actions and reactions of fate will be confident that providence will always support him.

Only a foolish person who has no insight into the actions and reactions will feel that providence will forever support him. Providence never made that commitment to any limited entity. It always disappointed us. It will continue to do so for eternity.

Pornography

Viewing pornographic videos is as recent as the invention of electronic media. Before the prevalence of electricity, there was exposed nudity and vulgarity but only a few people facilitated it. These were mostly exceptionally vulgar poor people or very wealthy folk.

It was mostly the rich who got such facilities. Their money afforded luxuries and covered the liabilities of vices which an ordinary person could not afford.

In the drawings and scribbling found in caves, made by prehistory people there were hardly scenes of vulgar sexual acts. That indicated that sex was not as prevalent or that it was taboo for anyone to depict.

There are leaf and bark manuscripts from India, China and Japan which show that wealthy people in medieval times and before, viewed sexual acts. There are drawings of kings, princes and other members of the aristocracy, engaging in sexual acts with a wife, concubine or palace maid.

In the Valmiki Ramayana there is a vivid scene, where when Hanuman went to find Princess Sita, who was kidnapped by King Ravana, Hanuman entered a gigantic bedroom in which Ravana slept with numerous women.

At first Hanuman did not take it seriously. It was after midnight. Everyone slept in that large room where there were many nude women lying carelessly after having alcohol beverages and participating in sexual intercourse. After searching and checking their faces, Hanuman realized that he was in a prohibited area. For one thing he was an unmarried male.

He said to himself, "What am I doing? I look for Princess Sita among naked women sleeping with King Ravana? I am not in my right mind. In the first place the Princess, a dignified lady, who is morality personified, would not be in this place. Secondly I look at females who are exposed."

He checked his mind and body. He found that there was no sexual breach. He viewed a vulgar scene but it was as if in the presence of naked females he was an infant with no sex urge.

This story is told in the Valmiki Ramayana, an ancient literature. It verified that an ancient writer in India was aware of orgies. Sexual attraction is universal. Hardly a human is exempt from it. If one is not exempt from something, the sensible alternative if one does not like to be involved, is to regulate it as carefully as one can.

After the development of films, pornography increased but at first the ordinary person did not see these motion pictures. You had to afford it and be in particular locations. You had to get in touch with a few companies which took the risk. These companies were in large cities, like Paris, London, Copenhagen, San Francisco and New York.

The average video which you could see in a theatre was barely pornographic in the beginning of the video industry because censorship was conducted by religious people who did not allow nude scenes.

Soon after this there were stag films, which were pornographic videos with or without a story line, but such videos were also hard to procure.

Gradually over time the censorship relaxed. There was full nudity in theatre videos but only for short periods. For an hour video one may see one or two semi-nude scenes and that was all.

In New York City and other big cities one could see full blown pornographic videos but you had to be 21 years or older to gain entry. Since public opinion was against anyone going to those places you had to have courage to go to such areas.

Then came home shown media. This gave a great boost to the pornographic industry, because they could offer a video which one could view at home. One did not have to risk reputation by appearing in the condemned area where the pornographic videos were shown.

Now there is Internet. One does not have to order videos by mail. One may not pay a fee. Sexual activity is available for viewing. The present state of affairs is recent. It is irregular when we consider the history of human beings on this planet. It is recent but many become addicted to it.

Nature's sexual urge

We may investigate by first admitting that sexual attraction is natural. It is impulsive and enjoyable. That realized, we may transcend the love for it. If one has an enemy or an unmanageable nuisance and which when it overpowers one gives enjoyment, how does one deal with it?

Obviously that will take some thinking, detailed planning and long term tactical fighting. By direct confrontation one will not win a war against an enemy who has every area of one's life under control. One should understand the oponent. This is why there is a need to understand sex impulsion.

The first consideration is to remember nature's purpose for sexual intercourse. We may feel that the purpose is pleasure. Does nature care about that? If one checks closely one should accept that nature's reason for this is reproduction of the species.

In a case where there is forced sexual contact, where for instance the woman involved dislikes the man and dislikes the act and gets no pleasure from it, and is emotionally distraught, still a child may be produced. This shows that nature is only concerned to give the result of reproduction. If this is a fact then the question remains as to why there is pleasure in sexual intercourse. If nature is so interested in reproduction, why did nature tag an enjoyable intense pleasure experience with intercourse?

To answer that we need realize that without that intense energy, nature could neither encourage reproduction, nor cause it to happen. The main cause for the pleasure is the generation of enough power in the body to expel semen from the male form and to cause reception in the female body.

Does this mean that a human male is disinclined to family responsibility? Some males are. Some evade responsibility for children and a partner. Pleasure is desirable, for sure, but responsibility, having to work to support family, is not liked by all. Some men willingly service responsibility but many avoid it.

In the animal kingdom, most males wander from place to place, eating whatever they need. They do not assist the females with progeny. A stag for instance does not contribute to the upkeep of his fawn. He ejaculates semen. He leaves and wanders here and here without fathering progeny.

In the animal kingdom, the males have the sex urge. The females have a fertile period which is called estrus. During the heat females are receptive to sexual advances. At other times, they do not allow males sexual entry. It so happens that many female species cannot be raped by a male. The males have no arms and hands which can hold a female for forced penetration. If I was in an animal form, rape may be impossible to commit. Subsequently when a male has the sexual urge, it is seen that some animal males masturbate. Some expel semen as nature itself causes the animal body to go into sexual frenzy.

Thus if this same type of experience comes on in the human form, at least we can understand that this is the operation of nature's system. This is not you. This is not me. If it were, why does the male bull sometimes have an erection and then ejaculate semen? Why does a billy goat sometimes try to mount another billy goat?

My point and I hope one is getting the idea, is this:

We must first understand how much of the sex urge is nature's operation. How much is the individual's desire. If there is confusion, if we cannot sort what is desire, and what is urge, we cannot transcend nature's influence.

Pornography / Curiosity

There are many reasons and motives for viewing pornography. One is the curiosity one may have about sexual organs and their usage. But curiosity is there in every aspect of inquiry except that in the case of sexual affairs, the mind becomes inflamed with desire.

If for instance, I have a desire to see dead bodies at a morgue, I may go there. Once given permission by the officials, I may see corpses. But such a curiously will more than likely disappear after the first viewing. Most of us would never return to a morgue after one visit.

Why is it that if I have a curiosity about seeing sexual parts, I will repeatedly return to the place in which I am allowed to view? In some countries there are red light districts which are legally open to the public where one can go and observe members of either sex in sexually exposed positions. Amsterdam, Holland, is one such place. When I was in Amsterdam some years ago, I went to such a district. There would be a showcase to a store front. It would have a curtain. A woman would have her face by a part of the curtain. If one signaled, she would reveal herself. One could pay to see her assume various sexual activities.

If after hearing about this, I went there, you can understand that. But if I told you that I returned there several times and paid hundreds of dollars to view exposed females, and that I was eager to return and am saving money for the expensive trip, then one may question my sanity. But this is exactly what happens.

For the morgue one visit was enough, but for the sexual exposure, one may never have enough.

What curiosity?

In the human species, sexual organs are not usually seen in public. In fact even in private, people have a tendency to cover sexual parts with clothing. But there are exceptions. About two years ago, there was a story where a woman who had a 14 year old son was found to be sexually exposed in her home. The problem was that her son's friends went to that home every day to see the nude woman.

She lived in city where there were no laws regarding how one may dress in the privacy of one's own home, even before one's children. The police could do nothing about it. Why were the boys going back to that home where a woman the age of their mothers was sexually exposed?

But that is the exception. Usually women will not be sexually exposed before family members what to speak of being before 14 years old friends of their sons.

Naturally if you cannot see something on a regular basis, curiosity about it may be there. Formerly before the days of books with photos and diagrams, hardly any human being saw a sexual part of an adult human being. Besides the person's body part, many people never saw any other adult sexual part but today even children may view photos of sexual organs on Internet.

In the Middle Ages, even a husband who had children by his wife, may not have seen his wife's sexual part. At the time, many people thought that sex intercourse should be in the dark and that you had sex but you never exposed yourself to viewing.

We may consider that electricity was not generated then, but still generally even in the day-time people did not usually have sexual activities and many never even thought of viewing sexual parts.

If you find drawings and paintings from the Middle Ages, one will see that mostly, at least in Europe people wore much clothing. Women would be covered from the neck downwards. There was not so much exposure in casual wear as we see today.

In the tropical climate, we find that people hardly wore clothes even before modern times. And this includes women but somehow that exposure does not have the same sexual connation it has today. Seeing an aborigine woman with just a G-string and seeing a modern woman on a city street of New York for example, dressed with a G-string is a totally different experience. The culture of either of the women is vastly different. Because of the lack of modern facilities and fabric, the aborigine had no choice in the matter, but the modern woman has more fabric than she needs. Her decision to wear a bikini is made on a totally different premise.

It goes back to the question of the curiosity we have for sexual organs.

What is the organ through which one's embryo body was expelled from the mother's form? Are you so curious that you would force the woman who delivered one's body to expose herself so that you can see where one's body was developed and the passage through which it passed into this world?

Do you wonder about the shape and form of the sexual organ of the opposite sex because you want to see that facility of pleasure? Why even after seeing one such part, one is still not satisfied, especially since every sexual organ is so similar? If one is interested in motor cycles, would one goes to a cycle shop and inspect every cycle in the store even though each bike has the same design?

Considering this, anyone can understand that sexual organs are a danger because they cause an ongoing desire. Curiosity about them causes desire which causes more desire. The only way to deal with that is to put a damper in the mind on its curiosity. One should train the mind to forget the memories of sexual exposure. No one can do that but the person himself or herself, because that occurs merely between that person and his or her mental energy.

Pornography / Privacy

Someone sent a note about being involved in pornography viewing for some years now, but we should realize that pornography on the Internet is an extension of pornographic viewing in the mind, in dreams and on the astral level. Pornography on the Internet is not isolated. It is a continuation of a habit which we practice in the privacy of the mind.

When one fantasizes about sex in the mind that is pornography. Human beings did that for as long, perhaps, as human beings have had minds. The media is an extension of daydreaming. The mind itself is a TV and Internet in its own right.

Our addictions to modern technology began long ago as addictions of certain behaviors in the mind. Unless we confront these habits we will never control the offshoots of it like TV and Internet.

Suppose I served a priest but I felt sexual desires. Suppose I looked at pornography and was observed and exposed. Subsequently I lost my position in the clergy. I decided to reform myself. I set myself in a situation where I had no access to TV or Internet. Still it does not mean that my problems ceased.

Unless I can stop the mind from hashing over, dwelling upon, conceiving and thinking of sexually related ideas, my flimsy effort to cease seeing sexual ideas through media, will mean little or nothing in terms of my ceasing the habit.

The small habits of the mind, which become full blown with the help of TV and Internet, must be curbed if I am to successfully cease the vices.

It is reduced to the habits of the mind

It is reformed by restricting the thinking habits of the mind, by catching the mind in the act of conceiving of what is undesirable and taking internal mental action to divert the mind to another topic or to stop it altogether. The change which we can establish is the change of the habits of the mind. We should tackle these from the mind's weakest point

There is a hint given by Krishna in the *Bhagavad Gita*:

ध्यायतो विषयान्पुंसः	dhyāyato viṣayānpuṁsaḥ
सङ्गस्तेषूपजायते ।	saṅgasteṣūpajāyate
सङ्गात्संजायते कामः	saṅgātsaṁjāyate kāmaḥ
कामात्क्रोधोऽभिजायते ॥२.६२॥	kāmātkrodho'bhijāyate (2.62)

dhyāyato = dhyāyataḥ — considering; viṣayān — sensual objects; puṁsaḥ — a person; saṅgas — attachment; teṣūpajāyate = teṣu — in them + upajāyate — is born, is created; saṅgāt — from attachment; saṁjāyate — is born; kāmaḥ — craving; kāmāt — from craving; krodho = krodhah — anger; 'bhijāyate = abhijāyate — is derived

The act of considering sensual objects, creates in a person, an attachment to them. From attachment comes craving. From this craving anger is derived. (Bhagavad Gita 2.62)

क्रोधाद्भवति संमोहः	krodhādbhavati saṁmohaḥ
संमोहात्स्मृतिविभ्रमः ।	saṁmohātsmṛtivibhramaḥ
स्मृतिभ्रंशाद्बुद्धिनाशो	smṛtibhraṁśādbuddhināśo
बुद्धिनाशात्प्रणश्यति ॥२.६३॥	buddhināśātpraṇaśyati (2.63)

krodhād = krodhāt — from anger; bhavati — becomes (comes); saṁmohaḥ — delusion; saṁmohāt — from delusion; smṛti — conscience + vibhramaḥ — vanish; smṛtibhraṁśād = smṛtibhraṁśāt = smṛti — memory, judgement + bhraṁśāt — from fading away; buddhināśo = buddhināśaḥ = buddhi —discerning power + nāśaḥ — lose, affected; buddhināśāt = buddhi — discernment + nāśāt — from loss, from being affected; praṇaśyati — is ruined

From anger, comes delusion. From this delusion, the conscience vanishes. When he loses judgment, his discerning power fades away. Once the discernment is affected, he is ruined. (Bhagavad Gita 2.63)

The technique given by Krishna lies in the first sentence, where we read about the act of considering sensual objects.

As soon as we can get this considering process observed and curbed, we may release ourselves from a vice. The mind is weak when it first begins a consideration. At that point one can suppress it. If one fails to do so, the mind increases influence. Then one helplessly subscribes to its ideas.

One should realize the mind in its act of considering. One should curb it. One can either promote a vice in the privacy of the minds or act to undermine and eliminate it.

Just as when I enjoy sexual ideas, there is no one with me in the mind. I enjoy alone and that develops into a full blown pornographic habit, just so I can cease the sexual ideas in the mind in private, and no one but me will note this. In the privacy of the mind I can act to hurt myself or to advance my interest.

Pornography / Ancestral pressure

Pornography is directly related to ancestral pressure, whereby ancestors who cannot get embryos, crowd into the psyche of persons on this side of existence in the hope of getting bodies through sexual indulgence. There is no other means of getting a body except through sexual interplay. For an embryo to develop there must be a mixture of male and female sexual fluids.

In the hereafter an ancestor does not have to be conscious of this fact. He or she does not need to believe in reincarnation. Regardless the process of nature develops even on the psychic side of life. It causes persons who need bodies to urge us to have sexual intercourse.

Suppose I make an arrangement with a woman whom I do not like, and with whom I feel no sexual attraction. I make an arrangement for this lady to view pornographic movies with me. In the arrangement, she is to meet me during her fertile cycle, when she is most likely to become pregnant. I would also agree to have her cycle checked by a gynecologist to be sure that the ovulation is accurately depicted. We also arrange that even though we do not like each other, we will cooperate financially, socially and otherwise to raise the infant produced.

Since neither the lady nor I are fond of each other, the pornographic viewing may take care of that. When viewing pornographic films some persons lose the dislike for each other, and become inclined for sexual affairs. As agreed, I meet the woman. We view three pornographic videos and became so sexually excited that we forget we even made an agreement. We indulge to our heart's content. We part ways. The woman returns in two months to report that she is pregnant.

From this story, you can see that the result of pornography was progeny. Nature's allowance for pornography, if not interfered with, would lead to pregnancies in fertile females who indulge with fertile males.

But why is an ascetic or religious person drawn into viewing pornography?

The answer is simple. Such persons are breaking a law of nature, which is the law of reproduction. If one has responsibilities for family, it is hardly likely that one would have time for pornography. Most adults even if they like pornography would not view it if they had children, unless they could do so without the children's knowledge.

Pornography assails those ascetic and religious people who do not have family responsibilities, who for one reason or the other are not actively engaged in caring for children. There are exceptions, but this is the generalization.

The ancestors are in the sex urge. Their idea is for the generation of embryos. We can have the sex pleasure. They are interested in the progeny aspect.

But think about it from another angle. Think of the time when one will be gone from the present body and will be an ancestor. How would it be for you if the would-be father looked at pornography but took no steps to raise a family? How would that be?

It would be fine if he looked at pornography so long as you got the embryo body and was regarded responsibly by him.

If they knew that one's viewing of that material, would lead to masturbation and effective contraceptive methods and not to the development of an embryo, why would the ancestors urge one to see sexually explicit films?

The answer is that when one becomes a departed ancestor, one may not see every possibility on this side of existence. One does however feel it from the emotional level. One feels the urge for sexual expression. In fact that urge in the parent or parents, acts as one's body at that time.

Pornography / psychic pattern

Someone brought it to my attention that pornography may not be ongoing in every case. In some cases, the need for it comes on suddenly with thoughts and desires for sexual exposure and viewing. Then after sometime of fulfilling that desire, it goes away, only to come back again after 2 or 3 days.

But this is the same way that sex desire operates, even in the cases of people who are duly married and who are aware of morality, based on their assumed religion. Sex desire has a cyclic operation.

And what is not cyclic? We live on a planet that is governed by cycles. Can we change that? Can we alter tidal currents? Can we stop solar flares? Can we alter the earth's rotation? Can we changed the cycle of seasons?

Can we alter the menstrual cycle, which is an inconvenience for females?

The pornography addict who finds himself or herself with a cyclic need should realize that sex desire is cyclic even for persons who have no pornographic vice.

The question has to do with decreasing the impact of the cycles of need. The cycles will not be eliminated but their impact may be reduced if one takes actions to curb the self from viewing pornography.

Sex desire does not stop merely because a man or woman attempts celibacy or monastic vows. Nature is not respectful of such aspirations of a human being. One should try to decrease and not aggravate or increase nature's influence.

Pornography - a way out

The question as to why one is pulled into pornography repeatedly, even though one knows that it is psychologically unhealthy and is undesirable, is answered in one word: reproduction.

The confusion about sexual pleasure is merely nature's way of confusing the issue in our minds. The real reason for sexual pleasure is reproduction and the assumption of responsibility for progeny.

So long as nature is concerned with reproduction and species survival anyone in any creature form will be faced with sex desire. Sex desire is not me. It is not you. In the human species, it is nature's way of reproduction.

There is no point in arrogantly taking all blame for a pornographic habit. If you or I was in control there may be no sex desire or it may be something we could suspend or use at wish. But it does not work in that way. Which human being can say that he or she caused the puberty in his or her body? Which woman or man can say she/he caused menopause or impotence?

How should I respond to sex desire? The question cannot be: How can I absolutely and surely control sex desire?

Full control is not possible for a limited being.

How can one decrease the sexual urge?

Does one have ancestors?

Did one's body come about without the participation of ancestors?

If one has ancestors and if any of those persons need embryos, one must expect sex desire. How else would those departed persons return physically into the world except through sex desire?

Are you reproducing children and taking responsibility for them?

If one is not, then how are you using the sexual energy? If one has no children to nurture, who is the target of one's affectionate energies?

These factors explain in part why sex desire will continue in this world. One secret of this existence is the fact that after losing a body when one lives in the hereafter, one converts into being a sexual urge. One torments the relatives who are descendants. Everyone does it, or more accurately, everyone who is not liberated is force to do it.

I may be the wealthiest man on earth, but if I become paralysed, someone may have to clear my urine and stool. I could not do it. I become a convalescent regardless of pride, regardless of whether I want to be someone's ward. When one is evicted from the body, one will eventually be converted into a sex urge. Then one will in turn do exactly what the departed souls did, which is to become sexual urges in someone's body.

If you view a pornographic scene, the desire to be sexually involved with persons in the video may arise. One may become attracted but since it is a video one's attraction cannot be fulfilled. One may experience a strong urge for intercourse. The body itself, in such a condition of arousal, may force one to masturbate. The sexual fluids which are expelled from that, are not placed in a womb environment. The ancestors who comprise the sexual urge will be frustrated. Subsequently, they may reenter one's emotions and again haunt one with the urge when one's body again accumulates sufficient sexual fluids for a discharge. That is nature's way.

The desire to see a pornographic video is the desire to be more sexually involved, which would normally lead to a pregnancy but which in the case of videos lead only to a frustrated sexual experience as masturbation. The solution, at least nature's satisfaction, would only come if one was to get a partner for intercourse.

Religion cannot free anyone from this. Ancestors who need bodies do not need religion. After all some were religious in the immediately past life. The religiousness led them nowhere but back into a focus for another body. What they need are embryos. The only way for them to get that is to harass relatives whose bodies are capable of reproduction.

The misery this: We do this to one another as we take turns having bodies and then being departed souls and then having bodies again. Hence committed couples should be responsible for progeny. So long as there are bodies on this planet, and so long as there are souls needing human forms, anyone who has such a body will be influenced by sex desires unless that person reproduces and participates fully in nurturing progeny. There is no way around this. The way out of this is to accept family responsibility and to actively participate in nurturing infants. That is the healthy and moral way to expend sexual energy.

Arrogance / coreSelf

On the question of human arrogance, one should consider that it is natural. One emerged from the mother's body with arrogance. It is a gift of nature. The first thing an infant usually does, is to cry. The next urge expressed is the one for food. As soon as food is supplied, there is the urge for comfort and security.

Life begins with making demands on the world, the sun, moon, climate, parent, government, on every person or thing that would be required to bring a sense of security to the infant. The infant is not concerned if the whole world is inconvenienced in providing that.

Remember the statement. He was born with a silver spoon in his mouth. Basically that means that he was born into a world that was responsive to his insecurities, a world which catered to every need. This is arrogance but before we rile against it, let us admit that it is part of nature.

Arrogance earned for itself an ugly portrait. But why? If we all had silver spoons gentle and lovingly placed into our mouths, full of cream, honey and nurturing care, at birth, none of us would think that arrogance is out of place. But since that is not the way it works, we hurl insults at arrogance.

Since the world did not respond by providing each child with a silver spoon, those children who were so deprived, got some objectivity and saw that some wealthy kids were a presumptuous arrogant lot.

The child was born but his mother died during the delivery, the frail lady. Her body was stressed to that extent. The child cried immediately, saying in his own way, "Where is my mother? Where are her breasts? Where are her loving emotions which urge her to respond to my every need? "

The nurse did not respond. She lifted the infant. She stuck a comforter in his mouth. The infant took the comforter but he thought, "What a hard nipple I got from my mother? How unfortunate? There is not a drop of milk to be had from this breast?"

It is all arrogance of course. Where did the infant get the idea that his mother owed him a soft nipple and milk?

He could not have carried that from his past life. In the past life, he passed from his body in old age where he long forgot what it was like to suckle the breast of a mother? Where did the idea originate?

Arrogance comes from nature. We have absolutely nothing to do with it. Our energy, the energy of the coreSelf is involved in expressing it, but the core itself is not the source of it. It is the existential accessories of the coreSelf which create arrogance. The coreSelf's fault if we were to point a finger, is to be the willing contributor of energy for boosting nature's arrogance.

If one thinks that the coreSelf is the cause of arrogance, one will never solve the problem nor come to terms with inconveniences in life. First track arrogance to its roots in nature and then find a way to decrease its influence on the coreSelf.

Arrogance / past life aspirations

Some arrogance comes from past life aspirations, whereby in the present life we were unfit for or were disqualified for certain things which we feel we deserved. In each life, one piles up a set of aspirations so that at the end of the body, those hopes and ambitions form into a collective energy in the subtle and causal forms.

At the time of death these aspirations subside as energies and regress into the subconscious mind which is really a storage of desires.

During the interim between losing an old body and getting an embryo, those aspirations may not be realized consciously. They do however surface in the person as an urge to take birth in a particular place. But it so happens that providence may not honor the urge. Here is an example.

In my immediate past life, when the time came to leave that body, some desires of mine formed into a collective subconscious energy. At the time I instinctively looked for parents who could assist me in taking an embryo. At first I looked for yogi parents but most of these persons were in India. That was not desired, because if I were to take another body in India, it would not help me in the desire to reach the English speaking global population. I searched for English speaking parents. Finding these was frustrating because most of these were not interested in yoga. In fact most were hostile to the practice.

Destiny was hostile to my finding both yogi parents and English speaking birth environment. In the end I had to settle for the English speaking environment and forsake the idea about yogi parents. But this meant that I would have to endeavor aggressively to fulfill my life, because in my infancy, adolescence and young adult periods I would have no facility for yoga practice.

This is where arrogance emerges. It is there because one may have this feeling that one should get all that one needs for the fulfillment of desires. But providence will rarely fulfill one's desire wholeheartedly. In my case, even though I was dissatisfied with the non-availability of yogi parents, I was humble about it. But that is rare. Usually one becomes arrogant. One misbehaves in childhood, refusing to assist one's parents and being mischievous.

In yoga practice humility is a positive factor. If one gets a less desirable birth, it is good for yoga progress. In my case I benefited from it. I had no reason to be arrogant merely because life did not accommodate every desire.

To come to terms with subconscious energies of dissatisfaction, one may meditate and reach such energies in the subtle body. One may quell such feelings. It is merely a matter of understanding that one is limited. Even the divine beings, when they take human forms, go through hassles. There is not a single case of any divine being either from the Western or Eastern religions, who was not inconvenienced in some way or the other, when taking human birth and participating in physical history.

Have you heard about Jesus Christ, how his parents hid him and sneaked about. They lived as refugees. Jesus was born in a donkey/goat shed. The word manger is used by the Christians but that simply means an animal barn. His crib was a straw bed. Another thing about his birth which is glossed over is that his father Joseph was not his biological parent. In fact his mother was pregnant but not from a sexual act with the husband. This may be explained as miracles but that explanation does not remove the contrariness of the circumstance.

Have you heard about Krishna's parents? Actually today if you ask a woman to birth her child in a house, she may be upset about it. Krishna was born in a prison cell. It was a stone prison, because we are told in the story, that when Kamsa came to investigate the delivery of Devaki (pronunciation Day-wuh-kee), he found a girl instead of a male infant which was predicted by astrologers. Kamsa was annoyed. He commented that even the astrologers and oracles were unreliable. But to make sure that he would be safe and sound and not be killed by the child, he grabbed the infant. He took its body and dashed it to the stone floor of the prison. The infant was female, because Vasudeva switched his male child for this girl whom he stole from Yashoda, a woman who was not in the prison but who gave birth to a girl at the same time that Devaki birthed Krishna. Krishna was born in a prison cell.

Even the girl whose infant body was killed by Kamsa, was frustrated in trying to take birth. She was a parallel personality of Goddess Durga. At the time of the destruction of her infant body even she was subjected to assassination in that birth. She brought it to Kamsa's attention that he was a fool, because in terms of religion, Kamsa worshipped Durga. Now he killed the infant body created by and for that same deity.

Yes, there is reason to be arrogant. It is natural to want the world to serve one's needs and to be at one's beck and call but it is also unreasonable, when one considers one's limited range as a tiny living entity.

Inadequate childhood?

Inadequate childhood occurs when one has a mother and father who are unable to provide sufficient schooling and counseling while one is in childhood. In the *Bhagavad Gita* Krishna spoke of the preferred birth for a yogi. Arjuna used the terms *yogāccalitamānasaḥ* and *yogasaṁsiddhiṁ* in verse 6.37. Krishna used the term *yogabhraṣṭo* in 6.41.

अर्जुन उवाच arjuna uvāca

अयतिः श्रद्धयोपेतो	ayatiḥ śraddhayopeto
योगाच्चलितमानसः ।	yogāccalitamānasaḥ
अप्राप्य योगसंसिद्धिं	aprāpya yogasaṁsiddhiṁ
कां गतिं कृष्ण गच्छति ॥६.३७॥	kāṁ gatiṁ kṛṣṇa gacchati (6.37)

arjuna — Arjuna; uvāca — said; ayatiḥ — indisciplined person; śraddhayopeto = śraddhayopetaḥ = śraddhayā — by faith + upetaḥ — has got; yogāccalitamānasaḥ = yogāc (yogāt) — from yoga practice + calita — deviated + mānasaḥ — mind; aprāpya — not attain; yogasaṁsiddhiṁ — yoga proficiency; kāṁ — what; gatiṁ — course; kṛṣṇa — Krishna; gacchati — he goes

Arjuna said: What about the undisciplined person who has faith? Having deviated from yoga practice, having not attained yoga proficiency, what course does he take, O Krishna? (Bhagavad Gita 6.37)

प्राप्य पुण्यकृताँल्लोकान्	prāpya puṇyakṛtām̐llokān
उषित्वा शाश्वतीः समाः ।	uṣitvā śāśvatīḥ samāḥ
शुचीनां श्रीमतां गेहे	śucīnāṁ śrīmatāṁ gehe
योगभ्रष्टोऽभिजायते॥६.४१॥	yogabhraṣṭo'bhijāyate(6.41)

prāpya — obtaining; puṇyakṛtām — of the performer of virtuous acts; lokān — celestial places; uṣitvā — having lived; śāśvatīḥ — many, many; samāḥ — years; śucīnām — of the purified person; śrīmatām — of the prosperous person; gehe — in the social circumstance; yogabhraṣṭo = yogabhraṣṭaḥ — fallen from yoga; 'bhijāyate = abhijāyate — is born

After obtaining the celestial places where the virtuous souls go, having lived there for many, many years, the fallen yogi is born into the social circumstances of the purified and prosperous people. (Bhagavad Gita 6.41)

Thus those of us who feel that we are or that we should be great yogins, and those of us who feel that we are or should be great wealthy religious people, would by preference desire one of these births. However it so happens that Krishna listed that as being rare, particular the birth in the family of enlightened people.

Krishna said that such a birth is difficult to attain, *durbhataram*. *Dur* means *duh/dus* or something that is hard to get, a rare circumstance. That means that if one takes another body one will hardly get that birth. What should be the attitude in the next body? Should one resent disqualified parents, and be unappreciative because they are not an ideal family?

In the present life, I took birth in a situation which was not conducive to yogic advancement? Does that mean that after relinquishing this body, I will get a better birth? Only a fool will think that he or she will definitely get a better opportunity. For that matter one may degrade to something lower.

Merely being yogis, or devotees or yogi devotees is no guarantee for a better birth. Was I not a devotee in past lives? Yet I got the present less than ideal birth? How was that? Why should I think that the next opportunity will be different?

In this life I spent time in the ashram of two religious organizations. In both of them there were children, who were born in those environments. Some dislike what they endured in the organization. Why is that? It means that even if one takes birth in a religious organization even then one may carry resentments for not getting this or not getting that in childhood.

One of the accusations of the children is that they were not properly prepared for life in the modern age and that they are handicapped in terms of job proficiently and social relating, due to being isolated from the general population. These are things to consider in soberness without being fanatically about religious affiliation.

Funny thing is that in one of these organizations, the spiritual master was sure to attract many persons who had college degrees but he was not sure to make certain that the children produced by members in his organization got such degrees. In fact he said that it was not important. To him only studying *Bhagavad Gita*, attending temple programs, following the disciplines of the society, were important.

It means that more than likely one will be resentful of the birth circumstance if that does not give one whatever one may need to live in the particular political and social environment of the time.

Since it is hardly likely that one will get a complete parental environment in the next life, how can one prepare oneself for the worse?

How should one set the mind so that after leaving this body and having to again take another birth, one will not be reactive to the situation?

It has to do with a sense of self-importance, with a certain arrogance, with expecting more than one may get, with thinking that one is special and that one's parents should give one this or that and that God should protect one and tend to every need.

Self-Selfishness

It is possible to think that one assists the self while one is selfish and destructive to it. We usually think selfishness is isolated and used only against others, but really, selfishness begins with a lack of genuine self-interest. Krishna brought this to our attention in two verses.

उद्धरेदात्मनात्मानं	uddharedātmanātmānaṁ
नात्मानमवसादयेत् ।	nātmānamavasādayet
आत्मैव ह्यात्मनो बन्धुर्	ātmaiva hyātmano bandhur
आत्मैव रिपुरात्मनः ॥६.५॥	ātmaiva ripurātmanaḥ (6.5)

uddhared = uddharet — should elevate; ātmanā — by the self; 'tmānaṁ = ātmānam — the self; nātmānam = na — not + ātmānam — the self; avasādayet — should degrade; ātmaiva = ātmā — self + eva — only; hyātmano = hyātmanaḥ = hy (hi) — indeed + ātmanaḥ — of the self; bandhur = bandhuh — friend; ātmaiva = ātmā — self + eva — as well; ripur = ripuḥ — enemy; ātmanaḥ — of the self

One should elevate his being by himself. One should not degrade the self. Indeed, the person should be the friend of himself. Or he could be the enemy as well. (Bhagavad Gita 6.5)

बन्धुरात्मात्मनस्तस्य
येनात्मैवात्मना जितः ।
अनात्मनस्तु शत्रुत्वे
वर्तेतात्मैव शत्रुवत् ॥६.६॥

bandhurātmātmanastasya
yenātmaivātmanā jitaḥ
anātmanastu śatrutve
vartetātmaiva śatruvat (6.6)

bandhur = bandhuḥ — friend; ātmā — personal energies; 'tmanas = ātmanas — of the self; tasya — of him; yenātmaivātmanā = yena — by whom + ātmā — self + eva — indeed + ātmanā — by the self; jitaḥ — subdued; anātmanas — of one who is not self-possessed; tu — but; śatrutve — in hostility; vartetātmaiva = varteta — it operates + ātmā - self + eva — indeed; śatruvat — like an enemy

The personal energies are the friend of the person by whom those energies are subdued. But for one whose personality is not self-possessed, the personal energies operate in hostility like an enemy. (Bhagavad Gita 6.6)

The key to understanding self selfishness is the term, personal energies. The Sanskrit is *ātmanātmānaṁ*. Which is *ātmana + ātmānaṁ*. But it is usually translated as spirit or soul. In this case however ātma means both the spirit and its psychological props. What are these props?

The adjuncts are the sense of identity, intellect, the lifeForce and memories. This is collectively called the mind and emotions. So long as we cannot sort between the coreSelf and the psychological adjuncts, we cannot discover and control the personal energies

Hardly a person would take a sharp knife and draw it across the skin of the body. People will not hurt themselves on purpose. But that is exactly what one does when one cannot sort the psychic aspects of the self. One hurts the self.

Can anyone remember the infant stage, when one runs carelessly, trips, falls and hurts the knee or hand? That occurs because one miscalculates how to operate the infant body. In the adult stage one is not likely to trip, fall nor run carelessly. One takes caution with the body for fear of hurting it.

As the body grows through infancy, one learns how to use it in the least destructive way. While as an infant one may step carelessly on a piece of broken glass, as an adult, one avoids a sharp object for fear that it would puncture the body.

One should protect the mind from self-injury. One should be familiar with the parts of the mind and the operation of its various aspects like the sensual energies, the calculating intellect, the emotional force and the willpower.

If one does not care for oneself, it is unlikely that one will care for anyone else. If one is selfish to oneself, one will be selfish with everyone else.

Get to know the self and its psychic accessories. By that one will be in a better position to regulate the mental and emotional actions, so that the self does not hurt itself.

Always read a verse or two of *Bhagavad Gita*. Take lessons directly from Krishna about the control of constituent parts of the psyche.

Two part mind

Even though it is difficult to sort the parts of the psyche, it is possible to begin that process from where you are. When studying the *Bhagavad Gita* one will find that Krishna listed parts of the psyche. For instance in chapter 3 verse 42, we get insight based on what was taught by the sages from the Upanishad period. Krishna said this:

इन्द्रियाणि पराण्याहुर्
इन्द्रियेभ्यः परं मनः ।
मनसस्तु परा बुद्धिर्
यो बुद्धेः परतस्तु सः ॥३.४२॥

indriyāṇi parāṇyāhur
indriyebhyaḥ paraṁ manaḥ
manasastu parā buddhir
yo buddheḥ paratastu saḥ (3.42)

indriyāṇi — the senses; parāṇyāhur = parāṇi — are energetic; āhur (āhuḥ) — the ancient psychologists say; indriyebhyaḥ — the senses; paraṁ — more energetic; manaḥ — the mind; manasas — in contrast to the mind; tu — but; parā — more sensitive; buddhir = buddhiḥ — the intelligence; yo = yaḥ — which; buddheḥ — in reference to the intelligence; paratas — most sensitive; tu — but; saḥ — he, the spirit

The ancient psychologists say that the senses are energetic, but in comparison to the senses, the mind is more energetic. In contrast to the mind, the intelligence is even more sensitive. But in reference, the spirit is most elevated. (Bhagavad Gita 3.42)

The problem with this statement, is that it is difficult understand because we do not have keen psychic perception. These words of Krishna do not come alive in our lives, except in theoretical way.

However we can start where we are with ignorance of the subtle components of the self. We can develop even though we are not as perceptive as we should be.

Take for instance, eating. In eating as in everything else, the self may have a dual mood, where in one part of the mind, there is a feeling that one should eat and in another part, there is a feeling that one should abstain.

We can know that the mind is dualistic. Once we admit that, the next step is to determine which part of the mind makes decisions in the moral and spiritual interest. If one can identify the destructive part of the mind, one may neglect that part.

If I am live alone if no one controls my meals who should I blame for a bad diet? Should it be the part of the mind which promotes self-destructive habits?

Even though one cannot integrate *Bhagavad Gita*, because one has no subtle perception, still one can progress in self-control by resisting the self-destructive part of the mind. Once one recognizes that one is negatively influenced within the mind one can ignore the mental sector and emotional influence which promotes or supports undesirable habits.

As soon as the self-destructive part gives an instruction for not eating on time, one should note the instruction and resist it.

Desire force

The operation of the mind is such that it is highly absorbent to ideas. This means mental and emotional absorbency. If you pour water on a roll of paper towels, the paper will become wet. If on the other hand you pour water on a roll of wax paper, that surface will repel the water and will not be affected. Unfortunately, the mind and the emotions are absorbent.

People abuse credit cards after absorbing desires for items which they may or may not need. Once they are exposed to these items through seeing the items or through hearing of them or even though seeing images of the items, they cannot resist. They charge the items.

The desires are a pushy force. They pressure the coreSelf from within the mind and emotions. Under that pressure, the core seeks relieved by acquiring money. If the money does not come easily, the core, in conjunction with the intellect plans various schemes. This even happens to religious people, yogis, preachers, sannnyasis, devotees and priests.

It occurs because of the absorbency of the mind and the emotions and our inability to control that. This was explained long ago by Krishna.

ध्यायतो विषयान्पुंसः
सङ्गस्तेषूपजायते ।
सङ्गात्संजायते कामः
कामात्क्रोधोऽभिजायते ॥२.६२॥

dhyāyato viṣayānpuṁsaḥ
saṅgasteṣūpajāyate
saṅgātsaṁjāyate kāmaḥ
kāmātkrodho'bhijāyate (2.62)

dhyāyato = dhyāyataḥ — considering; viṣayān — sensual objects; puṁsaḥ — a person; saṅgas — attachment; teṣūpajāyate = teṣu — in them + upajāyate — is born, is created; saṅgāt — from attachment; saṁjāyate — is born; kāmaḥ — craving; kāmāt — from craving; krodho = krodhah — anger; 'bhijāyate = abhijāyate — is derived

The act of considering sensual objects, creates in a person, an attachment to them. From attachment comes craving. From this craving anger is derived. (Bhagavad Gita 2.62)

The Sanskrit word for absorption used by Krishna is *dhyāyato.* This comes from a root word, *dhi (dhy)* and is usually found as the word *dhyāna*, which is the word from fusion meditation, the seventh stage of yoga practice. The mind has an absorbency which is difficult to control.

The inability to control this is so blatant in our lives that many religious systems were develop on the premise of avoiding direct control of the mind. Instead of instructing for direct mind control, many doctrines offer indirect mind control. We are advised: "You cannot control it directly. Do this to control it." "You cannot stop it from thinking and imagining. Do this instead."

The absorbency of the mind is a problem. The other bothersome feature is our inability to separate from the emotions. We cannot resist the influence of desires. We cannot cause a split between ourselves and the mental energy which is the conduit for desires.

First, one absorbs a desire. Then one is driven by urges to fulfill it. Then one must endeavor to get it even if that means dishonesty or compromise. If the desire is frustrated, anxieties arise. These cause inefficient use of psychological energy. One may become sleep deprived. One may dream about the desires and exert psychic energy for fulfillment. This may transpire even during sleep.

Psychic abilities

Always keep in mind that psychic abilities are functions of the subtle body. If the subtle body was not capable of a psychic act, such an act could not be performed. Everything is magic in that sense. For instance, as a boy, I went to mud flats by the seaside and by the riverside in Guyana. At the time there was little pollution. Many crabs and other aquatic life were in abundance. It was fun to observe crabs. As boys we caught crabs but it was not easy. Sometimes as one would hold a crab, it would pinch one's fingers drawing blood.

A crab can move in any direction, to the left or right or backwards or forwards quickly. How do crabs do this? Is there really a difference between a human being and a crab? Is the human being inferior?

It is the same thing with catching flies by hand. It is near impossible to catch a fly. The insect can fly up, down or in any direction. It does so swiftly. Even though it is in a lower species, its eyesight is better than a human's. A fly swatter which is made from screen will invariable and reliably kill or disable a fly. The reason is twofold.

- The fly cannot perceive the meshing.
- The fly relies on sensing changes in air pressure.

The screen allows air to pass through thus not causing a noticeable change in the air pressure on either side. The fly is not alerted and is killed.

Is the fly superior to the human being because of the insect's ability to avoid capture?

That question is faulty. In comparing a human being to a fly, we are comparing not the soul using the human or fly body but rather the life form which is used in each case.

The truth of the matter is that the fly body is superior to the human in flying capacity and air-pressure sensing ability. The crab body is a superior body in terms of maneuverability.

The self using the crab form can also use a human form if given the opportunity. The self using a human form, if he or she were to take an insect form would find itself to be superior in maneuverability.

Thus siddhi or mystic power has to do with the ability of particular body. Whatever you can do, which someone else cannot do or some other creature cannot do, is in a sense a siddhi or mystic power. Check to know if you would have that power if you had another body.

India has no monopoly on psychic development but India has a recorded history of psychic research. From studying the Upanishads and the Puranas for instance, one can see that India was always obsessed with psychic research. However Japanese and Chinese mystics also did such research. Some left records of their realizations. In the Western hemisphere, the Celtic people and others also did research.

The physical body of human beings in different countries is basically constructed in the same way. It is the same with the subtle forms. Thus we find that research in India, China, Japan and elsewhere has similarity. If you inspect the body of dead mammal in South American and you find a similar species in China, an inspection of the Chinese one will result in the conclusion, that the bodies are similar. It is the same with the subtle form.

We get confused because we think that we cannot assume another life form like that of a crab or fly but it is possible. The self is adaptable.

Chinese chi force

In China Taoist teachers left detailed records about their discoveries and recommendations of the subtle forces in the physical body, the subtle body itself, the causal one and also about the development and manifestation of a spiritual form.

There were even detailed diagrams about the kundalini lifeForce and how to reform, control and redirect it. These were done by Masters of Yoga in China, without any input from the teachers in India.

It is a fact however that the monk Bodhidharma left India and went to China to teach Buddhism. Finding people there to be weak in physical strength, he introduces a new discipline which came to be known as Kung Fu martial arts. I first learn about this in the Philippines in 1970, when I inquired from a martial arts teacher on a US Air Base about yoga practice. The teacher, Arthur Beverford, explained that Martial Arts practice serves as a preliminary practice for posture expertise and meditation. In other words, one who cannot begin yoga, but who is attracted to self-defense, would if that person mastered the practice of Kung Fu, naturally develop an interest in posture and meditation.

In the tradition of martial arts, one lived in an ashram of the teacher. Each day there was a meditation practice which got deeper and deeper as one advances. Eventually one realized that the best self-defense is a friendly attitude to one and all.

The Chi force is present in the body as the lifeForce, which is termed prana or kundalini in Sanskrit. Prana is the random energy in the psyche. Kundalini is the formatted energy. Prana is like static electricity which is everywhere in the atmosphere, while kundalini is like a lightning strike. In sexual orgasm one feels this flash force of kundalini.

I was in China in 2006. I went to four Taoist temples, but did not find a master. The residents were mostly novices. However the statues of the Patriarchs were very powerfully present. I was inspired by that.

Taoist masters are present in the USA, UK and elsewhere. There are books on the subject. If one is serious, one may meet a teacher on the astral level.

Fame = Envy

Fame which is something that is so much pursued in human society is in some cases the equal of envy. In some spiritual societies, I noticed how a person becomes preoccupied with fame, so much so that the person may do anything and everything to acquire it, even losing focus on the very reason one pursued spiritual life in the first place.

I knew some spiritual leaders who became so much absorbed with fame that everything they did from that point onwards was to acquire increasing fame, even if it meant that the spiritual progression digressed. It is very obvious in political leaders and in entertainment celebrities that fame carries the person away, but in the spiritual societies it is not that easy to trace it.

Fame may be considered as a commodity, like a pint of rice or a pair of shoes, except that it is a psychological product. It is good to think of subtle things as objects. Krishna explained.

बुद्धिर्ज्ञानमसंमोहः
क्षमा सत्यं दमः शमः ।
सुखं दुःखं भवोऽभावो
भयं चाभयमेव च ॥१०.४॥

buddhirjñānamasaṁmohaḥ
kṣamā satyaṁ damaḥ śamaḥ
sukhaṁ duḥkhaṁ bhavo'bhāvo
bhayaṁ cābhayameva ca (10.4)

buddhir = buddhiḥ — intelligence; jñānam — knowledge; asaṁmohaḥ — non-confusion, sanity; kṣamā — patience; satyam — truthfulness; damaḥ — self-control; śamaḥ — tranquility; sukham — pleasure; duḥkham — pain; bhavo = bhavaḥ — existence; 'bhāvo = abhāvaḥ — non-existence; bhayam — fear; cābhayam = ca- and + abhayam- fearlessness; eva — indeed; ca — and

Intelligence, knowledge, sanity, patience, truthfulness, self-control, tranquility, pleasure, pain, existence, non-existence, fear, fearlessness... (Bhagavad Gita 10.4)

अहिंसा समता तुष्टिस्
तपो दानं यशोऽयशः ।
भवन्ति भावा भूतानां
मत्त एव पृथग्विधाः ॥१०.५॥

ahiṁsā samatā tuṣṭis
tapo dānaṁ yaśo'yaśaḥ
bhavanti bhāvā bhūtānāṁ
matta eva pṛthagvidhāḥ (10..5)

ahiṁsā — non-violence; samatā — impartiality; tuṣṭiḥ — contentment; tapo = tapaḥ — austerity; dānam — charity; yaśo = yaśaḥ — fame; 'yaśaḥ = ayaśaḥ — infamy; bhavanti — are; bhāvā — existential conditions; bhūtānām — of the beings; matta — from Me; eva — alone; pṛthagvidhāḥ — multiple

...non-violence, impartiality, contentment, austerity, charity, fame and infamy, are multiple existential conditions, which are derived from Me alone. (Bhagavad Gita 10.5)

If one can realize that fame equals envy, one may be cautious in acquiring it. Since nearly everyone would like to have it, and only a few really can take advantage of it, it naturally breeds envy. One is better off diverting from it. There were many spiritual leaders from many of the various religions on this earth. Many were ruined in the effort to be known as servants, devotees, messengers, agents or sons of God.

Because the currency of fame can only be spent in human society, one is likely to turn away from God if one embraces fame. When one becomes famous, one runs the risk of ignoring God.

Fit into animal form

While on earth it takes years of discipline to master a skill, in the heavenly planets one does not have to practice to acquire a skill. The subtle body naturally does certain technical things, just as on this planet, a creature as lowly as a goat walks immediately after its embryo body is delivered from its mother. The human body is more advanced than that of a goat but the child is handicapped in infancy because it is partially developed at birth. Each species has particular constraints. For instance kittens remain blind for several days after delivery. This happens because the life mechanism in the body cannot produce the cat body in fullness at birth.

In the case of the deer or goat, the fawn or kid can walk as soon as it is delivered but in the case of the cat, even though it too has four legs, it cannot stand at delivery. It may be that since the cat is a predator, its lifeForce did not focus on the ability to run away, as in the case of the kid goat or fawn which are subject to predation.

It is a part of yoga to understand clearly that anyone may assume any other species. Pride in being a human being may hamper this understanding. One should make an effort to develop the insight to understand how one's energy can very well enter into any life form. Even if one cannot understand what the self is, one can understand the subtle energies, the psychological feelings. From that one can understand how one can assume an infant animal body.

Part 3

Nature is nature

One baffling feature when trying to make spiritual advancement is the dead weight of obligations. Arjuna was baffled by a negative influence when he wanted to fulfill obligations to the Kurus, the family in which his body was produced. Even with Krishna standing beside him, Arjuna was swamped by the obligations. He was weakened on the emotional plane. Such commitments have a power even over somebody who is close to God.

One reason why we are influenced by this, is the fact that we are ignorant of the composition of the consequential energy which is in the psyche. Usually we think that this energy is a cohesive force. In fact it is a composite energy, wherein one's personal account is mixed with that of others in the family in which one took birth.

During the time of development of the infant body, even before one assumes the embryo as a body, one is tagged with obligations to the family in which one would take birth. This means that one's fate is mixed with that of others. The question is: How to sort that? Suppose you find yourself with a bank account which has 16 holders. Suppose all 16 persons (yourself included), arrive at the bank simultaneously, desiring to withdraw money. Suppose there is not enough money in the account to share with everyone. What should you do?

Suppose you take a humble position. You instruct the teller, "Pay the others as desired. I will take what remains."

You assumed that some would be left, but instead the account becomes insolvent. The last of the 15 persons who went to the teller was told that no money was in the account. One did not know this. One is still positively hoping that there is sufficient funds. In any case, that last relatives ask the teller for a loan. The teller agreed and put that loan against the account.

You then approach the teller. You are told that you owe the bank a large sum with interest. This is how consequential accounts operates. They are not necessarily paid by the person who creates the obligation. In fact a consequential account may be paid by others who are circumstantial forced into assuming the liability.

Should we be resentful about this?

Of course not. Nature is nature. It will continue being nature no matter what we think and no matter what rules of engagement we feel it should enforce. Nature is not concerned with our ideas of fairness. Study the operations of nature. Work to suit so that you are least affected by its operations.

Special me

There is that feeling of that special me. From that I derived the 'life is not fair!' idea, as if life was originally designed to satisfy me.

All over the world, there are pockets of people assembling in groups, families, tribes, nations, religions and the like, all branding themselves as special groups. I grew up in Christianity where one becomes filled with the idea that one is tied to the only begotten son of God with stress on the word only, and that this God has favorites. His favorite people are supposed to be the Jews. Later on I entered another religion only to find the same syndrome of a group of people who felt that they were specially selected as devotees of God serving him under a special pure devotee.

Is this for real?

If you talk to the Muslims you may find that they feel that Muhammad is very special as the last prophet. There is no other prophet after Mohammad as far as they are concerned. They are the servants of God under the banner of Muhammad.

There are even more basic identity crises in families with a child feeling that his parents are special, provided of course they give what he or she desires. There is the husband and the wife who feel that they are specifically suited to each other.

We are in an Age when some discovered that the earth is not the center of the universe. Our sun is simply a little light off in a dark corner of the Milky Way. Our solar system is so important to this Milky Way, that if it were to vanish the rest of the stars systems would hardly notice its absence. And here we feel special.

We are on a planet which existed for many millions of years, before the emergence of primitive and modern man, a planet on which vegetation and wild creatures ruled supreme much longer than the human beings. And still we insist on being special.

Life is fair, but our perception is distorted so we feel that it is unfair.

A baby protrudes from its mother's birth passage. The infant cries, "Where is Mommy? Where is Daddy? Where is the world which should fulfill my every need?"

Coma

In Italy a father of a woman, was given permission to disconnect the medical apparatus which helped the lifeForce to keep his daughter's body alive for the past 16 years. The man spend years in courts trying to get this permission. Finally after 16 years of her comatose condition courts granted him to right to end her life.

What does it mean to be in a coma?

I remember years ago a friend who was in an Indian religious society, was in a car accident. He entered a coma for about two hours in which he remembered nothing. When he first became conscious he did not remember his cultural identity. Over time the memory surfaced.

I met him after he was dismissed from a hospital. I wanted to inquire of his religious belief. He was a religious fanatic. I ask him if he experienced anything during the coma. He said he did not. I then asked him if he was sure about this. I said, "What about the God of your religion. Did you not see that God?"

I asked because if one served faithful in the religion one is supposed to see the God and go to him at the time of death. He insisted that he had no experience of the sort and did not remember anything while in the coma.

What happens when a human body goes into a coma?

That question is answered daily for those who are put into unconsciousness before taking surgery. A comatose condition is very similar to that.

There are two types of comatose conditions. One has no objective awareness. In that the person involved is not aware of existence. It exists but it is not aware of itself. In such a condition even if its comatose body is wounded there is no suffering felt by the person. On this side of existence people who view that body may pity it, but for the person involved there is no suffering even on the psychic side of life.

The second comatose condition concerns having a comatose body and being aware of oneself besides that. In such a condition one may be aware of the condition of the body or one may not be conscious of it. If one is aware one feels trapped and restricted in the effort to operate the body. That would be like being in a car which is locked but being in there with no means of starting the vehicle or winding down the windows. One is trapped. One does not have the means of changing the coma. If one is locked in a car which has impact resistant windows, one cannot leave the vehicle. In fact even if one can see others outside the vehicle one may not communicate with them if the windshield and windows are made of Univision glass. That glass allows perception through the glass but only from one side. On the other side, there is no clarity. One may know that someone is outside of the car but one cannot communicate with the person. That other person cannot communicate with you and must make correct or incorrect assumptions about your condition.

If you ever have a dream in which you find yourself in the physical body but without the power to move it, that is a cataleptic trance. It is similar to a coma. It is being in the body without the power to operate it.

Another type of conscious condition in a coma, is where the person is not in the physical body which is in a coma but is outside of that body. This is similar to being in a realistic dream condition away from the physical form.

Comas are maintained by the lifeForce in the body, not by the person-self who uses the form. As such medical people who keep a comatose body alive assist the lifeForce in maintaining that body. They are not directly assisting the spirit person who uses the body. The lifeForce however is important because a spirit cannot transit from a damaged comatose body unless the lifeForce leaves that body permanently. This means that if one is in a coma one's lifeForce remains in the immobile body and one's individuality remains linked to that body by the necessity of the laws of psychic existence. These laws dictate that a person-self cannot fully abandon a body if the lifeForce remains in that form.

Abortion

Abortion means that someone is disenfranchised from getting a body. It means that someone lived as a birth situation and was evicted from it. Abortion does not mean the death of the would-be person. It means that his or her newly formed embryo was killed. Therefore he or she was deprived of the embryonic situation.

The person getting the body cannot be killed by an abortion or miscarriage or any other sabotage to the new body's formation. But this does not mean that abortion is not a faulty act. Aside from the laws of State, there is nature's way of action and reaction. If I take an action to cause someone to be disenfranchised from a birth opportunity, the question is not one of the State's reaction but rather nature's counteraction. The State is only important on the physical side. In contrast, nature is a serious threat. Nature keeps tabs on activities from millions of years prior. It can react unfavorably towards me at any time it chooses. My concern about abortions, miscarriages, deferred or prevented pregnancies, is nature's way of dealing with it.

Abortion is related to contraceptives which prevent pregnancy. Any action by a human being to prevent a pregnancy is restrictive if that action is successful in stopping the development of an embryo. Again I stress that I do discuss the death of the would-be personality but rather the death of his or her embryo or the prevention of the formation of a fetus.

Initiation of life

When is life initiated?

Unless one is a mystic or psychic and has objective awareness of an initiation point, the person involved in the formation of a body does not know when his or her life is initiated. I will give an example. Let us suppose that one is captured by a terrorist group which puts one's body into an unconscious state at the point of capture. They transport one's body to another country, where one becomes conscious in a dark room. Now suppose I gain entry into that place. I question you, "When were you captured? How did the terrorists transport you?"

You could not positively answer.

Who could tell the moment when his life as an embryo was initiated? Here is a reasonable question, "At what stage, beginning from the one-cellular state is the person who is to be an embryo, capable of feeling the pain of an abortion?"

That invokes another question as to why the question of initiation of life is being asked in the first place. It is an issue because the government is perplexed as to when an abortion would be termed as murder, the killing of an individual human being.

If we put aside the interests of the State, we may reason that at any stage of development an abortion is a situation of depriving somebody of a birth opportunity.

Going back to the example of the person who was kidnapped, suppose while he was unconscious, one terrorist severed his ear. If we ask when the ear was removed what will he say? He can only reply that he does not know. If we put ourselves in the position of the person whose embryo form is to be developed, we will find that he or she has no conscious recall of a beginning.

There are deep sea turtles which travel hundreds of miles to go to beaches of Pacific islands to lay eggs. Once they get to the beaches, they burrow to create areas in which they deposit and cover the eggs. During the laying period something happens in the brain of the turtles so that they go into a trance state. This was discovered by biological scientists. It would mean then if you were to ask one of those turtles, about the laying of the eggs, it would not detail the incidence.

Nature is in charge of pregnancies. Our conscious awareness of it is to an extent irrelevant. Some other biological and psychic mechanisms control pregnancies.

Womb Entry

At what point does the soul/spirit enter the womb? Is it at the moment of conception, the formation of a single cell?

We usually think of the soul's entry into the womb in physical terms. The human convention is to see everything in physical terms. However since the self is not a physical item and since in the hereafter, the self did not have a physical body, we would form erroneous ideas if we only consider the physical circumstances.

We should consider the subtle terms. The mother and father are on the physical side. Their sexual act is physical. There is no evidence that a sexual intercourse in a dream could produce a physical pregnancy. Therefore the physical side will not help us to figure in the subtlety of the disembodied soul.

Now since we understand that we must seek another plane of existence to be able to put the subtle soul into the equation, the question arises as to what plane that should be. It has to be a plane upon which both the mother and father has registry, a plane in which both parents have contact.

Let us look at another situation to get some understanding of this. A man I used to know was involved in looking at Internet pornography but it affected him. When we discussed it, I said to him, "Why worry about it? It is only images in motion. The image you view in the video is not a real human being. You cannot physically interact with the person in the video."

Fittingly he replied, "It may be a video but my energy makes contact with it. I am stimulated by it."

This answer shows that two items which are not in the same dimension can interact indirectly in another dimension. Stated differently the man was not in the same dimension or location with the sexually-exposed person who was videod but through the media he made contact with that person's energy. My point is that there must be some contact on some level, if a disembodied soul is to take a new body. It has to communicate on some level with its would-be parents.

We should cease looking for a physical entry point. In the case of the man who viewed the video, we should cease looking to see if the person in the video is physically with him. Why ask the question, "Where is the physical woman who stimulates you?" The question has no value. The point of contact or point of entry of the disembodied soul is not a physical one.

The other consideration we must take into account is that even though the departed soul has that tendency for having a physical form, it is not necessarily attracted to its would-be parents just for that. The initial attraction to the parents is merely an attraction which is a natural function of the human psyche. It is not a thought-out planned attraction in most cases. It is a strong irresistible attraction. We do experience a similar attraction on the physical side of life. Have you ever felt attracted to someone sexually and then see that person close-up and feel that you are not attracted, and then again feel that you are attracted to a part or parts of that person's body? How should we define that? This attraction occurs when a soul is disembodied. The person feels attraction to one or both of the would-be parents. It is spontaneous. It is not a planned attraction.

Sometime back, I walked on a city street. I found myself walking behind a woman. My mind and senses were irresistibly drawn to the woman's torso. Because my strides were longer than hers, after a time I walked ahead but when I glanced at her face, I lost the attraction. Why was that?

Suppose the opposite happened. Let us say for instance that when I glanced at her face, I became even more attracted and the woman also because attracted. Let us say that a relationship developed with her. Then there was a sexual intercourse. Then she became pregnant. Then a child was born. You can analyze from this that the physical child can be traced all the way back to my attraction to the mother's torso even before I knew the woman intimately. It developed from a subtle force of visual attraction. In this way we can learn how to begin tracking things from the psychic, emotional and mental dimensions. These occurrences, though abstract affect the physical outcomes.

Responsibility

What about the moral dilemma of an abortion? Is it always right to allow life to continue once it is initiated?

As far as possible, we should try not to interfere with the operations of nature. More or less our business is sense and mind control. It does not matter what I say or what I believe. If I do not exercise sense and mind control, I will be impulsive. I will be forced to take responsibility for reckless acts.

Who will punish me?

There are several agencies for enforcement. There is human society, the laws of the State. There is supernatural power which is questionable, since it is not a physical object. There is nature at large which causes disruption to human society by natural disasters, medical problems and the like. There are human beings who react like the man who shot his wife after finding her with another man.

This question:

Is it always right to allow life to continue once initiated, from the one-celled state onwards?

This question cannot be answered in a straightforward way because there are cases in which a woman is abused and is forced to have a pregnancy, then later the infant becomes a criminal element in society and harms even the woman who birthed it. Some children produced from sexual abuse become productive for the mother and society.

For general purposes, yes, life should go on once a pregnancy begins, but that is not a good decision for specific purposes. Each case is separate.

Once a yogi beggar practiced austerities in India. His main hang up was sweet foods. He was advised that it was best if he reformed that since it was his vice.

Deciding firmly in his mind, to stop the habit, he began to starve from sweets. From then on for about two years he did not take one single sweet. After that he went through a market and saw some gelebies, a syrup-drenched sweet. He ran to the vendor's cart. He grabbed and ate mouthfuls. The vendor was caught by surprise. Realizing what the yogi beggar did, the vendor took a stick and struck the yogi severely.

After this, another yogi of repute went to the vendor and chastised him, "What are you doing? He is a great yogin. Why do you beat him? You should instead give him the cart of sweets and whatever else his heart desires. You are an idiot. You cursed your family. Bad luck will surely find them."

The vendor became remorseful. He asked forgiveness.

In the meantime the yogi thief left the place and wandered off into a forest. He criticize himself, "What happened there? Hell, this sugar vice got stronger for those two years when I kept it from expression. Now it commanded my psyche to commit that crime on the vendor. I destroyed the man's income for today. Fie on me, I cannot control the tasting impulse, no matter what I do?"

In that case, the theft was different from a theft by a criminally minded person. Each instance must be reviewed. No one should steal from stalls but in each case, we should consider the details. Still the government has every right to make a general rule that if one steals from stalls, there will a penalty.

For our lifestyle and preference, as a general rule, from his sexual act, a yogi should allow an embryo to develop. He should bear responsibility for the child produced. This includes supporting the child and its mother's upkeep.

Liabilities - child's mother

When a man was about 58 years old he married a lady who was the age of his eldest daughter. From that relationship a child was produced. Is that approved?

Who should decide? He intended to have the infant. He supported the mother. Would I do a similar thing?

I would not plan it because I am apprehensive about the responsibility. But there is always the upper hand of fate in which case one should face up to the responsibility.

When a man has productive sexual intercourse, he becomes responsible not just for the child produced but for the child's mother. If he evades the responsibility, he must settle that with nature in the future. The liabilities for short sighted actions do not vanish into thin air. They remain in the reserve of cosmic energy and find the person later, even if it means thousands of years hence. Besides nature there are human beings who may be offended. If for instance I take a young woman for a wife, as the man did, I must deal with resentment from relatives.

The government may not care except for the child support payments, but the relatives, nature, and supernatural authorities, will be concerned and will see to it that the liabilities find me sooner or later.

Birth opportunity scrapped

Great people who had real concern for humanity, instructed that we do to others, what we would prefer for ourselves. That was something Jesus Christ taught. It means that if we look into the future, we can understand that we should not do anything foolhardy. The moral issue is both a government and a social one.

If one gets a birth opportunity, one desires to complete it. If the would-be parents deprive one, even though one is not in an objective position as an embryo, one will still feel the rejection. It will register in the mind energy as distrust and resentment.

Here is an example. Let us say that I am to be born as the son of Mr. and Mrs. Wilson. After six weeks of pregnancy when Mrs. Wilson discovered that she was pregnant, she decided that she did not want the child. After consulting Mr. Wilson, she got an abortion. That birth opportunity was scrapped. The Wilsons were well-to-do people. They had ample money and status. In any case my psychic energy was transferred to some persons who knew the Wilsons. This was a family, whose wife served the Wilsons as a cleaning lady. Because she had a close relationship with Mrs. Wilson, my energy shifted into her body. After a time that servant developed a pregnancy. Nine months after I emerged as her son.

What happened to the resentment about being rejected from Mrs. Wilson's womb? Simple. It surfaced in my attitude towards the servant. I always felt that she was not well-to-do. I longed to be living in the house of Mr. and Mrs. Wilson.

The point is that if someone is deprived of a birth opportunity that person will carry resentments towards the lost parents as well as towards even the people who assist like the servant. In addition, the Wilsons may face rejection and hostility in their next birth opportunities.

The lesson is that whatever we dish out to others today, will certainly circle back to us in the future.

Moment of conception

At what point does the self enter the womb?

Is it at the moment of conception, the formation of a single cell?

No, the attraction of the soul to its would-be parents occurs before there is a sexual intercourse. It occurs by social contact on the emotional level. There is a type of compatibility which causes the departed soul to become unified into the emotions of the parents or of at least one parent. At that time, the departed soul enters into the subtle body of one parent, either the mother or father. In a bee colony at any time, the queen has hundreds of souls in her body in embryonic cells. They are in her body. She, that particular spirit which functions as the queen bee, is also in that body.

The bees which have embryonic cell bodies, acquire those as they are attracted into the cell forming process in the queen bee's form. They are there while the egg cells are developed. The individual cells becomes their habitats. Once the development of a cell reaches a certain stage, the psyche of that bee influences the formation of changes in the cell such that the particular bee form will have certain unique characteristics once it develops into an insect form.

The individual soul in that bee form, that self, has little to do with this formation, except that it is done on the basis of its psychic tendencies.

Understand that when you become a departed soul, you will not be in a position to stipulate what sort of body you may have. It is not that you, as a disembodied soul, would say, "I want this kind of body." It is not like ordering a product. It happens naturally by concourse of nature.

When one needs a body one becomes part of nature's flow of attractions and rejections. The moment of conception may be a big event on the physical side but it is part of the concourse on the subtle level. Orgasm for example is a big event for the parents but it is not the same for the disembodied person who would be the child. That person does not experience it in the same way.

Orgasm is not important except for its function of releasing sperm in males. The pleasure aspect of it has little to do with making babies otherwise women would not be implanted with semen by using syringes only. In fact, the semen could be extracted in a surgery and it would still be viable for a pregnancy.

The departed soul cannot get a body unless it enters into the emotions of the father. We may contest as to how and when or where it may do that, but we must accept that as the psychic entry. My emphasis is that the disembodied spirit enters the body of the father before conception.

Lazyman's meditation

A very simple meditation which may be done without even rising from bed, without doing postures and breath infusion, involves going to the back of the head to escape from the dominance of the sensation-seeking aspect of the frontal lobe of the brain.

This meditation is perfect for those who have the lazy blues early in the morning. Ideally one should rise early, do exercises and then meditate for at least half hour if not more. If one is disinclined to this, one need not even sit on a bed, nor rise to do anything for that matter.

One can remain in comfort but switch the mind's attention to the back of the head. One can do this without stressing the mind, because early in the morning the mind may be disinclined to seek sensations outside the body. It may refrain from hashing over the challenges it will meet during the day.

At that time one may shift attention to the back of the head. With eyes closed practice the method below.

- Within the mind, turn the forward mental force to the back of the head.
- Pull one's attention backward in the head.
- Turn to the right inside of the head. Turn to the left inside of the head. Take these two actions alternately. Do this slowly so as not to change the sense of comfort.
- Listen to naad sound resonance inside the head.
- Listen to naad sound resonance at the back of the head.
- Listen to naad sound at the right or left backside of the head.
- Listen to buzzing or hissing sounds in the head.

At some point in the past and again in the future, all living beings on this planet will be in a condition that is exactly like the mental experience felt while being stationed existentially in the back of the head. They will no longer have access to the frontal energy for detecting varied sensations as we do now. Just as when one turns to the back of the head or draws the attention to the back, there is no external sensing through the face, so in the future, at some time, we will be in such a condition for a considerable length of time. That will happen when the material universe no longer provides facilities like those we have now. There will be no physical manifestation. All limited souls who did not transit to some other universe or some other dimension where they would have manifested forms, will remain in a state of existence without the variety of sensation which we usually see, hear, touch, smell and taste. What sort of existence will that be?

It really does not matter. What matters is the ability to remain calm and satisfied in that condition and not to hanker for manifestation at a time when it would not be produced for millions of years.

Limited contribution of a spirit

At first the soul/spirit is aware but it is not aware of all biological operations taking place in the manufacture of its embryo. Even now as an adult body, one is not aware of all operations in the body. One is oblivious about digesting, manufacture of blood, repair of organs, healing of damages to cells and other matters. Many operations take place without one's attention. One's presence in the body is necessary for these things to take place but one's objective participation is not required for completion of most events. Even while sleeping the body repairs itself. Neither the spirit who has the mother's body nor the spirit who would become the embryo are needed in the objective sense for the creation of an embryo. Nature operates these functions using energy from the consciousness of the spirits, but nature does not need their objective participation.

Sometimes due to brain damage, a person falls into a coma. After some weeks after the brain healed, the person becomes aware. It is obvious that objective awareness is not needed for repair of the body. It is not needed for formation of the embryo. Still our presence is needed because nature cannot make the adjustments nor further the development without a spirit's presence. This means that because a spirit is not connected there is no healing process in a dead body.

Self-worth

Self-worth is important in meditation. If it is not there one should cultivate it. In everyday dealings self-appraisal has value, but in meditation self-worth is more than aphorisms about self-esteem. One should develop self-worth in the deep levels of the mento-emotional energy. One should move away from the surface of the mind.

There is a story in Krishna's instructions to Uddhava in the *Uddhava Gita*. Krishna explained the life of the woman Pingala. She was in the sex-sale business. One night after getting disappointed repeatedly by potential customers, she became totally disgusted with her miserable plight. Krishna recommended that total disgust. Pingala lost self-esteem. She turned herself towards the Supreme Being and built confidence in a relation with that Supreme Person.

Many of us live a dual lifestyle; one part is for social betterment and the other is for spiritual advancement. Sometimes the two segments clash. The social interest wants to rule and wants the spiritual self to be under its control. In meditation we make an effort to discipline the social part, but it is resistant. Dominance by the social part converts into low self-esteem. There is a danger that if we build confidence on the social side, we will become habituated to working socially and may mistake progress there as spiritual life.

Lack of self-esteem on the social side may put the entire self in a negative mood. Too much self-esteem on the social side may completely delete meditation, and make one feel that one advances in the spiritual direction while in fact one is stagnant there. Somehow by the grace of guru and with deep insight, one should balance this, so as not to be in a happy delusion on the social side

In the *Bhagavad-Gita* there is a question of Arjuna that concerns this issue.

अर्जुन उवाच	arjuna uvāca
अयतिः श्रद्धयोपेतो	ayatiḥ śraddhayopeto
योगाच्चलितमानसः ।	yogāccalitamānasaḥ
अप्राप्य योगसंसिद्धिं	aprāpya yogasaṁsiddhiṁ
कां गतिं कृष्ण गच्छति ॥६.३७॥	kāṁ gatiṁ kṛṣṇa gacchati (6.37)

arjuna — Arjuna; uvāca — said; ayatiḥ — indisciplined person; śraddhayopeto = śraddhayopetaḥ = śraddhayā — by faith + upetaḥ — has got; yogāccalitamānasaḥ = yogāc (yogāt) — from yoga practice + calita — deviated + mānasaḥ — mind; aprāpya — not attain; yogasaṁsiddhiṁ — yoga proficiency; kāṁ — what; gatiṁ — course; kṛṣṇa — Krishna; gacchati — he goes

Arjuna said: What about the undisciplined person who has faith? Having deviated from yoga practice, having not attained yoga proficiency, what course does he take, O Krishna? (Bhagavad Gita 6.37)

कच्चिन्नोभयविभ्रष्टश्	kaccinnobhayavibhraṣṭaś
छिन्नाभ्रमिव नश्यति ।	chinnābhramiva naśyati
अप्रतिष्ठो महाबाहो	apratiṣṭho mahābāho
विमूढो ब्रह्मणः पथि ॥६.३८॥	vimūḍho brahmaṇaḥ pathi (6.38)

kaccin = kaccid — is he; nobhayavibhraṣṭaś = na — not + ubhaya — both + vibhraṣṭaḥ — lost out; chinnābhram = chinna — faded + abhram — cloud; iva — like; naśyati — lost; apratiṣṭho = apratiṣṭhaḥ — without foundation; mahābāho — O Almighty Kṛṣṇa; vimūḍho = vimūḍhaḥ — baffled; brahmaṇaḥ — of the spirituality; pathi — on the path

Is he not like a faded cloud, lost from both situations, like being without a foundation? O Almighty Krishna: He is baffled on the path of spirituality. (Bhagavad Gita 6.38)

If one gives attention only for spiritual life, one may lose status in the social world. If one does that and does not complete the spiritual practice, Arjuna inquired of the consequence.

If one develops too much self-esteem on the physical level those obligations may consume one's life. Then one would lose on the spiritual side.

Conversely if one goes over completely to the spiritual side and neglects convention, one may be demoted socially, and then what? Does one endeavor for yoga practice now because one failed to complete it in a former life? Is someone neglecting yoga and tending only to social convention because that person has an instinct that feels that too much yoga may cause social failure?

Psychic pressure for embryos

There is a constant pressure for bodies in all species, including the ones which became extinct either through human action or through natural disaster. This psychic pressure is ongoing.

When did it begin?

It was always there. It is perpetual. There will never be a time when that pressure is absent. There are trillions of coreSelves always needing various types of bodies for fulfillment.

This means that no matter where life occurs in any physical dimension, there will be the creation of some type of sperm cell and ovum for furthering such development.

If one fills a metal tank with air pressure, and if one compresses the air sufficiently, there will be the likelihood of an explosion. In the same way there is always psychic pressure for bodies in all life forms. All forms make an endeavor to procreate.

We are not sex crazed because we want to have pleasure. It is because nature itself is sex crazed for the purpose of constant reproduction. Once one discovers sexual pleasure, one craves it, but our discovery and subsequent craving has little to do with nature's urgency.

In some species, one unit splits into two-parts, resulting in two new bodies. In those species there is no sexual intercourse for reproduction. Of course those are simpler species. But the point is that the pressure is felt in every life form.

Nature is hardly concerned about achievements. We desire to make historic impact but nature ignores the achievements and continues with its urgency of reproduction. It cares little about our desires. It keeps on making the effort for reproduction. The psychic pressure for that affects us continually.

The sperm cells and ova are there for the purpose of fulfilling nature's mission of reproduction. If a form is aborted, nature continues the mission regardless. The spirit whose embryo is aborted, will again be drawn into the physical reproductive process. The miscarriage or abortion is a setback for that person, but he/she will again be drawn back into the process by nature's necessity. In that sense abortion has little useful function because the person who is deprived of a body, remains with reproductive energy until there is another opportunity for embryonic development.

Mind control

A large part of mind control is not control of the mind, but rather understanding how the mind operates. Do not try to control something which you do not understand. First study the activities and method of the mind. Then make a scheme for control.

Bhagavad Gita challenges us to befriend ourselves by taking control of the mind. Krishna gave details about the construction and control of the mind. One cannot have consistent mind control if one does not study the mental process.

After a day's work the mind will by necessity, hash over what took place. This cannot be stopped merely because one has a certain religious affiliation. The mind will retain the involvements and hash over the same. The more involved one is, the more the mind will insist on reviewing related memories.

How to control this?

One must agree to study how the mind does this. Study the mind in particular because different minds deal with hassles in a slightly different ways. Get details about the mind just as doctors first acquire details about a person's illness before suggesting treatment.

Even for a common disease like diabetes, doctors take numerous tests before prescribing medicine. Thus even though there are general methods of control, still a specific process should be used for one person and something else with great or little variation should be for someone else.

The first step is to agree to give the mind time when you get home in the afternoon. Sit down with a note pad. Attempt relaxation. Note what comes to mind. Notice that I suggested an attempt at relaxation. This is because true relaxation cannot occur if the mind is filled with memories. One may not relax but one should make the effort to do so. The nature of the mind is that as soon as one makes the effort, it will present pictures, images and sounds from memories. Since the mind behaves like this, one can take advantage of it by noting what the mind presents.

Once you know what the mind is occupied with, you may sort the information. Make a list of what can be done immediately and what should be postponed for another day. Make this list and emphatically decide that you will tend to whatever you can immediately complete.

This consideration will release an energy which will neutralize the mind's desire to hash over the items. Some resistant items will remain just as a stain remains on a fabric even after it is washed.

Make note of the persistent troubles in the mind. Once you isolate something that is persistent, act to resolve or avoid it. If one cannot wash a stain from a fabric, it is a good lesson in what type of chemical to avoid in the future. Those associations which are permanent irritants in the mind, should be side-stepped in the future.

An example is horror movies. There are many people who get nightmares after seeing horror in media. Even though the nightmares continue for years some people repeatedly view media.

They should avoid the videos. Why complain that the mind is stained with unwanted association? That is the nature of the mind. You can prevent the register by avoiding what is undesirable.

Benefit of Naad

For those who find the naad sound to be boring, the question is:

What should be one's attitude to naad? What should one derive from it?

At first when meditating on naad at least for the first six months of steady daily meditation, one should expect nothing from it. One should do the practice because it was recommended. This six month period will give the mind and the self time to appreciate naad and to relinquish the need for a result. The hankering for a result is itself a cause for not getting a result. Naad listening will eventually reach the intellect and influence it to switch into being a means of supernatural vision.

If one waits in naad, if one waits patiently without hankering, one will find that in the frontal part of the head the intellect will develop psychic, supernatural and spiritual perception of other dimensions. At first this vision will open up to heavenly worlds and other places which are near to this physical dimension. Later it will reveal spiritual places.

However these visions develop of their own accord. They cannot be forced. It is similar to a hen sitting on eggs. The hen cannot force an egg's development. There is absolutely nothing the hen can do to bring about the development of her chicks, except to sit on the eggs. That sitting provides heat which is the climate necessary for embryonic growth. When one listens to naad one cannot force supernatural vision but it will develop from that listening because that produces conditions under which the intellect is transformed into spiritual vision.

Use of spare time

Spiritual life is very similar to economy. Most adults deal with economy, the acquirement and spending of money. Some have more money than they require while others are always in want and never can make ends meet. We must also learn to budget the emotional and analytical energies. More or less the human being is a combination of emotional and analytical potency. The emotional part is involved with affections mostly. The analytical part is concerned with scheming and plotting.

If we fail to properly budget this energy, we suffer in various way. For instance if one does not scheme and plot, if one leaves everything to chance, one may find that one's life is filled with frustrations. If one does not properly apply one's emotions in relationships, one will be left in isolation without anyone to care about, and without anyone to be loved by.

In spiritual life some become stagnant. That is similar to a person who makes a livelihood selling items in a market but who is unable to increase his income in that way. He started his business making a profit of about $300 per day. Ten years after he still makes that amount even though inflation caused the expenses to increase. That is stagnation.

Some of us made a great stride in spiritual life at a particular time. Then we invested that energy to gain respect from the public. This is like a businessman who made a sizeable profit some years ago and who invested it to expand his business and to manufacture a product which was in high demand. As a result his profit increased year after year.

The lifestyle affects the rate of advancement. If I have a lifestyle and a career which is counterproductive to spiritual life, my advancement will be minimum. I should not become annoyed, either with myself or with others about this. Rather I should study my methods to find a way to improve the situation.

Suppose I work at a business which is hostile to spiritual life. Suppose I have a lifestyle that is abrasive to spiritual practice. Obviously I will absorb counterproductive energies. Do I have a choice? Suppose I need the money from the employment? Suppose I enjoy the lifestyle even though it is hostile to spiritual practice?

Obviously the first thing is to surrender to that providence and make a plan for the least absorption of bad energies.

It is not that if I move into a spiritual community I would be better off. That is not necessarily true. When Arjuna wanted to leave battlefield work, killing work, which is outright abominable, Krishna objected.

In chapter one of *Bhagavad Gita*, Arjuna had many considerations about the pros and cons of the battlefield situation. He wanted to find a way to either get away from it or to do it in the least harmful way.

The first step is learn how to use all spare time one is allotted by providence for spiritual development. Yes, providence does make demands that one should fulfill certain cultural obligations, but the same providence watches to see how one uses spare time. Even if it is five minutes per day. It is time. How is it used?

Years ago when I was employed, I always carried a book of spiritual information wherever I went. If I was at a job, I would have a book in my lunch kit. During even short breaks which were ten or fifteen minutes, I would read a spiritual book. In that way my spare time was used for spiritual cultivation. Sometimes during lunch breaks of thirty minutes or more, I would rest the mind, meditate or do another spiritual practice. If other employees were hostile to it, I would pretend that I was tired. I would act as if I fell asleep, while in fact mentally I meditated. In that way I did not attract hostility from those who disliked spiritual life. I simultaneously used my spare time for spiritual thinking and meditating while others socialized.

Realizing the self

Details about yoga practice are given in *Yoga Sutras*, as well as in *Bhagavad Gita*. The problem is that these text books about yoga are precise. Still one should know that the details are in those texts. Have confidence about that. If you get a manual about smelting gold, the book will be useless if one has no gold ore and have never seen pure gold. But even if one has the manual and even if you get some ore, it will still be difficult to use the instructions if you cannot get certain chemicals. The process of yoga has many parts. Unless one can get the self in order, one cannot successfully practice.

After sorting anxieties, solving some and leaving some for another day, a tired mind should be rested. This feature of resting the mind in the most efficient way is part of yoga practice. If mastered, this would bring one to the stage of definitely knowing and realizing that one is not the physical body, that one is relatively free to use the subtle form, which is part of the self composite.

There are many people who heard of reincarnation or who were told by a teacher that one is not the body. Some persons read of that in the *Bhagavad Gita*. Many have no regular experience as being completely separate from the physical body. They proceed with spiritual practice on the basis of faith. There is a verse in the Gita which appraises such people.

अन्ये त्वेवमजानन्तः
श्रुत्वान्येभ्य उपासते ।
तेऽपि चातितरन्त्येव
मृत्युं श्रुतिपरायणाः ॥१३.२६॥

anye tvevamajānantaḥ
śrutvānyebhya upāsate
te'pi cātitarantyeva
mṛtyuṁ śrutiparāyaṇāḥ (13.26)

anye — others; tu — but; evam — thus; ajānantaḥ — not knowing; śrutvānyebhya = śrutvā — hearing + anyebhya — from others; upāsate — they worship; te — they; 'pi = api — also; catitaranti = ca — and + atitaranti — transcend; eva — indeed; mṛtyuṁ — death: śrutiparāyaṇāḥ = śruti — hearing + parāyaṇāḥ — putting confidence in as the highest

But some, though they are ignorant, hear from others. They worship and by their confidence in what is heard, they also transcend death. (Bhagavad Gita 13.26)

But if one aims to be an accomplished yogi, one does not want to remain in this category of spiritual seekers. One should experience the self as distinct from the body on a consistent basis. The interesting thing is that one is separated from the body on a daily basis but one does not objectively realize that. It is not that one has to separate but it more that one should realize when one is involuntarily separated from the physical system.

Whenever the physical body sleeps, the subtle one is desynchronized. This may occur in one of two ways:

- a separation with the subtle body moving away from the physical form
- a separation with the subtle body remaining interspaced into the physical one.

This may be compared to an appliance remaining in a house and being unplugged from an electrical outlet and taken outside the building. In either case, the appliance is not connected to the electrical outlet but when it is outside the building, it is at a greater distance from the outlet in the house.

Sometimes during sleep the subtle body remains interspaced in the physical form, just as if it were not separate from it, just as a radio on a shelf in the house seems to be part of the house, while in fact it is a separate item.

In other experiences the subtle body is desynchronized to such a degree that it is not present in the physical form, even though it has an energy connection to it.

What am I indicating?

It is that self-realization begins when one realizes that one is separate from the physical body. This begins by experiencing the subtle body as different to the physical one. There are many persons who heard about the soul's status and who explain that to others without ever realizing the self as separate from the body. When I say that one is separate from the body, I speak of the subtle body as being distinct from the physical one. However, one is not the subtle body just as one is not the physical system. If you cannot experience yourself as the subtle body, it is not possible for you to know what the coreSelf is, because that is super-subtle. The first step in self-realization is to experience the subtle body apart from the physical form.

Since those two forms separate during sleep, the first accomplishment is to be conscious during that daily experience.

Whenever one rests the body, whenever it sleeps, one should hold some aspiration for realizing the separation of the subtle form. This idea should be prominent. The conventional way to take rest, is to go to sleep. For a yogi, the way is to remain silent in the mind, in the consciousness, and to observe as much as possible the process of how the psyche goes to sleep stage by stage.

The lifeForce in the body controls the sleeping mechanism. It is similar to a timing system which disconnects power from appliances. There are electronic systems which secure buildings, where a system shuts doors and secures other functions automatically. Similarly in the psyche there is the lifeForce which operates a system of shutting down the functions in the body. For yoga, we are required to observe those operations.

How does one do this?

The first step is to develop the desire to realize this.

The second step is to know that you cannot realize this unless you are attentive.

You must show an interest on the subtle side, just as you developed an interest in physicality.

Rest in Peace

Any type of spiritual practice is best done early in the morning before sunrise. In fact any activity is best down when the physical body is rested and the subtle body is refreshed. Even after one is evicted permanently from a material body one is required to take rest before assuming a new embryo. On tombstones there is a common marking which means *Rest in Peace*. After a life of chasing ambitions, whatever mentality and emotions remain needs rest before the next round of challenges in a new body.

Higher worlds

Naad practice is best done early in the morning. In addition one gets better results from practice if the subtle body is rested and air-surcharged. To surcharge it one should do pranayama breath infusion. This is not a matter of belief. One should test to see if breath infusion is effective. Do it early in the morning for three months. One difference between yoga practice and other systems of religious exercise is that yoga demands that you test as you proceed. If there is no result, why do it?

The subtle body is the means of gaining supernatural vision to see into higher dimensions. It is necessary to discover how it will develop that vision. It should do so while one uses the physical system. One should not have to wait until after one is separated from the physical body permanently. If one cannot get insight into the astral levels which are near to this physical world, how would it be possible for one to get vision or any type of perception into spiritual levels which are much higher?

Managing inconveniences

Every ascetic has to deal with unfavorable situations. We must apply intelligence when we find ourselves in unfavorable circumstances. There is no point in making a bad situation worse. If meditation or other spiritual exercise aggravates people whom one must rely on, then it is best to forestall or hide the practice for the time being and wait for the circumstance to change. None of these good or bad social circumstances will remain forever. One need not despair when fate puts one in a bad way. One should not get excited when things are favorable.

When I came to the United States in 1967, I already made efforts to retrieve my spiritual practice which digressed after taking a body from a materialistic family. I struggled to reestablish yoga. I enlisted in the US Air Force, a social environment which at the time was not conducive to yoga. There were many fellow crew members who were into narcotics, sexual access, music, drugs and alcohol but none had the yoga interest. Somehow by providence I found a teacher on an air base in the Philippines but over all I hid the practice. To avoid disclosure, I hid myself in a metal locker to meditate.

Some barracks were open, so that you could see from one end to the other but there were metal lockers assigned to each person. Some days I would sequester myself in a locker and remain there without interference. One should figure how to salvage spirituality. When one has a family, there may be interference but one should find a way to procure time for spiritual life.

Use the intelligence. Do not act in a counterproductive way by offending persons whom you must rely on. Having to listen to a radio is disturbing. When I was in the Air Force in the Philippines, sometimes I drank alcohol just to patronize others whom I was stationed with. It was their habit. If one did not take a drink now and again it was considered to be a hostile attitude. For peace sake I indulged. Sometimes there would be narcotics like opium which use to come from Thailand. There was marijuana. I took a toke now and again just to be friendly.

There was the need for sexual access. This is not good for an ascetic but when one is faced with some unfavorable things, one must sometimes participate for the time being. As soon as one is freed from it, one should resume the spiritual quest.

In the material world every circumstance cannot be favorable. This place is not for one's convenience. One should cull some time for spiritual focus even when the situation is unfavorable.

Music and video can be degrading for a person who practices meditation. If one must listen and view media, do so with the understanding that it may have negative effects and may retard the spiritual practice. Make methods to defeat the mind's interest in whatever is counterproductive.

One method is to use a mantra and chant in the mind. One other method is to observe how the mind pursues undesirable sounds. If the mind hears a melody several times, it maintains a recording of the pattern. When it again hears that it internally rehearses the sound. By studying this one can understand how the mind operates. One should discover how the mind procures sense fulfillments like sounds and how the mind becomes enthralled by that.

Naad sound

The importance of naad sound is its natural occurrence. It is not based on something a human being creates on the basis of what he heard. In chanting mantras, one has to create the sound. In the case of visualizing a deity, one must create an image in the mind. Naad is itself a subjective item. It is subtle undoubtedly but it is real. It comes from the spiritual side. Focus on naad is a definite means of getting in touch with transcendence. If one reads the instructions given to Uddhava one will see that Krishna recommended it. He listed it as part of the meditative procedure.

Normally we are not attracted to naad. Someone prefers to hear music or to chant a mantra than to listen to naad. Some say that is an impersonal sound. Krishna did not say that to Uddhava. Normally we are not attracted to it. That is the first thing we should realize. Why are we not attracted to it? How can one increase the attraction? How can one cause the psyche to desire it and to be satisfied being absorbed in it?

After the mind relaxes one may not think of listening to naad. Instead the mind may select something else to be preoccupied with. The procedure should be that as soon as the mind relaxes sufficiently, one switches the attention to naad sound which is heard mostly in the back of the head.

Blank stare practice

There is a meditation practice where one meditates with eyes open. There is also a blank stare practice which is used to develop and usher in the senses of the subtle body.

There is a practice where one sits and stares into nothingness without a particular focus, just allowing the eyes to stare but withdrawing the mind from the vision of the eyes. This causes the mental system to switch into the subtle body, where one experiences the vision of the subtle body which is different to the physical sight.

If this is practiced, there is sometimes a flicker of energy where one sees a glow of light and then one experiences that one can see glowing forms of light, even of dense objects like trees. Even trees are then seen as their subtle bodies and not as dense wood. We talk about spiritual life and about the spirit soul but do we actually experience visions of spiritual bodies? Usually we do not. Usually it stays in the realm of belief, but through such practices one experiences the subtle side. This subtle side is not the spiritual side but it is a beginning of breaking away from physical perception, something which most of us are limited to throughout our lives.

Identify the outward-going energy

Each meditation technique has non-obvious methods but usually what works for one person may not be effective for another. The honest way to develop oneself is to practice painstakingly and to get oneself out of the habit of wanting the process to be easy. The easy method attitude caused many seekers to fail in practice.

If one is a born psychic then psychic things comes easy but if one is not, the alternative is to develop over time without wanting to have it as easy as a psychic. Some people have subtle experiences even in childhood, as if they were born in that way while others even after years of meditation practice still do not get psychic clarity. Each person is endowed differently but if one endeavors with the right method one may eventually get psychic access.

To track something that is transcendental or abstract, requires first of all some attention to the transcendental or subtle side of existence. The first hurdle to climb is to confront the mental tendency which insists that one dedicates one's attention to the physical side. A few nights ago in a dream dimension I was with some persons whom I used to be with in Trinidad some 30 years ago. These persons were in bodies which were about 45 years of age at the time. Now they are deceased. One man said, "We had no idea this would happen to us. We should have listened. Now we are on the subtle side with nowhere to go. We cannot come back into the world because most of our descendants have no children. Up till now, we experienced no heavenly world as suggested in the Bible. What should we do?"

I replied, "Why worry about it? There is never any sense in worrying over things which are beyond control."

After this some deceased women appeared. They were the age of my mother while I was in Trinidad. They said, "How were we to know it would end like this. We trusted Christianity but there was no Christ once we died."

I told them, "Christ does exist but if He did not assist while you used a physical body, it makes no sense that he would do so hereafter. What can Christ do if one's focus is the material world? Break that focus and then perhaps Christ may have an effect."

The point is that we should change focus from the physical to psychic. We should do so while using the physical body. The strong focus into the material energy for whatever reason keeps us time bound.

How does one break this focus? One should meditate and practice withdrawing the sensual interest from this world. It is the interest and that alone, which causes one to be physically obsessed. In meditation one should identify the energy which pours out of the mind into the physical environment. One should capture that energy and retract it into the psyche. Naturally the habit is to put the self into physical involvement. That should be reversed. In meditation one should identify the outward focusing energy. One should arrest and retract it into the psyche. This energy is the energy of thoughts, the energy of perception, the desire to see outside the physical body, to hear outside of it and so on. Mostly it pours out of the head and chest of the physical body. For those who are intellectual it pours out of the head mostly. For those who are emotional it may pour out of the bosom mostly. In either case one should sit silently to identity and retract it. Do not feel that God will do this for you. You should do it. God left instructions in his intellect yoga explanation (buddhi yoga) in chapter two of *Bhagavad Gita*. The commitment for practice is with you.

Honest practice

One came into objective awareness with a leaky psyche. This is the first realization. One has a defective psyche. There is an idea that once we were perfect and now we are imperfect. Well that is nonsensical.

First realize that one is in a defective condition. Once one does this one will be more willing to work for improvement. Stop feeling or thinking that God will drop one's freedom on one's lap. He will do nothing. If for many millions of years past he failed to act, why would he do so now?

God does not need to help one bit more than he did by sending instructions with others or by leaving instructions in the *Bhagavad Gita*. We have to rise to the occasion and do whatever is necessary to get free from the defective psychology which we found ourselves to be.

The trick of tracking the moment of slipping into sleep is to develop psychic sensitivity. Because we are grossly aware, we do not have this sensitivity. It can be developed by being more attentive to the psychic side.

The problem is that to do so one has to decrease one's interest and particularly the intensity of interest in the physical side of life. There are two aspect to this, one is simply the interest and the other is its intensity. Intensity means the flowing force of the interest.

Each yogi should identity his or her interest in this world and then gage the intensity. One should apply a braking force to decrease it and eventually reduce it to nil.

Once this is reduced, one can apply the interest to the subtle side. In the case of the reservoir, merely plugging the hole permanently is not the solution because if you allow the tank to fill and if one does not use some water in the tank, it will overflow. In the same way as one conserves the energy on this physical side by withdrawing interest here and by reducing its intensity, one should direct the conserved interest to the subtle side. As one does this, over time, one will develop psychic perception.

More than likely it will not happen overnight. It will take place over a period of time. How long does it take to develop a human embryo? Everyone knows it is nine months but it is nine months after there is a productive sexual act. It may take nine years or nine days before there is unification with that sexual act. Psychic development takes time. One needs confidence in the practice. One needs patience to wait for the development which will come from the practice.

As one curtails the interest for the world, particularly as one decreases its intensity, there will be a proportionate psychic sensitivity. Do honest practice. Be willing to forgo some mundane interest. Reduce the intensity of interest in physical displays.

Last resort sounds

The best thing is naad sound because it is not produced by a human being. It comes from the other side of existence, the transcendental side. It is found in advanced meditation that naad sound is traceable to the transcendental side. It causes the yogi to develop supernatural and spiritual vision.

However if one cannot have naad sound because of the social environment, then some type of devotional or meditation music could be used. But one should not rely on that. After all what will one do if one loses the body, how will one get an electronic sound device hereafter? Will one find that in the astral world? Yoga is safe because it depends on one thing, the psyche. You can know for sure that one will have that after death of the physical body.

One who leaves the body and who is attached to gadgets may, after leaving the body, transfer to an adjacent astral dimensions in which there are sound producing devices. It is possible. However a yogi should not aspire for such astral places.

Early morning naad

High-pitched sound on the right, left or back of head is naad sound. There should be no doubt about it. It is not magic. Still, there is no reason to doubt it. To cause it to be magic, one should surcharge the subtle body with fresh subtle air. That is why pranayama breath infusion is necessary and is listed as the 4th step of yoga. If one does not surcharge the subtle body, naad sound may be boring, depressing or enjoyment-less. Because of the low energy in the subtle body, consciousness will be of a low frequency. When naad sound enters it will be heard in the low frequency which may be depressive.

To get the best out of naad, do breath infusion early in the morning. Immediately after sit and listen to naad. The quality of it will be attractive. It will bring peace of mind.

The location of naad should be known. Most of the time, it is near the right or left ear. At other times it will seem to be from all directions at once. In any of these circumstances, one should focus on it.

In some experiences it has a core or middle zone which is like a circle of about ¼ inch diameter. One should focus on that. One should enter that.

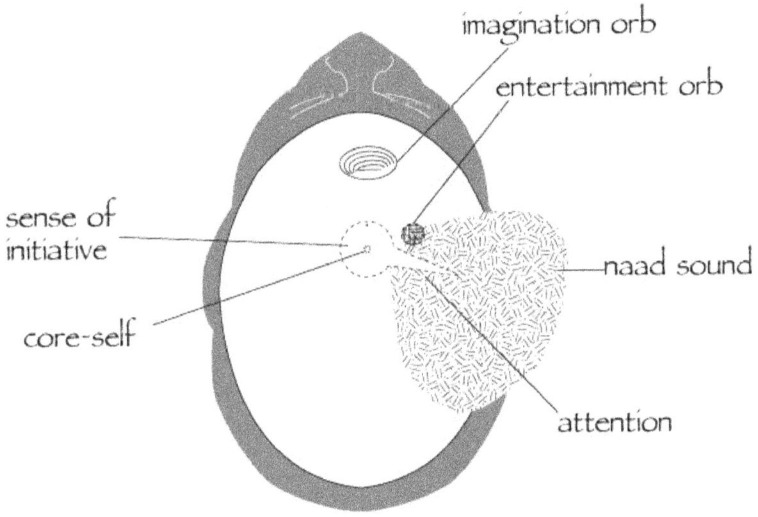

Quality of naad

At first naad sound may not have an attractive listening quality but as one deepens the meditation by steady practice, naad is noticed to change into a quality which attracts one's attention.

Take note of the force of the attention. Note that when listening to naad, one performs a switch in the direction of the attention. This attention force is the sense of identity that we use once we are in touch with a subtle object.

Why is that attention always peering forward into the frontal part of the brain? Why does one have to pull and redirected it to naad?

What is the pulling force? Why does one have to exert willpower and directional energy to cause the attention to turn about and focus on naad?

Self-realization is more than hearing from a spiritual master or reading about the teachings of Krishna. The effort at meditation brings one closer to getting firsthand experience of the subtle reality which surrounds us.

Attention composite

Just as a businessman or money-hungry person makes detailed observations of how he acquires and spends money, one should make detailed observations about the distribution of the attentive energies. Be very particular about it. In this way, one may realize the influence of the various subtle organs in the psyche.

The attention force as one normally experiences it is polluted. It is a composite energy, a mixture of intellect, emotion, sensual quest and bare identity. Each of these can be sorted but only after one acquires mystic clarity. For now one is confused about this, but if one practices sincerely, one may develop the insight.

Naad singular focus

Normally when one sees light, sunlight for instance, one assumes that it has a transparent color. If one directs sunlight through a prism, it shows various colors. The eye is unable to sort the combination. In the present state one cannot sort the various parts of the psyche which are in the mind. Instead it seems to be one energy. Beginning where one is with the polluted mental force, an attempt to focus on naad will result in one of three things:

- singular focus on naad
- singular focus on ideas in the front part of the head
- split focus which is spread to naad and to ideas in the head

This helps. It is part of the journey of getting clarity as to the psyche's operations. Three factors are involved:

- an observing iSelf
- an attention force which links the iSelf to what is observed
- an object of focus, in this case either the ideas in the head or the naad sound

We can develop this meditation by considering the iSelf. What is it? How is it connected to the attention force?

Can it reach an object of focus without using the attention force?

When by chance without effort, one finds that there is singular focus on naad, one should take advantage of the change in the noisy mental atmosphere. However along with this advantage, one should make a note of the flavor and musical pitch of naad. One should check the intellectual powers and the thought-force area in the frontal region of the head. Both the *Yoga Sutras* and the *Bhagavad Gita* instruct that a yogi should apply *nirodhah* to the mental and emotional energies. This means a complete checking of the whimsical automatic noisy operations of the mind, which are called *chittavritti*. When one finds that the *chittavritti* ceased of its own accord, one should note the state of the mind, so that one can learn to identify that state internally and also learn how to invoke and rely on it. One should train the mind to become addicted to that state, giving up its concerns for the noise show which usually occupies the mind.

When naturally without effort one finds the observing self focused on naad, one should remain in the focus and also make detailed observations of that condition, so that one can positively identify that and also be able to locate that at other times.

Many pious as well as the criminal-minded people, devotees of Krishna as well as followers of other divine beings like Jesus Christ, are versed with physical geography. They know how to move about physically. They know how to procure items for physical wellbeing. How many of them know about the psychic geography? If one is serious about a spiritual world, one should be familiar with it, just as one is acquainted with this physical environment.

Do not feel that God will give divine sight. Arjuna got divine vision because he had a mission to serve God in righteous duty as a member of a political family. That vision did not stay with Arjuna. Even when he had the vision Arjuna lost his bearings and could not tell where he was during the apparition of the Universal Form. If anything, one has to cultivate divine vision. One must make the effort to get it. Krishna left directions on how to develop it. If one rejects the directions and create other ideas, what will be the situation?

The directions for yoga practice are there. Why not follow? Why reject and propose that it is difficult? Give some time to it. Make the effort.

When making an effort to reach naad if one finds that the effort is unsuccessful and that one only reaches into the frontal part of the brain where the thoughts, sounds and pictures are created for absorption, one should conclude that the mind has a low charge of energy. It is natural to feel frustrated when one attempts to meditate. In fact many persons abandon meditation because of this.

There are three main ways to deal with this:

- ignore the ideas which flash in the mind
- confront the ideas and make an effort to terminate them
- confront ideas and sort them, dealing with meaningful ones and blanking out whimsical ideas

The other important attitude to assume is the one of:

I-cannot-meditate-until-I-relax-the-mind.

One should understand how the mind operates so that one can get an effective strategy to control it. One should observe its habits and find methods of curbing it.

What will happen if one practices ignoring the ideas in the mind? Will the mind cease crazy thinking patterns and memory simulations? Or will the mind continue regardless?

If one practices confronting the ideas and makes the effort to blank them, one should check the mind's resistance. Does the mind reenact a thought pattern immediately after one blanks it? Does the attention again move into the frontal part of the head in expectation of more thought flashes? Does the self forget its goal of pursuing naad? Does it remain in pitch black mental darkness in a void state?

If one confronts the ideas and sort them, dealing with the meaningful ones and blanking the whimsical ones, what does one do with the meaningful ones? Where does the energy of the whimsical ones go? Can one silence the meaningful ones and return to naad focus without interruption from the analytical ability of the mind and from the constant presentations from memory?

Split Focus

When meditating if one finds that there is split focus between naad and mental ideas it means that the attention energy is not strongly attached to either the frontal part of the brain or the naad sound. There is no strong influence coming from the senses or the memory, or even from the lifeForce.

Inner sensual concepts and feelings come from the lifeForce. Outer ones come from the procurement grasp of the senses, which hunt for objects of interest outside the body. Each student has the burden of sensual addictions to confront and eventually eradicate. One should defeat the sensual interest. Each person should work in the psyche to overcome the sensual addictions.

If one finds that the attention is equally pulled to both naad sound as well as to the mental noise in the front part of the head, then know for sure that the attention is in a state of indifference. But it will not stay in that state. Usually the attention reaches that state due to stupor, mental fatigue or just a repulsion from the frontal part of the head.

In any case, the objective would be to place the attention on naad sound. There should be some mental action where one turns the attention to the right or left and focuses it into naad sound or where one retracts it into naad sound.

This effort should result in one losing track in the frontal noise area of the head, such that memories, sensual information from outside the body and urges to use the body, cease.

Part 4

Kundalini location

The lifeForce or bio-psychic battery, the kundalini, is rooted at the tailbone of the spine. The sexual aspect of it is surcharged from the perineum area. Even though initially, raising of kundalini is done by the help of the sexual aspect, ultimately it is the aspect at the base chakra *muladhar* which must be curbed. Even though that is not as sensational, it is the root element *(mula).* In fact the sexual aspect will always enslave us if we do not get the root aspect under control.

After a yogi achieves what is called *urdhvareta,* he gets the authority to approach and fully subdue muladhara base chakra. So long as muladhara is not understood and as long as we are hypnotized by the sexual aspect we will be under the subjugation of kundalini. Enjoying kundalini by manipulating the sexual aspect is not the same as full control of it by a siddha. Books like *Hatha Yoga Pradipika* gave muladhara as the root chakra. If one feels that kundalini is rooted in perineum, it means that one is identifying kundalini as sexual potency. However, the definition from yogic tradition only places sexual potency as an aspect of kundalini which is curbed by celibate practices in special yoga techniques.

Detailed study of *Bhagavad Gita*

We should be aware of at least two bodies. Actually there are at least four or more types of bodies which we use but initially we should think of two bodies, otherwise the conversation would be confusing. One reason why languages developed was for clarity in communication, one human being to another. Language helps to remove vagueness, misunderstanding and other types of confusion.

Initially in yoga practice one endeavors internally to differentiate between the subtle and the physical bodies. One must also get clarity regarding how the subtle body receives energy from the physical one and how the physical is motivated by the subtle one. When you hear someone say that the soul transmigrates, try to understand what is being said. Actually most persons who say that, even most of the established gurus are mistaken. The reason is this. The actually thing which transmigrates is the subtle body. In fact without a subtle body the iSelf cannot transmigrate. It is only when the self is housed in a subtle body that it can transmigrate from one material form to another. By itself without a subtle body it cannot transmigrate in the material world. In fact the spirit cannot even sense, detect or even know a physical body unless it first energized into a subtle form. We need this clarity. It is not enough to believe what a teacher says. We should realize the truth through mystic experience.

Suppose I tell you that I travelled from London to Berlin at 500 miles per hour. You would immediately understand that I used an aircraft. You would not think that I ran at 500 miles per hour over land and sea, nor that I flew like a bird. The fact of the matter is that the aircraft moved at that speed, not the human being except that the aircraft carried a stationary human being who sat in it with seat beats. We need information about the various bodies so that we are not harboring misunderstandings about the self and its conveyances. The capability for travelling at 500 miles per hour belongs to the aircraft, not to the human being. Even if we strap a jet engine to a human body and propel that through the atmosphere at 500 miles per hour, the human form would not survive if it was not encased. The capability for moving from one old or damaged body to a new one, belongs not to the self but to the subtle body which the self inhabits.

If one studies the human situation, one will see that mostly we came to this level called modern civilization by studies. It did not happen by chance or by nature. If it were left to nature we would still be cave people for the most part. The development of the human being came by deliberate study, not by all the population but by the leading minds. As we applied ourselves to the natural world, we may do so to the supernatural and spiritual realities.

Take a look at *Bhagavad Gita*. Arjuna wanted to get some basic idea of why he should commit himself to duties as a prince in a ruling family. Just for that he listened to a lecture and saw a supernatural apparition. It is complicated. Some people feel that a detailed study of *Bhagavad Gita* is unnecessary, but I disagree.

Subtle body control

Asana yoga postures have value because the subtle body is hell bent on having physical forms. If it were not for that tendency of the subtle body we would not be in a physical environment. It is not something that we desired on the spiritual level of existence. The physical plane came about because of our affiliation with the subtle form. Suppose one has a donkey, which is hitched to a cart. You ride in the cart as the donkey pulls it. The donkey's force is harnessed for you through leather straps which are tied to donkey's body. In that case whenever the donkey goes one will go. If one is unable to control the animal, one will have to go wherever it selects.

As a human being you wish to travel on a smooth path. One is not interested in other donkeys nor grass, but since one cannot control the animal one has to go wherever it takes one. In the same way we transmigrate not by selection but by the tendency of the subtle body. Until one controls that one will enter life forms on the basis of the urges of the subtle form.

Because we are under the control of the subtle body's needs and habits, we cannot control it by willpower. We must study its habits. Then as we gain leverage we may adjust it.

Since the subtle body is focused into the physical world, especially to acquire physical species, we should begin controlling it by gaining control of the physical body. This is an indirect method but it is effective because we are not in a lordship position just yet. Right now the subtle body has us under its control. Just as for a slave, it is foolish to rebel, if he knows that the rebellion will fail and the master will retaliate severely, it is best to study the master's habit and figure a strategy.

Why does asana postures give us some control? The reason is simple. The subtle body is attached to the physical system. Suppose you want to control a donkey. If you find that you cannot direct the animal from in the wagon which it is hitched to, one may find other methods such asking one's friend to walk ahead of the animal with a bucket of oats. Or perhaps one may ask one's friend to take a she-ass ahead of the animal on the path. The point is that if you cannot control the subtle body directly you should begin where you are and control it partially.

Subtle world pleasures

Asana postures give control of the physical system. Since the subtle is attached to the physical, one may gain indirect but effective leverage of over the subtle body. Postures are not a waste of time, otherwise they would not be recommended by Patañjali and even by Krishna who mentioned it in chapter six of *Bhagavad Gita*.

To gain a handle of the subtle body, one may begin with control over the physical system. In the subtle world, the pleasures are so intense that it is hardly likely that we can begin by controlling anything there.

There are many who feel that they will gain control if only they could get to heaven. This is mostly wishful thinking. The subtle situation is so intense that it is near impossible to control anything there. The pleasures are so overwhelming that even the best pleasures in this world are more or less like displeasures in comparison. There was a nice example of this in the life of Buddha. One of his younger relatives was reluctant to leave family life because he was recently married. He had an attractive young woman for a wife. His enjoyments with her were incomparable as far as he was concerned. When he was explained to Buddha that it would not be possible for him to abandon her and enter the monk life, Buddha revealed some girls from the heavenly planets. After displaying those celestial women, Buddha asked the young man if he would leave the family life to enter the monk discipline, provided that he would get one or more of those heavenly ladies. The man consented and left the home life.

When Buddha asked him what he taught of the beauty, love and pleasure of the earthly woman, the guy said that she was worse than a monkey when compared to what he saw in the heavenly world. One should not think that in heaven one will have control. If one cannot control the physical system, one certainly will not control anything in the heavenly world. One will be overwhelmed.

Physical / subtle interaction

Yoga postures make the physical body less resistant to the energy which is supplied to it from the subtle form. When the resistance of the physical form is decreased, the subtle body doles out less energy to maintain the physical one. The result is that the subtle body is able to use more of its energy for its own sake. This increase in the energy in the subtle body, is experienced by the person as increased psychic perception.

Let us study this by using the situation of an electric circuit. If you create an electrical circuit which uses a small generator as the power source and if you apply too many appliances to the circuit the generator will cease working.

On the other hand if you add just enough appliances to keep the generation from failing, you would have in effect limited the use of the generator's power. If for instance you remove one appliance, then the other appliances which were getting the minimum amount of current for their ideal operation, will begin to work more efficiently.

In this example the subtle body is like the generator, and the appliances are like the various organs in the physical body. If for instance we damage a person's lung with a chemical gas, the subtle body cannot keep the physical one in order. The subtle body will cease interactiong with the physical body. We will declare the physical one as dead. When the subtle body ceases working in reference to a physical form, the subtle one does in fact, remains in the subtle world but its connection to the physical one is terminated, just as when a breaker is flipped or when a fuse is blown, the power supply is disconnected from the appliance and the appliance no longer functions.

If instead a surgeon fixes the damaged lung, there will more efficient usage of that lung. The subtle body will not have to supply excess energy for its operation. If you can do postures and if these improve the condition of the physical body, the subtle one will appreciate that. One may experience that appreciation as increase psychic perception.

Subtle body loves physical form

Postures make the physical body receptive to subtle energy shifts. This should be rewritten as:

Postures make the physical body a more efficient mechanism, such that the subtle body can operate it with the minimal energy, and thus the subtle body maintains a higher charge of energy.

There is another dimension to this, which is the effect of the postures on the subtle body. There is a direct effect. When the physical body acts, usually the subtle body mimics the behavior. When the physical body walks, the subtle body does the same. It would be impossible for one to move the physical body without moving the subtle one. The two forms are interrelated.

If you join a blender to the circuit, and if you turn it on, the current from the generator will flow through the blender's wiring. Thus in a sense the operation of the blender is also the operation of the current from the generator. You cannot run the blender unless the generator powers it. In fact just as a physical body may be incapacitated, so a blender will simply sit on a shelf if one does not plug it into a circuit and turn on a switch, which allows current to flow. The operation of the blender alerts us to the fact that there must be a current supplier. The movement of a physical body tells us that there must be a subtle form which motivates it.

During postures, one moves the physical and subtle bodies. The idea that postures only directly affect the physical body is false. In fact one cannot do a single act with a physical body unless one uses the subtle one to energize for action. When one does postures in the physical body, the subtle one simultaneously commits the same movements.

When one does postures, one improves the condition of the subtle body. Even so however, the main benefit is in the physical form. The subtle body is so focused into the physical form that if you improve the physical body, that will have a greater impact on the subtle one than if you were to work on the subtle body alone without affecting the physical form.

Psychic perception

Psychic perception means the extra-sensory functions of the subtle body. We currently use some functions of the subtle body. The physical body operates because it is enthused by energies of the subtle form. However, many of the abilities of the subtle body are muffled by the physical one. When those other capabilities are used, it is called psychic perception.

The relationship between the physical body and the subtle one is similar to the relationship between a glove and the hand which is inserted into it. The glove appears to have life but if you take the hand out of it, the glove will exhibit no activity. When the hand is in the glove, the movements of the glove indicates the life of the hand but it appears that the glove itself has life. As far as the hand is concerned, it enjoys the protection of the glove.

For the sake of protection, the hand uses the glove but the hand loses some sensitivity when it is gloved. If the glove is removed the hand can directly hold items and can directly get information about heat, cold, softness, and hardness. Unless we get some experiences with the subtle body directly, we cannot understand it. So long as we are totally reliant on the physical form, our idea of the subtle body will remain incomplete.

Psychic perception is important because it is frees one from the limitations of the physical body. It makes one understand that there is a subtle form which is superimposed into the physical form and which will live beyond the physical system.

In the example of the glove, we can say that all human beings are born with gloves on their hands. With yoga practice there is an effort to remove the glove. To get confidence in the ability to survive the physical body, one should experience the subtle body by itself without its unity with the physical system. When this is done it is called psychic perception. If you remove the glove and touch a surface directly, that is compared to psychic perception.

Subtle body recognition

Psychic perception is the first step of confidence in knowing that one has and can use a subtle body. After all why do we speak of spiritual life if it will manifest only after we leave these bodies at death. Why is it that we have no spiritual perception and must wait until death to get it? That makes no sense.

Strive for spiritual perception now. Begin with subtle body perception which is not spiritual perception but which is a step in the direction of using a spiritual body. Many hints are given in *Bhagavad Gita* about spiritual vision and about types of supernatural perception. Arjuna was awarded supernatural perception and saw the Universal Form but that vision did not contain within it the ability to see the spiritual form of the four-handed divine beings. For that higher vision, Krishna gave Arjuna another vision after terminating the supernatural perception which gave Arjuna sight into the plane of existence of the Universal Form. From this we can surmise that these visions are different. Each requires the use of a different non-physical body.

The first step is to access the facilities of the subtle body. At present the average human being and even the average spiritual seeker, cannot correctly sort the subtle body from the physical one. Scriptural knowledge and allegiance to a spiritual teacher, will not necessarily allow anyone insight into the attributes of the subtle body. However the confusion between the subtle and physical needs to be eliminated. We can gain clarity in the matter by turning attention to the development of psychic perception which is the use of the subtle body when it is freed from having to power the physical form.

Because the subtle body is presently preoccupied with supplying energy and attention to the physical system, the subtle form is unable to operate its facilities in full. This can change if one reduces the energy consumption of the physical form.

Astral details

The subtle body is frequently not under control of the self. The subtle body acts independently, going its way, such that during dreams and astral projection one is unable to stop it from drifting through dimensions. In a dream when approaching a window, one may desire not to crash into it but one may be unable to stop the astral form from moving towards the window. This means that once deceased, one may not control the subtle body.

The statement made about being like a ship cut loose from its moorings applies. The physical body is like an anchor or like a hitch connector for the subtle body. The self relies on the grossness of the physical plane to stabilize and restrict the subtle body.

In the subtle world, in the dream world, everything is wayward and flimsy for the most part. One is unable to control the psyche there unless one is an expert mystic. This has little to do with religion. People who are religious suffer from the same problems with the subtle body just as they do with the physical form in terms of its health, it needs for pleasure and other such demands.

In some dream states and astral realms, any attempt to make a sound results in no sound being manifested. In those places the sound ability and hearing sense are absent. To understand this, we may consider going to the bottom of a pool and trying to alert another diver of a danger. Because the water does not allow human voice transmission talking to the person would not be effective. Sound is transmitted in water but not in the same way as it does in air. Unless the physical body is equipped with a special sound device it cannot emit sounds in water which would travel through the medium of that liquid.

There are many dimensions. Each has special facilities, special advantages as well as disadvantages. During astral travel, one may become aware of someone who is in another dimension. If one tries to communicate with that person, one may find that there is no response because the perception may be available only in a one-way direction, whereby the other person has no cognizance and hence would not respond due to lack of perception of anything besides the dimension which he is in.

While in a dream state or in an astral projection it is possible to see someone's astral body while that person is physically active, this may be confusing for the astral projector because his insight may not reveal that the astral form of the person seen is mimicking that person's physical system and is not independently acting in the astral world. That person is physically focused unlike the dreamer who is psychically or astrally obsessed.

This means the physical person is unaware of the astral one and cannot know that the astral one is cognizant of both astral and physical acts due to the fact that the astral body of the physical person mimics exactly what the physical body does. The physical person may have ideas about the astral observer but those thoughts would not be coherent and would not reveal that the dreamer is perceptive. The physical person may dismiss the thoughts as being only ideas in the mind.

Physical objects have subtle forms. In the astral world there are many persons who lost the physical body and who did not take a baby form for one reason or the other. Many live in a mockup situation which they created mentally out of subtle elements and which looks exactly like their lifestyle before death. Sometimes one meets a long departed relative in the subtle world. One finds the person living in a subtle residence which is a replica of the residence the person inhabited before the physical body died. Such persons may remain in those astral buildings for as long as it takes for them to contact the next parents to get baby forms.

Subtle body improvement

The difference between a subtle experience while using a living body and the final subtle experience before leaving a just-about-to-be-dead body, is the fact that when the body is healthy you return to it by the impulsive operation of the lifeForce. When the physical body dies, one is desynchronized from it forever.

While the body is alive, one resynchronizes into it after sleeping sessions or after dreams but when the body finally dies, one is unable to do so. The system which causes a person to awaken on this side of existence in a living body, loses the power to use that body when the body dies.

In that sense we are dying and going to the hereafter every time the body sleeps but we do not realize this. All the same one will not improve the perception of this merely by the death of the body. If one is unaware of this now, if this is vague and ill-defined, it will be like that if the body dies. This is why it is important to improve subtle perception now.

We use the same subtle body now which we will use at the time of the physical body's death. The subtle status will not suddenly improve merely because the physical access is terminated. The subtle system will be the same. If we do not improve it, if we do not become conscious of its operations now, the same ignorance will prevail at death.

Nothing clears up merely because of death. It did not clear up in the past. This is why we can assume that we have the same vagueness and ignorance as before. Now that the body is healthy and we can consider this and endeavor to remove the ignorance we should make efforts to improve the subtle system, the psyche.

Unless we find some way to interfere with the subtle form in our interest, it will continue in its impulsive way during life of the physical form and also after death.

Hereafter communications

The communication is ongoing between one person's mind and another's. The problem is the interpretation. When the thought of one person hits the mind of another, the receiving mind may buffer, accept or change the message. The coreSelf usually receives the information after the mind processes it. Because of this reliance on the mind, one is in a fix to get clear transfer of an idea from one person to another.

There are several issues.

- How does a coreSelf receive information from its mind?
- How does it use the mind to transmit thoughts or ideas?
- Is it possible for a coreSelf to transmit directly to the core of another person, bypassing the minds altogether?
- Is it possible for the mind of a person to transmit thoughts or ideas independently, without being prompted by the coreSelf?

Some people assume that the self is detached from the thinking processes of the mind, that the self exists independently. They question if the self is the recipient of ideas and thoughts.

Even between two persons who are in the same dimension, for example in this physical environment, there is confusion, even if they are in the same room using the same language, even from the same cultural background.

A person with psychic sensitivity would have no problem communicating with someone who is departed. If that psychic was to lose his or her body, the person would be able to send messages or to speak into the mind of any person who is physically based.

However, usually, departed persons are unable to communicate with family and friends. They do however remain in close contact with such acquaintances. That is how they capitalize on their pious activities and again take birth through family or friends.

Even though the conscious mind of a departed person may make no coherent contact with anyone who has a physical body, the lifeForce is able to communicate with the lifeForces in the bodies of relatives and friends. It is the lifeForce connection, which enables the departed soul to appear again as the child of a man and woman who has an obligation in the family.

One who leaves a body soon comes to accept the astral situation, just as when people migrate or are forced to leave a country, willingly or unwillingly, they soon adapt to the new location. There is a tendency for convenience. This operates on the principle of adjusting situations or being adjusted to situations. Due to that, persons who are quarantined in the astral world because of losing a physical body, soon learn how to live there in that purely psychic existence.

In the astral world one can invent things on the spur of the moment even to create a climate of preference, all by mental power. If in this world, I told you that I created a house mentally and that its temperature was always the same optimum climate which I prefer, you would not believe, but in the astral world that is possible because of the powers in the subtle body and due to the responsiveness of the astral substances. People, after leaving a dead form here, may create horrible or very nice or even mediocre environments for themselves on the purely psychic side of existence. However, that does not last, because the subtle body hankers for physical participation. Hence the need for physicality through development of an embryo.

The other headache people face when they are in the astral world is its flimsiness and its super-temporariness. In the astral existence, even though you can create many things mentally, the duration of those things is quite limited according to one's mental capability. It is such there that an object one may create will disappear as soon as one's mind is unable to keep the conception of it or as soon as one's mind loses the focus on that conception.

In this world if you build a house and provided no one burns it down or bulldozes it, it will remain standing for years, even if one does not live in it and even if one forgets about it. Even though the house could not be built without one's mental ideas about it, one's desire for it and the labor in producing it, still once it is built it is no longer reliant on you. If you leave it and forget about it, it will still exist. It will not disappear into thin air. But in the astral world, once one's mental idea relaxes, the house would immediately disappear.

This is one reason why one became attached to this physical situation. One values its permanence in comparison to astral reality.

Right now millions of dollars are being poured into sending probes into outer space only for the reason of finding another physical planet which could support human bodies. Nothing was found even for millions of miles away. Scientists are worried that we would have nowhere to go if a meteor hits this planet or if there is some other disaster like a nuclear war or a planetary ice age.

Behind this big worry is the fact that unless we can transfer from the astral world into an environment like this, we as a race of beings would be frustrated if we are left with only the astral level.

They are many people who think that they would be better off in heaven. Some think that they would do better going to live with Jesus Christ. Others think that it would be better to live with Krishna or Shiva or whoever. Some others think the same about a paradise where the last prophet resides. This is mostly irrational because the truth is that until we can wean ourselves from the need for physical existence, the flimsy subtle body, the causal body and the very super-flimsy spiritual form will mean a disadvantage for us.

If you cannot realize the subtle body, there is absolutely no chance of realizing anything that is subtler. We are condemned to the state of always wanting physical forms. A human being is so built as a living unit, that he or she will continue taking confidence from believing in this or that God even though in fact, the person does not qualify for living in the realm of that divinity.

If one cannot master the subtle existence which is adjacent to this physical world, it is hardly likely that one would remain in any such heaven even if one got a glimpse of it while using this physical system or at the time of death. We have to individually become transformed before heaven would become a permanent reality. The attachment and need for physical existence has to be removed before one can progress to any subtler place permanently.

In the majority of cases, one relies on relatives to get one the next body. There are exceptions as for instance when one takes a body on the basis of a friend. Usually one takes a body on the basis of a relative and even if it finalizes that one emerged as a son or daughter of a former friend or of a relative of a friend, it is usually done through a relationship with a family member who contacts and maintains an association with that friend.

Always try to see this matter from the position of the lifeForce in the body. Why? Because the lifeForce has the upper hand in regards to the physical form. For instance sleep is mostly controlled by the needs of the lifeForce and so is sexual indulgence and many other functions of the body. Even in the *Bhagavad Gita* there is a verse which alerts us to the fact that a self-realized person does not get involved with the eating, sleeping and other routine functions of the psyche. But there is more to it than that. The atma or iSelf does not conduct the functions. They are produced by the lifeForce.

In canto four of *Srimad Bhagavatam* in the story of Puranjan, Narada explained that in the end, it was the lifeForce which was important. The soul and the intelligence, along with all other subtle mechanisms of the psyche were reliant on the lifeForce to make a decision to leave the body. For that matter, the coreSelf was unable to do anything but to follow the lifeForce when it left the body.

This means that mostly, we transmigrate on the basis of the selections of the lifeForce and its habit is to rely on relatives. It does not matter what I think or what you think. The lifeForce has the tendency to rely on relatives. It will do that after it leaves the body.

Observe an infant and one may understand the lifeForce. The infant, even though his or her self had a body in the past, has no awareness of the previous status. It acts in a way which makes it obviously that he or she is dependent on its mother or guardian. This posture of the child is the posture of the lifeForce.

In the story in the *Srimad Bhagavatam* regarding Ajamila, he appealed to his son at the time of death when he was frightened after seeing ghost police who wanted to arrest his subtle body. Ajamila had friends just as we do, but still he called his son. That is the posture of the lifeForce. It has its own way of operating.

There are exceptions where a person takes a body on the basis of a connection with a friend but in most cases, it is done on the basis of the relatives of the body. Stated differently, the actual item which pursues the next body is the lifeForce. It does this on the basis of its own way of operation, not on the basis of what the person thinks or conceives.

The system of relatives, that network of genetic connections, is conducted by the various lifeForces for the most part. What has the coreSelf to do with it, except that it has to accept liabilities for social actions when nature decides to dish out reactions and make compensations?

Naad / sound of bells or crickets

Naad is a sound which comes from the other side of existence, the transcendence. If one links to it, that makes it easy to reach that side. The big value of it, is that we do not have to chant it. We do not have to create it. It is there. We need only link to it. When one links it causes the development of supernatural and spiritual sight.

By an instinct of good fortune, one may have a habit of listening to naad. That is a valid meditation. Sometimes when hearing naad, people get bored because they are in a lower state of mind while hearing it. Naad is enriching but if one hears it from a low mental state, it may be boring.

Just as if someone is anemic, that person has to take proteins to regain health, so if one listens to naad one's consciousness becomes enriched. One moves up bit by bit to higher planes of consciousness. The quality of one's consciousness is upgraded more and more as one listens.

The basic level of naad is similar to the ring of tiny bells (ding ding ding ding ding or a continuous eeeeee). This is its lowest plane of manifestation but when the mind is on a low plane of consciousness, this does not have a pleasant or endearing ring. However if one moves up in consciousness, it has an attractive tone. While listening one may be distracted by external noises or by memories or mental images.

The meditator should train the mind to take naad as a priority sound, such that the mind develops a habit of ignoring other sounds which it is attached to but from which it derives no upliftment.

While listening to the base level of naad, it may change to other more pleasant and secured tones. This change signifies a change not in naad but in one's existential position. As one changes from one level of existence to another, one perceives the tone of naad that is heard by persons who exist in those other dimensions.

Intellect Yoga

Intellect (buddhi) yoga as given in *Bhagavad Gita* is a practice which was taught by Krishna to both the jnana yogis and the karma yogis. When taught to the karma yogis it is presented as an advanced course but to the jnana yogis it is an intermediately course.

Karma yogi students like Arjuna got that skill through the practice of elementary meditation and with that psychological proficiency, they applied this to their life in the cultural world, as government officials. The proficiency of this shows by the person's detachment when as an official, he deals with citizens. Krishna requested Arjuna to exhibit intellect yoga proficient during the Battle of Kurukshetra. The meditative yoga practice of a karma yogi ends with this intellect yoga. Its result in his life is highlighted by detachment and impartially.

The course of jnana yoga is not for socially active people. Jnana yogis are not involved like government officials. They master intellect yoga and then do more advanced meditation practice. They are not culturally involved. Hence they have time to do deeper meditations which requires complete detachment from social circumstances.

One should regard any type of yoga, except Patañjali yoga or ashtanga yoga, as yoga plus something else. First we begin by defining yoga. To do so we refer to Patañjali. He gave an eight part system which is ashtanga yoga.

Bhakti yoga is bhakti + yoga. Intellect (buddhi) yoga is intellect + yoga. Jnana yoga is jnana + yoga. Atma yoga is atma + yoga and so on. In this way we will be clear when we use these terms. If we agree that bhakti yoga is bhakti + yoga, then what is bhakti? The answer is that bhakti is bhakti. The next question is: Can someone reach perfection by bhakti alone. The answer is that scriptures give examples of persons who did just that, persons like the gopis.

Then there is another question, why do yoga and then apply it to bhakti if one can reach perfection by bhakti alone. The answer is that it would be foolish to do yoga and apply bhakti if one can reach perfection by bhakti alone. Therefore we accept that only those who will fail at bhakti by itself should do yoga and then do bhakti.

But then there is another question as to why even bother with yoga. The answer is given by Krishna when he defined the purpose of yoga as ātmaviśuddha.

तत्रैकाग्रं मनः कृत्वा
यतचित्तेन्द्रियक्रियः ।
उपविश्यासने युञ्ज्याद्
योगमात्मविशुद्धये ॥६.१२॥

tatraikāgraṁ manaḥ kṛtvā
yatacittendriyakriyaḥ
upaviśyāsane yuñjyād
yogamātmaviśuddhaye (6.12)

tatraikāgraṁ = tatra — there + ekāgram — single-focused; manaḥ — mind; kṛtvā — having made; yatacittendriyakriyaḥ = yata - controlled + citta — thought + indriyakriyaḥ — sense energy; upaviśyāsane = upaviśya — seating himself + āsane — in a posture; yuñjād = yuñjāt — should practice; yogamātmaviśuddhaye = yogam — to yoga discipline + ātma — self + viśuddhaye — to purification

...being there, seated in a posture, having the mind focused, the person who controls his thinking and sensual energy, should practise the yoga discipline for self-purification. (Bhagavad Gita 6.12)

Therefore if one finds that his or her bhakti is not getting perfection, that person may do yoga for purification of the psyche (atma), the psychological energies. Then when yoga is successful in that purpose, he or she can apply bhakti and get the desired success.

What is intellect yoga?

That is the application of yoga practice to curbing and purifying the intellect. The Sanskrit is *buddhi* yoga. It has to do with that one aspect only, the intellect. It concerns nothing else. It is the process of curbing the intellect by meditation techniques.

The mastery of the 5th stage of yoga, *pratyahar*, and the beginning practice of the 6th stage, dharana, concerns intellect yoga, the curbing and subjugation of the intellect in the subtle body.

Independent mind

Is it possible for a coreSelf to transmit directly to another core of another person, bypassing the minds altogether?

Is it possible for the mind of a person to transmit thoughts independently, without being prompted by the coreSelf?

Presently due to our condition, it is not possible to communicate directly nor to by-pass the mind apparatus. This is because the coreSelf is surrounded on all sides spherically by the attention energy, then by the analysis energy, then by the organized and random sensual energy. Each core is surrounded by that. When one self tries to relate to another, the relating self expresses itself through the medium of those energies and the self who is being contacted only receives the information through the layers of his or her energies. In every way, each communication is conditioned. If a person can purifies the surrounding layers, then it would be possible to express purely but even then, unless that person was in a world in which everyone else was that pure, the communications would be distorted since everyone else would be subjected to their impure psychic means of receiving the information.

To explain the surround energy, Krishna said.

धूमेनाव्रियते वह्निर्
यथादर्शो मलेन च ।
यथोल्बेनावृतो गर्भस्
तथा तेनेदमावृतम् ॥ ३.३८ ॥

dhūmenāvriyate vahnir
yathādarśo malena ca
yatholbenāvṛto garbhas
tathā tenedamāvṛtam (3.38)

dhūmenāvriyate = dhūmena — by smoke + āvriyate — is obscured; vahnir = vahniḥ — the sacrificial fire; yathā — similarly; 'darśo = ādarśaḥ — mirror; malena — with dust; ca — and; yatholbenāvṛto = yatholbenāvṛtaḥ = yatho (yatha) — similarly + ulbena — by skin + āvṛtaḥ — is covered; garbhaḥ — embryo; tathā — so; tenedam = tena — by this + idam — this; āvṛtam — is blocked

As the sacrificial fire is obscured by smoke, and similarly as a mirror is shrouded by dust or as an embryo is covered by skin, so a man's insight is blocked by the passionate energy. (Bhagavad Git*a* 3.38)

इन्द्रियाणि मनो बुद्धिर्
अस्याधिष्ठानमुच्यते ।
एतैर्विमोहयत्येष
ज्ञानमावृत्य देहिनम् ॥ ३.४० ॥

indriyāṇi mano buddhir
asyādhiṣṭhānamucyate
etairvimohayatyeṣa
jñānamāvṛtya dehinam (3.40)

indriyāṇi — the senses; mano = manaḥ — the mind; buddhir = buddhiḥ — the intelligence; asyādhiṣṭhānam = asya — if this + adhiṣṭhānam — warehouse; ucyate — it is authoritatively stated; etair = etaiḥ — with these; vimohayatyeṣa = vimohayaty (vimohayati) — confuses + eṣa — this; jñānam — insight; āvṛtya — is shrouded; dehinam — embodied soul

It is authoritatively stated that the senses, the mind and the intelligence are the combined warehouse of the passionate enemy. By these faculties, the lusty power confuses the embodied soul, shrouding his insight. (Bhagavad Gita 3.40)

The mind can transmit thoughts and ideas independently but only because it accesses the energy of the coreSelf. It so happens that the core in its present condition is unable to stop the mind from absorbing power. Could you imagine the sun stopping us from taking its heat? It is not in a position to exhibit such control and similarly in the conditioned existence we are not positioned to stop the mind from using the self's energy. The mind is not reliant on the self for promptings. In fact most of the promptings come from the feeling energies, memory and intellect.

Samadhi process

Unless one practices repeatedly for many years, spontaneous long-duration transcendence focus states (*samadhi*) may occur infrequently and not by command. Only by repeated practice and repeated study of the operations in the psyche, the chittavritti interactions with the intellect, memory, sensual energy (kundalini) and sense of identity, can one master it to do as desired. Otherwise it is a matter of good luck.

Consistent practice is not about controlling what happens. It is about studying how consciousness becomes altered, and then learning how to put the self into a position which facilitates higher experiences.

A simple feat like conscious astral projection is difficult to master and difficult to make happen. When someone says that he can induce transcendence focus, my tendency is to harbor doubts. If someone cannot remember the subtle experiences in dreams every night when the astral body separates from the physical one, that person's claim to higher states should be questioned.

One consideration is that to be in transcendence one must shift or be shifted to a higher plane. One's consciousness must de-focus from this level. By Krishna's mystic power Arjuna shifted but later when Arjuna asked Krishna to do that again, Krishna said that originally it occurred by special yoga. Krishna did not repeat the magic. Please read the *Anu Gita*. Yogis who shift to higher planes do so on the basis of consistent efforts or their existential superiority as in the case of Krishna.

If a yoga guru said that after practicing a certain method for forty days, one will enter into a high transcendence, we may question that teacher about the details of the method. When Krishna went to Upamanyu Rishi and asked for a method of speaking to Shiva, the Rishi gave a technique which was effective in a set number of days. In *Srimad Bhagavatam*, Dhruva got a set process. He got directions from Narada. It is best to study the instructions and see if one can follow the methods.

Recently in Florida, a man did bhastrika pranayama breath infusion under my supervision. He entered a transcendence stupor during two successive early morning sessions. He remained in it for about three minutes the first day and then for about two minutes the second day.

With each person it is different. Of course stupor transcendence (jada *samadhi*) even though it is a type of nirvikalpa *samadhi* is transcendence in spiritual ignorance which lacks insight and discernment.

In the 1960s and 1970s Yogi Harbhajan Singh taught bhastrika breath infusion to many persons. Some attained transcendental states in every session. It is not a secret. It is based on doing intense breath infusion and then arching the small of the back, so as to release the charged kundalini shakti into sushumna nadi subtle spinal column. Kundalini then rushes into the brain. When it strikes the intellect, that adjunct is shifted to a higher plane, even to the brahman level. But kundalini cannot remain near to intellect because of its habit of living separately at the lower end of sushumna nadi. One must repeat the practice daily and then over time, according to the amount of subtle impurities one removes, one can cause kundalini to come up permanently.

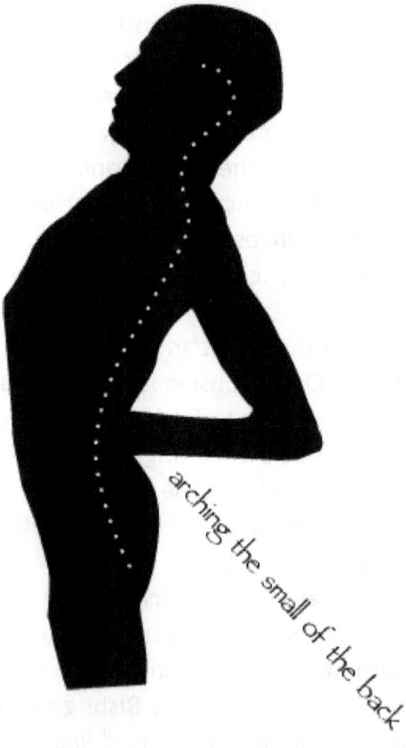

To learn of the habits of kundalini, one should read canto four of *Srimad Bhagavatam* where the classic description is given by Narada to King Prachinabarhi in the story of Puranjan, where kundalini is represented as Protector of the Queen. One should also read the *Hatha Yoga Pradipika* which I published as *Kundalini Hatha Yoga Pradipika*.

There are different definitions of transcendence states. Patañjali listed two categories but if one checks his *Yoga Sutras* closely one will see that there are many types of those two big headings.

For the ultimate or highest transcendence (*nirvikalpa* or *savikalpa*) according to Patañjali, one has to bring *chittavritti* to a complete halt (*nirodhah*). That means a disengagement of the coreSelf's interest in its adjuncts.

Kundalini location

Where is the kundalini situated when the subtle body separates from the physical one in an astral projection or dream state?

Kundalini is the essential motor which operates the physical form. If kundalini is fully separated from the physical system, that body will die. Of all the factors which must be in a physical body for its survival, none is as important as the kundalini energy, not even the coreSelf.

When kundalini is fully separated from the physical body that form is pronounced dead. When a body is in a comatose state or when a body is unconscious, it is operated by and kept alive by the presence of kundalini. Even if the intellect is disabled, still the body can live if there is a kundalini. If the observing self is not aware of the body, still the body will live, if the kundalini is active in it.

Kundalini must be kept connected to a living body once that body is created, or else there will be death. If someone is revived from death and is again conscious in a body, it means that kundalini was not fully disconnected from it. A full disconnect of kundalini causes the organs of the body to be in a condition from which that body cannot again be used by kundalini. Hence kundalini, when it finds itself without a body, develops a craving for another physical form and enters into conditions of physical life where a new body can be created around it and for it. These conditions of physical life are the energy of the parents of that would-be embryo form.

Where is the kundalini situated when the subtle body separates from the physical one in astral projection or in dream states?

Obviously, the answer is that the kundalini must be located in the physical body when the subtle separates from the physical form. If it is not connected into the physical form, that physical body will die. The coreSelf will discover that it cannot again awaken physically. On this side of existence people will realize that the body is dead. They dispose it.

Kundalini's predominance

If kundalini is part of the subtle body why is kundalini not stationed in the subtle form when it separates from the physical body in dreams or in astral projections?

Kundalini is created initially in the subtle body. But Kundalini has an attachment to the physical life which is created around it in the body of the parents.

There is a difference between the kundalini in our bodies and that in the bodies of the angelic beings who are permanent residents in the heavenly locales. Their kundalinis do not have the inclination for lower births in physical bodies. Their kundalinis do not have the tendency to be physical. Our kundalinis are differently oriented and have the desire for physical bodies. Even if we go to heaven we would not remain there permanently because of this tendency in the kundalini.

Since our kundalinis have that tendency, when it formulates a physical form, it is attached to that form and is not easily released from it. Once a physical body is created, the kundalini takes a position in the root place within it. This root place is the original starting point of the form when it was in the father's body as a mere sperm. While the physical system lives, kundalini does not leave the root place, even during astral projections.

Kundalini is a permanent component of the subtle form but it is essential to the physical system as well. This is why when there are bad dreams, one awakens quickly in the physical body. It is because the physical system is the pivotal point of one's existence while one has a physical form.

Once the physical body dies, however, the kundalini is forced to remain only in the subtle body but it does so with a longing for a new physical form and with resentment for being deprived of the physical system. This becomes an obsession. Thus one again takes birth through other parents after a long or short period living as a ghost, according to availability of parents and according to one's submissiveness to nature.

Unless one can purify the kundalini, one cannot be elevated to any other place, not even to the heavenly worlds which are close to this earthly place in vibration what to speak of a spiritual world which is far removed from this place in terms of its frequency level.

The other thing to consider is this:

Even though the subtle body can survive with just a little energy from the kundalini force, the physical body must have much energy from it, otherwise it will suddenly collapse and die. This is because kundalini operates the lung system. The heart is the motor pump in the body but the lungs are the main fuel source. Food is a supplementary fuel source. Kundalini has to stay in the physical body to keep it breathing, but it does not mind doing that because its orientation is for physical life, especially for sexual intercourse.

There is sexual intercourse in the heavenly world. In fact in that world the sexual intercourse is much more pleasurable and intense but the kundalini prefers physical indulgence because of the denseness of such contact. Thus again unless we can change the habits of kundalini and get it to be elevated in its needs, we will be condemned to taking birth repeatedly just as we did before.

Kundalini is not concerned with the hope for salvation. It is not concerned about which God one worships. Its main concern is to continue in the course of repeated birth and death. Unless something changes radically in the individual psychology, one will again take another body, just as haphazardly as one took the present one.

coreSelf / mind communications

- How does a coreSelf receive information from its mind?
- How does the coreSelf use its mind to transmit thoughts or ideas?

First we need define the word mind. Mind is a compartment, a psychological space area. Its location is the head and chest of the body. It is mostly felt in the head, but it pervades the entire body. Mind is a container, a compartment in which we experience thinking and feeling.

In some usages of the word manas, which means mind in Sanskrit, the mind is defined in a different way as the senses, for instance, or as the intellect for instance.

Here however I use the meaning of the mind as a compartment in which thinking and feeling takes place. If one has a cell phone the case is the container of the components. The gadget is called a cell phone but the inner parts have different names such a microphone and screen. The mind is the container. Within it there are thoughts, feelings and other subtle objects.

For this definition I will rephrase the questions:

- How does the coreSelf receive information when it is in the mind?
- How does the coreSelf use the components in the mind to transmit thoughts or ideas?

Within the mind there are thinking energies which manifest as images. The intellect however is viewed as a video screen in which images are seen, sounds are heard, and thoughts are constructed and displayed.

In yoga one realizes that the core is surrounded by an energy. This energy is experienced as attention or will power. It is experienced as a sense of identity, as ego, as an iSelf or as an observing identity.

Since the core is surrounded by this attention energy, it stands to reason that anything which reaches the self must travel through that energy.

In the space of the mind, in the compartment that is the mind, there is a coreSelf which is surrounded by the attention energy. Besides that there is an intellect which reasons and presents conclusions to the self. In the intellect, thoughts are created either by promptings of the self or as ideas which came from memory or which are formed by what is perceived by the senses.

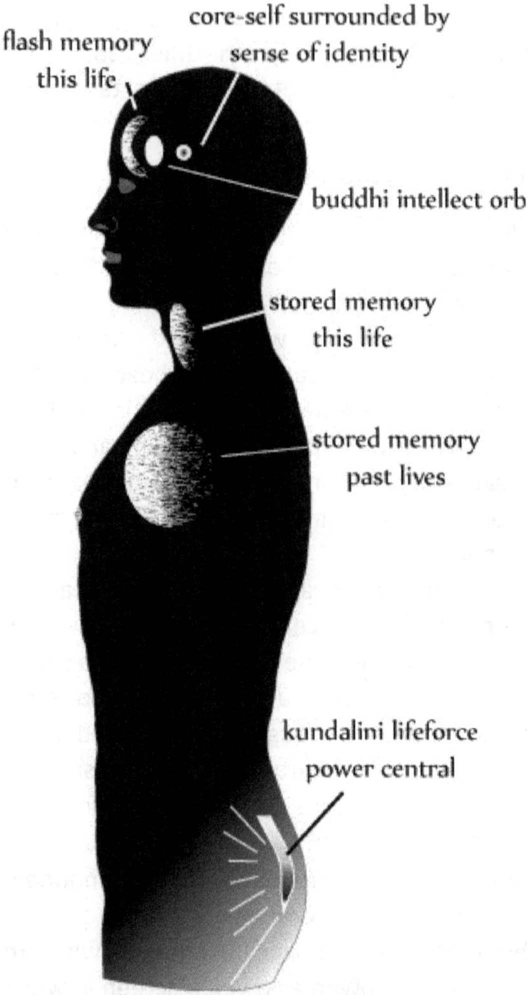

The self receives this information because the information travels to the core through the attention energy. It travels rapidly. It travels so fast that usually the self does not perceive the transit. To the self it is instantaneous.

Within the compartment of the mind, the self interacts through the attention energy and perceives what is drafted in the intellect. If we remove the intellect or disable it, the self would not perceive thoughts, images or ideas. This is what happens when someone is in a coma. This is what happens in unconsciousness. By using a drug, doctors can disable the intellect which results in the self being deprived of perception. Under the circumstance, the coreSelf is present but it is subjective only. One may exist without being objective to oneself, without knowing oneself.

The self inadvertently uses the components in the mind to transmit thoughts or ideas? This happens by an involuntary process. Ask a four year old child to explain how he or she walks? The child cannot explain this satisfactorily because walking takes place by involuntary actions of the body. One exceptional child may study the muscular operations and give an explanation.

When the self wishes to communicate, it sends an interest though the attention energy. When this energy strikes the intellect, the intellect creates thoughts and sounds, which then motivate the body to act.

Just as one uses gadgets which one did not create and which one cannot manufacture, so one has a mind with automatic mechanisms. One cannot understand the psyche but one can use it. Just as when one speaks into a phone it captures the message, converts it and then transmit the converted frequencies, which is received by another phone which in turn converts what it receives and which issues a sound similar to the one initially spoken, so the mind operates.

In summary:

The coreSelf as a component within the mind, views mental and emotional constructions on the screen of the intellect, which itself takes cues from the senses, the memories and the feeling-energy of the lifeForce. When the intellect is hit by energy from the memory, senses, lifeForce or attention energy, it creates depictions accordingly.

Physical/subtle confusion

Someone shared that he was in bed during the night, when he found himself floating above the bed. He could see his wife's shape beneath the blankets, but next to her his body appeared to leave an impression in the bed but was completely invisible to him. His first thought was one of panic, that he was dead. But that seemed to disappear because a peculiar logic said that since he could not see his body it could not be dead. He felt he had a body that could float in air.

This experience may be repeated when one leaves a physical body at death. Because one is not familiar with the operation of the subtle body, and due to focusing on the physical side during the life time of the now dead body, one is left with a feeling of life as being only physical. Hence when one finds the self with only a subtle form, one feels that subtle existence is physical.

This astral projector automatically thought of his partner. Similar concerns arise at death, where one thinks of a relative, most likely a spouse or child. This thinking though natural is the main cause of taking another body haphazardly without due consideration of what will happen to that new form in terms of its parents and life opportunities according to the time and place in which it takes birth.

The panic of being dead, occurs as a regular incidence for those who loose physical bodies. Why panic? Because generally one has made no preparation for being deprived of the body. One developed no connections in the subtle world of the hereafter. When death comes, one panics because one is locked out from many reliable relationships in this world and one developed no connection with anyone in the psychic situation hereafter.

The dreamer above felt a particular logic of the intellect. Using the conclusions presented by that, the panic feeling went away as he felt that his floating body was his physical form. This was of course an inaccurate logic used by the faulty intellect. In the first place the floating body was not the physical system. It was his subtle form.

The body of his wife which he saw was not her physical form but was her subtle form which was interspaced into her physical body, which he could not see due to his subtle body‘s eyes being limited to a certain subtle dimension.

Silver cord

If kundalini stays behind in the physical body, when the subtle body is separated in astral projections or in dream states, what force operates the subtle body at that time?

During astral projections, kundalini stays in the physical body. It has no choice. Its fusion into the physical form begins as soon it is unified into the emotions of one of the would-be parents. It must stay in the physical body until the physical apparatus dies. However kundalini is required for operating the subtle body as well. During astral projections when kundalini stays in the physical form it sends energy for the operation of the subtle one.

Some mystics admitted seeing a silver cord connecting the displaced astral form to the physical one. This silver cord which is a subtle energy pulsation, is energy of the lifeForce being sent to the subtle body. At the time of death, the kundalini force is shifted fully into the subtle body and operates in it without connection to the physical one.

The kundalini gives energy to the subtle and physical bodies simultaneously. When the physical one dies, the kundalini has only the subtle body to energize. During astral projections and in dream states, the kundalini delivers energy to the separated subtle body through an astral tubing, as a silver-blueish cord.

To further identify how the lifeForce which remains behind in a sleeping physical body, operates, consider this:

Jack went to a horror movie. Later that evening, when he fell asleep, he found himself in a cemetery in the city where he lived. The monster in the movie appeared. Jack became so frightened that he screamed in the dream. He turned to run away. Just then he awoke in a cold sweat as his physical body.

In this example Jack as the subtle body was retracted into the physical form by the kundalini force. It instantly retracted the silver cord because it sensed danger through the fearful feelings which flushed through Jack's subtle body.

Predominance of lifeForce

- Since kundalini is subtle in what form/nature does kundalini rise?
- Kundalini is very attracted to the sexual propensity, how is it different from sexual energy?
- How does kundalini ascend through the chakras in the spine?
- How does kundalini become energized or de-energized?
- If when the subtle form is separated from the physical one, the lifeForce remains anchored in the physical system, does that mean that the mind too remains in the physical brain? What of the analytical powers of the mind? What of the coreSelf?

These are the main parts of the psyche.

- coreSelf (atma)
- sense of identity (ahankar)
- intellect (buddhi)
- mind chamber (manas)
- lifeForce feeling energy (kundalini)
- sense detection organs (indriyas)
- memory (smrti)

These comprise the psyche or subtle body. That subtle body is a container for the components.

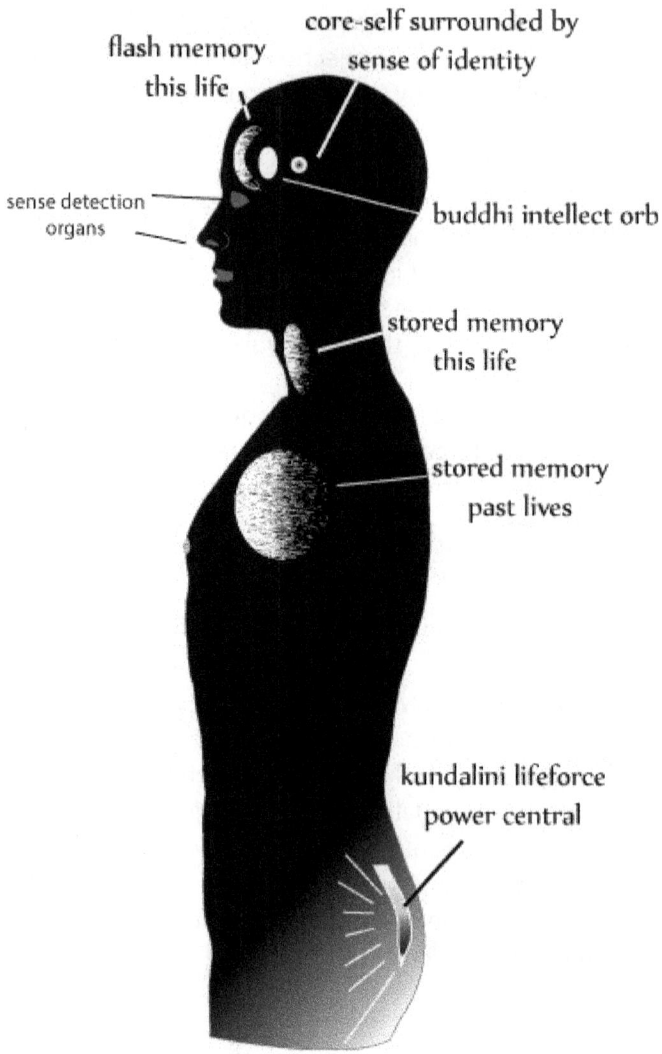

Of these the only one which is very crazy over a physical body and which remains anchored in that body throughout the life of that form and which never leaves that body until the time of death is the lifeForce.

The intellect is centered on the coreSelf. When the core is displaced from the body, the intellect becomes displaced. It leaves the physical body when the subtle body leaves the physical form. The self also leaves the physical body when the subtle form is separated. The only one of these components which stays behind in the body is the lifeForce. In the story of Puranjan,

Narada explained to King Prachinabarhi that the city policeman, the guardian of the psyche, the lifeForce, protected the material body single-handedly without assistance from any other component in the psyche.

If however the body dies or if the organs age beyond repair, the lifeForce is forced to vacate the form. Then and only then will it become completely dependent on the subtle form for a residence. But even then, unless it is highly energized and reformed, it will assume an embryo.

Currently, while one has a healthy physical form, the lifeForce instinctively pursues its next parents. This is the primary reason for sexual attraction.

Kundalini yoga certification

Some students who become certified in kundalini yoga instruction, abandon the practice or do it infrequently. It begs the question as to how someone can get a certification for kundalini yoga and not be in the habit, whereby the practice continues no matter what?

We must accept that a certification does not mean that the certified person is a persistent yogi. Certification is good. The ambition to acquire it, along with the training received is an asset. The problem is persistence.

To get a certificate one has to be at the place of the teacher who trains, at least for a few weeks if not more, but once the trainee leaves, what association is required for supporting the practice?

I will explain this by citing something personal. This happened in 1973.

I lived at Yogi Bhajan's kundalini yoga ashram in Denver, Colorado. As things worked out I had to leave Denver. Before I left, an ashram leader from Kansas City visited the ashram. He invited me to come to the Kansas City since he needed assistants. His idea was to open a vegetarian restaurant. In Denver there was such a restaurant which Yogi Bhajan opened and which was named *Hanuman's Restaurant*.

Thinking that I could help him and being snubbed by the other single men in the ashram, the person from Kansas City asked me to come. I made no pledge to him.

However I had to leave Denver to meet a friend who was stationed with me in the Philippines while I was in the US Air Force. That friend called and invited me to travel around the USA with him in a Volkswagen van. This was a popular thing to do at the time. Anyway I went to Kansas City, but on the way there, I nodded out at the wheel of my car. It overturned on the highway and was partially wrecked.

Although it was a good thing from the spiritual viewpoint, physically it was a hassle because a person who saw the accident called the police who came and issued a reckless driving charge. I drove the wrecked vehicle into a small town and paid a fine. After this for about two hours the damaged car ran but then its engine quit. It was just rebuilt before I left Denver. I then sold the car as a scrap metal. Catching a Greyhound bus, I arrived in Kansas City. The ashram leader was disappointed that my car was wrecked because he did not have a vehicle and had planned to use it. In any case, he rented a small store front and was busy trying to organize to open the restaurant.

In the meantime, my friend from Baltimore who wanted to travel in the USA arrived. After talking with him I decided to hit the road. Needless to say the ashram leader was highly annoyed and complained that he singled me out to assist him with the ashram and especially with the restaurant.

About three years later, I heard that he left the ashram and became a Christian, giving up the kundalini yoga practice. The point is that association is important. That ashram leader met a Christian woman and under agreement for being with her, he became a Christian.

In a way association is everything. We can hardly sustain any spiritual practice without association. In every spiritual group this is stressed.

Special note:

Though unfortunate from the physical angle, the automobile accident was auspicious spiritually. When the car left the roadway, it went into the air for a time. It landed on its top in a flat area. From the time the car shot into the air and overturned, my subtle body separated from the physical form and remained floating looking down on the scene. I saw the physical body crumpled in the smashed car. At the time seatbelt laws were not mandatory and hardly any driver used them.

As soon as the vehicle landed on its top and stopped moving, my astral form was again fused into the physical body. I got it out of the car, rolled the vehicle over and started it. The police officer drove up and presented the reckless driving citation.

Kundalini / sexual energy

If one is deprived of the material body kundalini will be all psychic. Otherwise so long as one has a physical body, kundalini is subtle partially. The subtle body can exist without a physical form for some time, but it has this need to experience physicality. It is equipped with the capability to use physical energy.

When kundalini loses a physical form, it maintains its ability to run such a form. As soon as it acquires an embryo, it develops that form. When one has a nervous sensation or when one has a sexual sensation that is the power of kundalini.

Kundalini is attracted to sexual potency but not for the reason of mere enjoyment. It is for the reason of survival. Through sexual potency there is reproduction. Kundalini has interest in physical life. It invests in sexual energy since that is the main gateway to reproduction. Kundalini is itself the principle which generates sexual energy. It is the enjoyer of that energy.

Kundalini movement

Because it is forced to by the accumulation and thrust of physical and subtle air energy, kundalini ascends the spine or moves into another part of the body during kundalini yoga practice.

Normally kundalini will rarely move up the spine. There are cases where a person who sat for a long period and stood up experienced the rise of kundalini. Others experienced it while walking, sitting, lying on a bed or by doing another activity like climbing at a high altitude.

However during pranayama breath infusion, the accumulated air energy hits the kundalini at the base of the spine and affects its condition in such a way as to make it move. This movement is called the rising of kundalini. It is really a movement from its root place at the base of the spine.

It is important to take the mystique out of kundalini by understanding that the world pursues sexual pleasure which is a manifestation of the aroused kundalini.

Kundalini regeneration

Kundalini's regeneration is the same as the body's regeneration. It is the same as sexual energy regeneration. If for instance one has an intense sexual involvement and much depletion of sexual force, one feels exhausted. To regenerate, one must rest and eat nutritious foods to accumulate the hormonal fluids. Kundalini is regenerated during resting periods. It is enhanced by food nutrients and fresh air.

Once the physical system dies, kundalini lives on subtle air and no longer relies on physical food, at least not until it grows an embryo. Kundalini is depleted by over-exertion, too much sexual intercourse, low protein diet, lack of fresh air, lung diseases and such factors.

Kundalini energy system

When Kundalini is expressed sexually, we interpret that as sexual force. Hardly do we realize that this is the same psychic energization which is required for spiritual purposes. When kundalini is expressed as exhaustion, we interpret it as tiredness, laziness and stupor. When kundalini is expressed as extrovert awareness we interpret that as enthusiasm, energization and keen awareness.

Kundalini has methods of regenerating the body. We become familiar with this system in the form of being awake and falling asleep. During sleep kundalini does most of its maintenance work for the body. We can assist it by giving more fresh air, by restricting the food we put into the body, by having prompt evacuation, by regulating the thoughts expressed in the body, by making sure that the body is properly dressed if we live in a cold climate where the body may be subjected to freezing. These are some ways in which we can facilitate kundalini.

If one does not assist kundalini it will penalize one for the neglect. If for instance one does not increase the fresh air that enters the body, it will be drowsier. The body will assume a more depressed attitude. If the body is not maintained efficiently its mental and emotional condition will deteriorate. That will affect what we achieve and how we aspire for fulfillments. This is because kundalini will have less energy to expend in the maintenance of the brain. If we express much sexual energy, kundalini's supply of energy will be diminished. It will have a lower energy supply. That will result in more drowsiness, sleep, discouragement for spiritual pursuit and a general malaise towards life.

The main body is the subtle one. Self-realization has its basis in realizing that subtle form. If one does not realize the self in the subtle body in dreams, one's basis spiritual life is nil. One may go to a church or temple. One may chant holy names. One may meditate or whatever. If one does not realize oneself in the separated subtle form, it means that despite the religious beliefs one self-realization is not progressive. To increase subtle views, one should give kundalini more energy. Kundalini's expression of energy into the separated subtle body is boosted if one gives it the extra energy. If not the recall of dream experiences, the awareness of the subtle body's separation from the physical one will be absent.

According to yoga the standard method of giving kundalini extra energy is pranayama breath infusion which despite its mystique, is simply a charging of the physical body with fresh air. That means the subtle body and the physical one. When one breathes both bodies are charged simultaneously.

There is sometimes an argument as to the most effective method for spiritual life. Someone says pranayama. Someone says chanting. Someone says prayer. Someone else says something else. The arguments are irrelevant because the real issue is what gives the result. If my method causes increased dream recall and consciousness of the separated subtle body, it speaks for itself. It does not matter which method is used, provided there are results.

Spiritual life, knowing that one is not the physical body, begins with the most basic experience of being separated from the body consciously. By convention if a body sleeps, people assume that the sleeper has no coherent consciousness. If a body snores, people assume that it is the self which snores. Is that factual in every case? The sleeper may not be present in the snoring body? The snoring activity may be based on the position of the neck and the way the kundalini maintains the body during sleep. If someone finds a body dead, the assumption may be that the person died while sleeping.

If it was absolutely true that the person sleeps every time his physical body slumbers, then no one would recall dreams. No one would have experiences of being separated from the physical system. The realization is that sleep is particular to the physical body. The subtle one does sleep as well. It may even sleep while the physical one does the same. Still the two bodies are distinctly separate.

A tired physical body does not necessary coincide with a tired subtle form. When the physical one is tired the subtle body may be energized. Or conversely the subtle body may be tired and the physical body may be energized.

Meditation protection

The mind is easily influenced but that observation should result in more care in dealing with it. One result of meditation is the self's knowledge about the mistakes, misjudgments and prejudices of the mind. In other words, once you notice that the mind is weak, the next step is to subsidize the mind in order to increase the application of willpower. Supposed you hire a servant to carry the heavy packages which come to your home. This will make it easy since you will not have to fetch deliveries.

Suppose the servant gets a hernia after lifting a package, what will you do? Obviously the convenience of having the servant will be offset by the expense of his medical care. At that stage one may reconsider. One's insurance company may make a stipulation whereby the servant may lift a maximum of seventy-five pounds and must get assistance for heavier packages.

Since the mind is weak, the coreSelf must subsidize it. We know for sure that we cannot use the material body forever. It will last some years, say fifty, forty or one hundred. The mind however will remain with us for millions of years. It is in our interest to assist it.

The mind will not become perfect overnight, nor by God's magic wand. With help from God through applying God's instructions from books like *Bhagavad Gita*, each person should endeavor to improve the functions of his or her mind

Since the mind is easily influenced the coreSelf will have to apply itself to monitor the mind. Meditation may give protection from being influence towards the negative, but only if the motive for meditation concerns that. Motive has much to do with what we derive from meditation.

Be reasonable with yourself. Some things which we do which are not helpful in meditation, are necessary features while living in the material world. Take for example listening to the morning news. If you live in a war-torn country and meditate there, you would be foolish not to be aware of the news as that may result in your death. In such situations, listening to news is important but it should be regulated and prioritize. We should not be lazy in scheduling what we must do for social well-being and what we should do for spiritual advancement.

We rise early and meditate for a certain time, then listen to news to get a briefing of what happened in the social world. We do both things without allowing one to eliminate the other. If there is political disorder, there will be no time for meditation. If one become too much absorbed in political affairs, one will have no time for meditation. We should limit interest in political concerns.

If one has a strong motive and if the meditation is fulfilling it will be self-sustaining. If it is not fulfilling, if one does not feel that one makes progress, it is likely that one will cease meditating. Buddha for instance began to meditate because he shied away from the hassles of life, incidences like old age, disease, death. That was enough to keep him meditating until he got enlightenment. If one's motive is strong, one will continue the practice. If it is weak, other habits will replace the need for meditation, unless one reinforces the resolve.

If one lives with people who are not concerned about meditation, who do not think that it is a big deal, one should not expose the meditation practice to such persons, but should instead be humble by meditating without their knowledge. Do not boast about it in their presence since they may feel intimidated or offended and then will exude a negative energy which may enter the psyche and depress one. It is better to live in peace with others by not mentioning meditation and doing it in one's private time quietly and secretly.

Morning bath

Cleanliness is one of the approved behaviors for yogis. But in the advanced states, this cleanliness takes precedence on the subtle plane. A yogi should focuses on psychological cleanliness. He should lose the obsession with physical cleanliness which is a hallmark of traditional religious principles.

Psychological cleanliness is done chiefly by doing pranayama practices. Just as in physical cleanliness the flow of water is necessary to flush dirt and debris, so in psychological cleanliness fresh air is necessary to flush negative subtle energies.

In higher yoga unlike traditional religion and external yoga, one clears internal pollution. That is the obsession. The morning bath which is a glorified and highly acclaimed activity in traditional religion, loses importance. It is done but only as a secondary activity. The yogi knows well that no matter how much he cleans the external parts of the body, if his psyche is not in order, if that is not cleansed internally, the external bath only contributes to false confidence and insincerity.

The afternoon bath however has importance to a yogi, since then he may clean the body after a day's activity and especially he should change the clothing and not reuse towels. Since the old vibrations from a previous use will affect the subtle body, the repeated use of a towel is not good for a yogin. If one can, one should use small towels once and then clean them. Using a large towel discourages cleanliness since one is apt to use it repeatedly for many days before it is laundered.

If the yogi takes a bath after the afternoon session of exercises, his body will remain clean during the night due to the fact that he is not involved in daily activities and is not socializing. In the morning the main duty for external cleanliness will be to thoroughly wash the mouth, the hands and the face. The main objective in the morning is to do postures, breath infusion and meditation and then make notations regarding the practice. However there is no rule that says one should not take bath. Everything one does takes time. If one has one or two hours in the morning for free time, how much will be used for bath. How much for meditation?

There is a stipulation concerning morning bath. If one does Deity Worship or attend a temple program one must by all means take bath. Hence the allowance about not taking bath has more to do with isolated ascetics who focus completely on internal yoga, and who do not attend temple functions and mix with the public.

Get in the habit of thinking of internal bath, inside the psyche. Water and soap is irrelevant for that. As far as the physical body is concern, prompt evacuation is more important than bath. Suppose one is a fanatic about bath but one's bowels do not move efficiently, then why the pride in such bath, since in the body the stool lingers?

Diet

In the evolutionary process of life, diet is always a factor. If you eat something it affects you. It does not matter if one is Baptist or Muslim, yogi or devotee. Whatever a person eats has some small or large effect on his or her behavior. We know that alcohol affects the behavior of the body. If I am a priest of the highest order or if I am the Pope of the Catholic Church even, if I sit and drink one pint of whiskey, it will affect me. I cannot claim that my system or religion is so great that even if I drink two pints of alcohol at one sitting, it will not affect me.

Diet can aid or negatively affect a person's spiritual life.

Each yogi should locate foods which enhance practice. We should avoid foods which are negative for practice. We should study how the schedule of eating an approved food affects practice. For instance vegetarian food is better for spiritual practice that flesh foods but if one is a vegetarian and one eats late at night that will be negative for practice. At first if one grew up on flesh foods, the change to vegetarian diet is a big accomplishment, no matter if one eats at midnight, but as one continues, one may realize that the midnight schedule is not the best for progress.

It is what I eat and also when I eat that approved food.

I grew up in Guyana. At the time the habits of some people was to have tea and bread in the early morning, a heavy main meal at noon and tea and bread again in the early evening. That was it. This I feel was introduced by the British in some colonial territories. It may be traced to the eating schedule they established during the times of slavery. Slaves are not permitting to eat when they like. They must accept what is given, just as animals which are confined by human beings.

Even if through slavery that schedule was imposed on my body's ancestors, still when looking at it from a yogic point of view, it is a good schedule. The food itself was not vegetarian. That part was bad, but the schedule is ideal for yoga practice. Later as a young man I came to the United States. I adopted the American standards which meant eating a main meal at night. Even vegetarian eating at night does not go well with meditation practice. Such practice is best at the wee hours of the morning. If the stomach is full and the intestinal system is occupied processing food, the mind and lifeForce will inevitably be occupied with that which will disrupt efforts at meditation.

But this is not a believe-and-be-saved religion. Each person should come to the conclusion for himself or herself and apply effective methods to curb counterproductive habits. It is about enforcing methods of improvement to accelerate practice.

Mind improvement

Improving the quality of the mind, refers to improving the quality of energy the mind uses. This is an entirely different approach to spiritual progress, but it is an old system taught in the *Yoga Sutras*, and in *Bhagavad Gita* and similar texts.

We may understand this by studying what happens when a person switches from a flesh eating diet to a vegetarian one. In the switch the energy source changed. Can a person's character change by changing the person's energy source? Will a person be kinder and less vicious if we change his diet?

A few weeks ago I was in Florida. Someone offered a meal which was described as veggie chicken. I never heard of it but I assumed that it was soy bean curd molded into the texture of chicken. My guess was correct. Since the host made special efforts to prepare the meal, I did not refuse it. But what is the fault with such a meal?

It is this. If in fact the vegetarian diet changed my character, why do I need to have a meal which has the connotation of flesh forms? The soy curds were molded into chicken legs. They were colored like fried chicken.

The meaning is this:

If I took to vegetarian diet and still feel that I must see and bite into the leg of a chicken, my character was not impacted by the vegetarian diet. Thus I will strive to resume flesh eating. The first step in that direction is to use the soy curd in the shape of the desired flesh.

If I gave you a method for improving the quality of the mind and if you find that your character remains the same and that the unwanted habits are reasserted, it means that the method is ineffective. It is either that the method is invalid or the application is incorrect.

According to *Bhagavad Gita* chapter 6 verse 12 and chapter 5 verse 11, the methods for psyche purification are yoga practice and the performance of cultural activities.

The process which we recommend is the one for mind improvement according to the yoga system, which means getting a higher grade of energy into the mind. The direct method for this is pranayama breath infusion. Once the mind is upgraded, the meditation can begin in earnest.

Hashing-over tendency

Evening meditation is different to the morning session. This is due to the change in energy when the sun sets. Evening mood is different in the atmosphere. Human beings have a change of attitude in the evening. As the planet rotates and the sunlight is spread to various regions, it leaves some regions devoid of sunlight. This changes the energy level.

At night the main problem for the meditator is the preoccupation with the day's activities. The mind operates on the basis of preoccupation, hashing over what took place. At night the mind seeks to reserve itself for thinking of what took place during the day.

Since the mind has this preoccupation tendency, it must be dealt with on a daily basis. One should do so without resentment for having to perform the task of disciplining the mind each day. Sometimes one gets the idea that one should not have to do this and that one should be free from having to hassle with the mind, but this feeling is misleading. One should ignore it.

Within human nature there is a feeling that everything should be suitable to each human. This is natural even though it is not possible. Nature itself gives this feeling. Nature itself frustrates this idea. We should understand this and ignore this feeling which will continue in human nature. Every child who is born, feels that the world, the sun, the moon, the planet earth, the weather, the nurse, the doctor, the mother, the father, everyone, should create suitable conditions for his or her development. This attitude should not be taken seriously.

In a child's body, I used to find that when it was time to dress on Sunday for going to church, I was not happy about it. It felt like a humbug activity. But when as a teenager, I was allowed to go to the cinema or to go to parties or to meet friends, I found great happiness in getting dressed for these occasions. Why is that? What is the difference? Where did the reluctance or encouragement originate?

A man who plans to meet a woman, whom he is attracted to, does not complain about having to comb his hair and dress attractively, before going to meet her. Why is this?

It is because his senses gladly engage in the activity in anticipation of the resulting pleasure derived from the woman's company. Similarly a woman who is about to meet a man whom she hopes to be her husband will go to great lengths, wear uncomfortable shoes and clothing and not complain about it. In fact she tolerates the inconveniences because she feels that her enhanced appearance will facilitate her union with man. Again why is this?

Why is it that we gladly go through difficulties for one type of accomplishment, while we turn a negative attitude towards other achievements and think that life is unfair in those regards?

Dealing with the stubborn tendency of the mind to hash over the day's activities may be a hassle but it is vital if one wishes for success and cumulative progress in meditation practice.

Settlement of mental ideas

This is advice on how to handle ideas before doing the evening meditation. The first part is to consider that the hashing over process is the preliminary or clearing stage of the meditation. This is so essentially a part that if one forgets to do it, the mind will remind one by engaging one in musing.

Usually as one sits to meditate, the mind begins hashing current views and unfinished business from the day's involvement but the self looks at these images and ideas helplessly and at a loss of what to do. It is like if you sleepwalked into a theatre or in front of a TV screen and began looking at a sequence of videos without even realizing that you were moved to a theatre seat or couch.

However eventually one will realize that one is engaged by the mind. One will gradually recover discrimination. At that point one should confront and sort the ideas.

Since the mind will invariably do this, it is best to beat the mind to its own game by doing this as the preliminary stage of meditation. The example of a nursing mother may suffice. Usually an infant cries if it requires milk, but if the mother is attentive, if she feeds the infant before he or she gets the food urge, the infant is better behaved, is less irritable, is less insecure and gains a reputation as a pleasant baby.

Similarly if one beats the mind to it, by first attending to the ideas, one will have more control over the sorting and processing of thoughts. The mind will be less insecure, less erratic.

Sorting the ideas means to put each in one of three categories.

- ideas which are settled but which linger in the mind
- ideas which are not settled but which cannot be settled except in the future.
- ideas which can be settled immediately.

An example of an idea which was settled but which lingered in the mind, is the case of the man who met his girlfriend for a lover's session. They met. They had the affair. They enjoyed. They were not seen by anyone. Since it was over there is really no need for them to think further about it. But since it was enjoyable, the mind rehashed it repeatedly in an attempt to re-enjoy a second, a third, a fourth, a fifth, a sixth time. This type of idea should be cleared because it will divert the mind from deep meditation

An example of an idea which was not settled and which can only be settled in the future is the case of the man who met his lover in a lonesome place and who was told by her that until her father was dead, they could not be married nor meet again.

In that case, there is no need for the mind to rehash the subject matter unless news comes of the father's death. Hence the mind should be diverted from thinking of the woman and the love affair. It should be conditioned only to be alert for news about her father's death.

An example of an idea that can be settled on the spot is the case of the young man who met a young lady in a lonesome place and who was told that her parents approved of the relationship. They were permitted to marry at any time. In this case to get this subject out of the mind, the young man needs to leave aside the attempt at meditation. Instead, he should go to the place of the young lady and with her parents' permission, take her to a Justice of Peace and take the marriage vow. Doing this will settle the matter. The mind will no longer bring up the issue in future meditations.

The whole point is that one should attend the mind, sort its ideas, put them into perspective and treat them according to urgency and the possibility of fulfilment. By doing this one frees the self from having to deal with hashing and rehashing ideas which frustrate meditation.

Contrast: morning/evening mind content

Due to the influences which prevail morning meditation is different to evening sessions. While in the afternoon one is concerned with ideas which recur from a day's activities, the early morning meditation is not plaque with as much mental chatter. Instead it is concerned with dream and subtle world experiences. Most beginners may not remember dreams.

Meditation means the elimination of ideas, at least that is the suggestion of Patañjali, but the mind is concerned with generation and preoccupation of ideas. If the mind is a cleared of ideas, it will immediate begin an investigation to find some cause for ideas.

This leads the mind in two directions, either to go to the memory and resurrect a skeleton of a past occurrence or to configure fresh information from the senses, by focusing though all or any one of the five senses.

In the morning we have the added advantage of having rested the material body and the subtle form. As such the mind space is usually quieter, less active in terms of pursuing random thoughts and more conducive to quiet blankness. In the afternoon this advantage vanishes, leaving the meditator to battle with involuntary thoughts which intimidate the self and bulldoze it with various sequences.

The key to a successful meditation is to first eliminate the thought patterns. If you only afford a five minute meditation period, what will happen? Will you get beyond mere thought clean-up? More than likely one will not. Still the effort to do this will result in success over time. With persistence, one should become more efficient at the clearing process.

Stuck in time

Last night in the astral world, I was with some persons whom I knew some twenty years ago. These were persons who left old bodies for one reason or the other. Each one lived in a dimension which is adjacent to this physical realm. Each lived in an astral residence that was a mirror image of the place that person resided before being deprived of the last body.

They were stuck in time, in the sense that their development, even their cultural development stopped at the point at which they were, when they left the last body. Each wanted to discuss the terminal illness of the last body. As far as the subtle body was concerned, it assumed the shape of the old adult form but it was relatively healthy having recovered from the terminal illness which affected the last physical one.

I wanted to share the fact of reincarnation but their minds were just as resistant to the idea as it was while they used the last physical system. There was no change in demeanor. I could not convey that they were departed. They knew that they were departed but the knowledge of it was mentally suppressed.

These persons await the next birth opportunity. Due to the conditions of their astral forms, they cannot enter into any would-be parental forms as yet. In time the conditions will change. Their astral forms will merge into the psyche of would-be parents. Then each will again come out as a baby, for a new history in this world

Early morning attitude

Morning meditation begins with the evening set up. If the evening set up is not under control and is not designed to facilitate the morning session, the morning program will not be as productive.

The morning attitude is based on the evening program. If the evening attitude is not a preparation for the morning session, the morning session will suffer.

There is a question.

What should I do to improve the morning session? How can I change my attitude towards the morning program? I am reluctant to practice due to a negative attitude towards rising early.

This negative attitude is a malaise suffered by most human beings. It is not particular to one person. We experience this due to the sluggishness of the body. Each person who wants to rise early has to be motivated. Many human beings suffer from this and yet many rise to procure a livelihood. Why do we do this?

If you understand what motivates you to rise, as for example when one has an important appointment or when one desires to meet someone who is dear, then one can study the behavior towards morning meditation and adjust the attitude.

This is personal. Nobody can do that for someone else. It is the relationship between oneself, one's motivational energies and one's objectives. If one studies that, one may develop a self-therapy which causes a change in attitude towards the morning sessions.

Preparation for morning meditation begins the night before. If the schedule and attitude was not set favorably towards early rising, the negativity towards it may increase.

One should recline to bed as early as possible. One should agree with the psyche that one will give the system sufficient rest. If one goes to bed late, there will be insufficient rest. The system will be grumpy about rising. To diminish or eliminate this grumpy attitude, one needs to eliminate its main cause which is late resting the night before.

A person who does not go to bed early and who still complains and asks for assistance with early rising, is impractical. No one can sleep at late hours, deprive the body of its needed quota of rest and rise early with a good attitude consistently. It is not possible.

We must agree to give the system sufficient rest. We must agree to rest as early as possible and to curtail night activities. If one cannot do this, one should stop complaining about late rising because the lifestyle promotes a bad attitude towards morning practice.

Someone was advised to rest early and the person was assured that if this was done, most of the negative attitude would go away. Being convinced, the person began practice. However the bad attitude towards early rising continued.

This may happen to an impatient person who fails to understand that early resting is more than just reclining in a bed early. Early resting includes relaxing the mind.

If one goes into bed early and thinks and thinks and thinks and if one is unable to rid the mind of ideas and memories then the only part of the system which will rest will be the limbs and some organs of the body. But resting includes the psychology as well. Initially a person who is prone to impulsive thinking, will not get the result of early resting. His mind will rebel at early rising.

If however that person is patient, over time, the early rest method will affect the mental system. He will experience a change in demeanor, from a negative to a willing one.

One should recline in bed early. One should free the mind from thinking impulsions. Then one may have an agreeable mind for early meditation.

Burial of a body

Burial of a human being may be for two reasons.

- disposal of the form
- preservation of the form

Explanation:

- disposal of the form

This is for the sake of hygiene, particularly because a dead body will decompose and upon decomposition will emit foul odors. People, who bury bodies in a shallow grave, find that animals which detect the body, scratch and exhume it for eating. In most cultures, the body is placed in a deep hole, the so called six feet deep.

A dead body is attractive to insects which lay eggs in or on the body. Those eggs produce larvae which consume the body. This caused human beings, even primitive ones, to develop hygienic means of disposal of the dead forms.

- preservation of the form

If one believes that the person is the body, when the body dies one thinks that the person is no more. This belief is the hardest one from the emotional perspective. Once that person is dead as per such a belief, one feels that one may do something to preserve the person. This is epitomized in cultures worldwide which mummified bodies.

Some ancient cultures went to such extent as to put servants with a deceased king so that in the afterworld, the king would have his entourage. They also felt that his body was to be preserved and that he was that dead body. There was a belief that if that body was mistreated his soul would be affected. In such a belief there is a dual concept.

- the person is his body
- the person is his psychology, which can separate from but never be fully disconnected from his body

If one believes that the person is the body, it makes sense that one should grieve for the body, and that one should do whatever is possible to preserve it.

If in addition to this one believes that there is the possibility of revival of the body, then it makes sense that one should be concerned with its decay. If one believes that the body may be revived through a resurrection, then it makes sense that one should protect the body from animals and from any other desecration.

Time regulation of dead bodies

If one feels that there is any chance that the dead body's condition will affect the condition of the surviving psyche of a person, then it makes sense that one should see to it that the dead form is kept in a certain condition which one feels is suitable for the benefit of the surviving psyche. For instance, sometimes we hear of a person not getting a decent burial. This means that people on this side of existence feel that the person was or is dishonored by not having a ritual funeral. In that case, it makes sense to purchase an ornate casket, build a mausoleum and do whatever is approved in the particular society.

In some cultures there are time spans for rituals after death. These stipulations state that after so many days or months certain things occur to either the dead body or to the departed psyche or to both. According to the belief system there are rituals designed to benefit the departed.

I remember years ago there was a conversation with a monk. Someone asked him about the resurrection of bodies as per the Christian beliefs. He asked a question in return, saying, "Which of the bodies of that soul should be resurrected?"

After he said this there was dead silence as everyone scrambled in their minds for the answer. And of course nobody could answer that question. If we take the question apart however it reveals our perplexity about death. It is a paradoxical question, because in the first place to a Christian there is only one body. The bible tells us that it is given to man to live once and then to die and wait for the resurrection. Therefore the monk's question was out of place because in Christianity there would only be one body.

Still the question is worthy of consideration, because we are not so sure that one can only live once, just as we are not so sure that one can live more than once. If I had numerous bodies, which one should be selected to be used at resurrection, since at that time, I am supposed to assume an eternal material body. Which one of my past life identities should I assume? Who will make that decision? Will it be as it is at present where I became aware of myself after my body was formed and I grew up to become a certain person who assumed a particular role in a society?

There is another related belief system which is that the person is repeated born and repeatedly dies, without having memories or understanding about the process. In that doctrine, I am born. Then I die or go out of existence, then inexplicably I am born again without understanding about the past birth and de-existence phase. This is repeated perpetually so long as life forms are produced.

Krishna made a related statement.

अथ चैनं नित्यजातं
नित्यं वा मन्यसे मृतम् ।
तथापि त्वं महाबाहो
नैनं शोचितुमर्हसि ॥२.२६॥

atha cainaṁ nityajātaṁ
nityaṁ vā manyase mṛtam
tathāpi tvaṁ mahābāho
nainaṁ śocitumarhasi (2.26)

atha — furthermore; cainaṁ = ca — and + enam — this; nityajātaṁ = nitya — continually + jātam — being born; nityam — continually; vā — or; manyase — you think; mṛtam — dying; tathā 'pi = tathā — so + api — also; tvam — you; mahābāho — strong-armed man; nainaṁ = na — not + enam — this; śocitum arhasi = śocitum — to mourn + arhasi — you can

And furthermore if you think that this embodied soul is continually being born or continually dying, even so, O strong-armed man, you should not lament. (Bhagavad Gita 2.26)

My view is this.

The psyche is separate from the body. The psyche survives the death of the body. Persons who are related to a dead body, should do whatever they can to assist the departed psyche. But I do not see how excessive rituals for a dead body helps the departed psyche. Even though one is attached to one's physical body, and will feel that attachment for some time after departing from the form, still activities for the preservation and care of that form on this side of existence, will not help once the psychic connection between the subtle psyche and the physical system is terminated. Ritual activities by physical people have little impact on the condition of those who are deceased.

What survives death?

From the angle of astral projection, the angle of the subtle body, if the physical body was buried, and if there is just a little soft tissue remaining, the departed soul cannot in any way use any part of that form, even the bones which may take centuries to deteriorate.

For that matter if a body was buried and it was not sealed in plastic or was not housed in a wet or dry chemical, worms and bacteria in the soil may gradually and surely digest all tissue in the body. In other words, that body will be utilized by other creatures, some of which are microscopic beyond human perception. As such those tissues would be claimed by such creatures as food. The departed soul could not stop this process, nor could he or she use the decomposing materials.

Of course the surviving relatives and friends may believe whatever they need to. The only connection between a soul and such a decayed body would be an emotional one of attachment to something that cannot be reclaimed. Gradually that attachment will subside. Some departed souls linger at a residence after leaving the body. Some do so for weeks or years but the attachment never results in repossession of the body. Hence it is futile for anyone on this side of existence to encourage a departed soul in such attachment.

The best ritual action is to do something to encourage the departed soul to go on to a new life either by taking another body here on earth or by going on to a heavenly world, if that is possible. We have no control over any heavenly world but we do have some say on this earthly side. As such we may facilitate a new body, a baby form, for that relative either by begetting one and assuming parenting responsibilities or by encouraging a family member or friend to do so.

For a departed soul, the old body which was left behind, the one he or she was evicted from, is merely a costly distraction. The real thing for such a person is the psychological energy which survives the physical body.

Rest in Peace

What is the rest condition hereafter? On one hand there is the fact of death, especially since all flesh decomposes. On the other hand there is rest? This begs the inquiry as to what item is at rest.

If I am my body and its flesh deteriorates, only leaving the bones, what does it mean for me to be at rest?

I would rewrite the statement follows:

Once the bones are cleared of flesh the departed person has absolutely no chance of repossessing the body. The surviving relatives are forced to accept this fact beyond any shadow of a doubt. This is similar to our position when a dear one enters a coma or is put under life-support machines in an intensive care unit. So long as the coma continues or so long as the body continues to respond to the medical machines, we would feel that there is a chance that person may again be that body and speak to us on this side. But if the coma ends with death or if the life support system fails to keep the body alive, we are forced to face the state of decomposition.

If the astral body completely separates from a physical one, there is no chance of that departed person using that body again. But on this side of existence, relatives may hope for the person to again be energized as the body.

The actual meaning of the soul being at rest, or of the statement **Rest in Peace (R.I.P),** is that the soul, after a traumatic life on this side of existence, is forced to relax those mental concerns when he or she loses a body. In fact, there is a resting period which the astral body enters before it assumes another embryo in the womb of the mother-to-be.

This has nothing to do with the condition of the body which was left behind. This is fully a subtle or psychological aspect. In this physical existence, we experience psychological fatigue as mental and emotional stress. We deal with this daily and we continue activities no matter what. But a departed soul feels his or her recent life as one compounded stress energy. The subtle body seeks relief from that by going into deep sleep.

Astral breath

The stoppage of the breath is a function which occurs on the physical side only. The subtle body does breathe but its air supply is subtle. When the physical form ceases breathing the subtle body continues to exist because its air supply is still available. This is experienced during lucid dreams, when we find that the subtle body continues to exist even though it is separated from the physical one. If the subtle body was 100% dependent on the physical, there would be no lucid dreams or experiences of astral projection.

However if a person is on this side of life, inevitably his or her idea about the death of someone is mostly dictated by conclusions from the condition of the physical body. To correct this we should consider the dream body as being just as substantial, or ever more so, than the physical one.

From the astral angle the statement above would be written like this.

First the physical body stops breathing, causing the subtle one to permanently separate from it. If that physical form is buried in the earth, the soft tissue will be the first part to deteriorate.

Is there a relationship between the decomposition of the physical body and the activities of the departed soul?

The answer to this is that there is absolutely no relationship except that a departed soul usually tries to repossess his or her physical body and is unable to do so, once the lifeForce in that body departed.

Can the departed soul perceive that decomposing body?

The answer is that usually he or she cannot because the means of perception into this world is no longer available. That means of perception was the physical body. Without it the subtle body cannot see physically.

The departed soul wanders on the astral level, in the ghost worlds, but does so because of being disoriented not by reason of flesh decomposition. Even if the body was cremated, even if the body was put into a tank of liquid preservatives, still the soul will wander. The wandering has nothing to with the condition of the body which is left behind.

The wandering is based on psychic confusion, psychic shock, because of losing a foothold on this side of existence and being in the hereafter without any detailed knowledge of the astral zones.

Cremation is only helpful to a departed soul in the sense that if he or she knows for sure that the body will be cremated; he or she will make no efforts to reawaken as that form. Usually a person tries to be the physical body on this side of existence. This occurs by lifelong force of habit of rising each morning after sleep as a living physical form. Once death occurs that wake-up process is permanently terminated. Still, some departed souls try to do it again and again for days or weeks and for the most for about one year, after a body dies.

Now let us say for example that I believe in cremation rituals. If I pass from the body, as soon as I become convinced that I did pass on, I will not try to locate and re-enter the dead form. I would assumed that my relatives complied with the cremation ritual. Hence I would make no attempt to reenter the body.

This is the only advantage of cremation. It has no other advantage for the departed person. On the human side cremation has the advantage of causing a discouragement of morbid thoughts, because in the case where the body is buried, some person may have bad dreams of it. Someone may want to open the coffin or mausoleum to see it. If it was cremated, such ideas would not surface.

Supernatural light at death

In the physical world, everything stays put for a time. Even though some things do vaporize here as soon as they are created, deterioration occurs at a slow pace. In the human and other animal species here, life may last for some years. In the astral world there are similar situations, but mostly people who depart from a body find the astral existence to be ghostly and flimsy, to be unsatisfactory. Most departed souls gravitate towards more physical existence.

One may see a divine or a supernatural light during the experience of being displaced from a body, but the vision may be a flash only. One may even enter into or be drawn helplessly into such light but still that does not mean that it would be a permanent experience. For those whom it is a permanent experience, they transferred to heaven or paradise. For those whom it is a flash experience, they will resume their usual dream bodies and experience themselves as subtle beings on the astral planes.

After being there for a time, a departed soul will again enter into the emotions of the would-be parents and will again develop another embryo to again be birthed in nine months as the infant of a woman.

According to the status of a person's consciousness at the time of departure from the body, his or her destiny is formulated in conjunction with time and circumstance. Here is a statement from Krishna.

यं यं वापि स्मरन्भावं
त्यजत्यन्ते कलेवरम् ।
तं तमेवैति कौन्तेय
सदा तद्भावभावितः ॥८.६॥

yaṁ yaṁ vāpi smaranbhāvaṁ
tyajatyante kalevaram
taṁ tamevaiti kaunteya
sadā tadbhāvabhāvitaḥ (8.6)

yaṁ yam - whatever; vāpi = va — or + api — also; moreover; smaran — recalling; bhāvam — texture of existence; tyajaty = tyajati — abandons; ante — in the end; kalevaram - the body; taṁtam - that that; evaiti = eva - indeed + eti — is projected; kaunteya - O son of Kuntī; sadā - always; tad — that + bhāva — status of life + bhāvitaḥ — being transformed

Moreover, whatever texture of existence is recalled when a person abandons his body in the end, to that same type of life, he is projected, O son of Kuntī, always being transformed into that status of life. (Bhagavad Gita 8.6)

In a strange warning however, Patañjali, author of the Yoga Sutras, warns all yogins about rushing into favorable influences at the time of death. See if you can decipher what he wrote.

स्थान्युपनिमन्त्रणे सङ्गस्मयाकरणं पुनरनिष्टप्रसङ्गात्॥५२॥
sthānyupanimantraṇe saṅgasmayākaraṇaṁ
punaraniṣṭa prasaṅgāt

sthāni – person from the place a yogi would then attain if his material body died; upanimantraṇe – on being invited; saṅga – association; smaya – fascination, wonderment; akaraṇaṁ – non-responsiveness; punaḥ – again; aniṣṭa – unwanted features of existence; prasaṅgāt – due to association, due to endearing friendliness.

On being invited by a person from the place one would attain if the body died, a yogi should be non-responsive, not desiring their association and not being fascinated, otherwise that would cause unwanted features of existence to arise again. (Yoga Sutras 3.52)

Patañjali alerts that death does not mean a change in nature's way of doing things. The same tomfoolery may continue. Just as we were invited into this world by someone from here, by would-be parents, and we found out the hard way through acceptance of a material body, that it is not all honey and roses, the same cycle of bright hopes and frustrated dreams would be our lot if we are not careful in the interim stage after being displaced from the physical body.

Heaven / hell

Religious people usually see death as a heaven or hell termination. This is because there is no idea of having to take another body. In a religious system where there is no admittance of reincarnation, the only possibility for a departed soul is a life with God or a life with God's antithesis. This is reduced to life in a paradise for the faithful or life in a hell for those who ignore or disavow the said God.

When reincarnation is figured, the calculation changes. For most human beings the future is life on an earthly planet or life in the interim state on a ghostly plane of existence. To go to a hellish place on a permanent or semi-permanent basis is just as difficult as it is for most of us to be in federal prison on a life sentence. Human beings as a mass are not that evil. Similarly, it is hardly likely that we will go to paradise permanently because we are not compatible with higher levels.

How many people on earth live in a circumstance where they do not exploit anyone and still have grand opulence? Heavenly existence is grand opulence without exploitation, while on earth usually wealth means exploitation of unfortunate human beings.

There is not a single human being who is wealthy and whose wealth is not tinged with exploitation of other humans. It just does not exist on this planet, but in heaven the opulence is there without exploitation. That is the difference.

To go to heaven permanently one has to develop a psychology which is compatible to living in a place where there is opulence but no exploitation. One may think that such a state of mind is desirable but is it?

Are we sure that we wish to exist without exploiting others?

Are we sure that human nature does not comprise a deep need for advantage and for governing others?

If we are sure and if that is our nature in fact, surely we are likely to go to heaven.

Vision at death

It does happen that at the time of death, some enter an astral tunnel. Usually the person finds himself or herself being pulled helpless into the tunnel, but it is usually a nice experience, just like sexual experience. Boy meets girl. They are sexually attracted. It all flows naturally and gives them pleasure and release. They are not in control of it but it is desirable nevertheless.

Such an experience may lead nowhere, just as a sexual experience happens but it does not change the person's status necessarily. People have such sexual experiences repeatedly and find that their bills are not paid by it, their hassles with one another are not removed by it. At death if one has such an experience, it may not change one's astral status. Immediately after the flash one may find oneself to be in the dream body, the same one used while one's physical form lived.

Sometimes there is a vision of an angelic being, sending out grace energy to the departed soul, but even that may not be something of much impact. Why? Currently the angelic beings radiate grace energies but we are not receptive. At death we may suddenly see a divine person who acts as a guardian angel but that does not mean that suddenly the grace will be effective. If it is not effective now, it may be ineffective at death. Why? Because we will be overpowered by the materialistic mentality and will be drawn into the earthly associations which captivated us previously. If on the other hand we respond to divine guidance now, it is likely that we may assume a divine form in the hereafter.

Death experience

At death a departed soul may transit to a hellish place or see hell-beings. Sometimes at death one is scared out of one's wits by frightening apparitions of hell beings who attack one's subtle body or by hell-beings who want to punish one or target one with resentments. Any of these things can happen. The departed soul has little or no control over the afterdeath experiences.

A more important consideration is to realize that since these experiences are not under the control of the departed person, the duration of the experience is not under that person's control either. Thus there is no guarantee that the person would remain in the divine experience or the hellish life.

In this life every human being experiences both positive and negative states of mind. There is no exception for this. Even Jesus Christ was described as having feelings of isolation when his material body hung on a cross. We can assume that in the interim period after death we may go through divine and hellish experiences alternately. We need not fantasize about something else. To control this one should develop an effective spiritual practice which gives results before death.

Part 5

Silence

Silence is a meditation practice used for bringing the mundane impressions in the mind to an end. It is a complicated practice but at some point it should be mastered, otherwise the trillions of mundane impressions in the conscious and subconscious minds will remain in the psyche and cause the self to be time bound. There are many methods of getting these impressions out of the mind but in the end a yogi must directly confront the memory compartments which hold the impressions. He should delete them from the mind.

It is even more complicated when we discuss the impressions in the psyche. In Sanskrit there is a word for these impressions which is *samskaras*.

The silence practice commences as soon as one masters the sensual withdrawal stage, *pratyahar*. At that time it becomes a need, because one has internalized and faced the unfavorable impressions which are stored in the mind and which has the power to motivate one with mundane ambitions.

Realizing that these impressions goaded one from within the mind to aspire for various desires, one loses interest in the problems in the external world and begins a final assault on the real enemies of the coreSelf which are the unwanted desire-energies in the psyche.

Silence practice exposes the unwanted desire-energies. They appear one after the other in the silence environment. The yogi can examine and destroy them sequentially. This is something like a legitimate government rooting out a guerrilla force. Unless the guerrillas are exposed, the government is helpless in its effort to eliminate them. But if the government can implement a plan which causes the guerillas to be targeted, the problem is solved.

If we can see the tiny seed impressions (*bija* - Sanskrit) which motivate us from the subconscious level, and if we can see in slow motion how these surface in the mental and emotional energies and motivate us to act in unfavorable ways, we could wipe out those impression and get free from self-destructive desires.

Astral lands

Last night I met some departed persons. They were with others who still have bodies on this side. This was in a parallel world where the astral body and the objects there feel physical. In such worlds, persons are of the belief that they live on a physical planet like this one but in fact it is not a physical place. However since the vibration rate of the energy there is exactly the same as the rate of the subtle bodies used, one does not realize that the materials there are subtle. While there, one has absolutely no recall of one's life on this side of existence.

While there I saw some persons whom I knew in this world but those persons had no recall of the acquaintance and did not recognize me or greet me as they would have in this world.

One lady there questioned me as to why I was reclined on her lawn. I apologized and explained to her that I was on my way to another property which I was in the process of purchasing. She then became friendly and asked me to have breakfast with her family. I agreed to take a small portion of the meal which she instantly prepared. In that place people can prepare meals instantaneously without heat or fire. If they desire, if it is in their mental scope, fires are produced instantaneously. The fires cook at a rate which is designed mentally by the person concerned.

The sense of possession of departed souls is just as strong as it is for the non-departed, except that the departed may instantaneously produce anything desired. The astral landscape and residence change in design by the whim of desire.

Even though the subtle bodies of the departed have powers of instantaneous production, and even though the environment is responsive to their mental whims, still some of them are unable to create freely due to being dependent on others. Those dependents are mentally limited so that he or she does not infringe upon the desires of the person who is the head of household. There are no children in that world. There was no sexual interest but there was an interest of nearness between persons who would have been lovers in this world. For instance a woman sat on a man's lap and maintained a connection with energy which came from his pubic cavity, but there was no sexual arousal in either person.

Fourth (4th) dimension question

When third eye chakra changes into a transparent opening or the shape of an eye, this means that the coreSelf shifted to a higher frequency. Sometimes the chakra may change into a rectangular opening like a transparent TV screen. If one looks through that transparent opening one will see into another world. Those other places may appear to be similar or dissimilar to the earth. In some experiences one may see into other places on this planet.

The third eye chakra may shrink. It may change colors (purple, indigo and light purple). It may cause a feeling of acceleration as if one travels faster and faster. It may be like a purple light at the end of a black tunnel which appears and disappears with an experience of receding and approaching alternately.

In most experiences what is seen or experienced does not disappear. What happens is that the viewer is shifted from the dimension due to a frequency change. The experience may continue as is but the viewer is shifted or is deprived of sensual access. Since the viewer is his reference, he feels as if the experience terminated while it may terminate only for him and may continue on the level where it exists.

In some experiences when everything disappears one may see swirling silvery small stars or pixelated energy in a dark-blue or black sky. It radiates a neutral bliss energy. This location is important. It is the chit akash, the sky of consciousness or the 4th dimension of existence. When this happens one may try to transit into it or one may try to link one's attention to it. This linkage if successful results in a transcendental absorption, a *samadhi*.

Lucid dreams

Astral projection is when the subtle body separates from the physical form. The astral one remains connected by an energy flow which if seen with subtle eyes will appear to be a whitish tube of pulsating energy. The astral body may remain near the physical one in an adjacent dimension or it may go far away in terms of subtle distance.

In the subtle world distance has more than one computation. A few are:

- subtle linear distance
- subtle dimensional distance

The *subtle linear distance* is observed within one subtle level. The *subtle dimensional distance* is experienced when switching from one subtle plane to another.

Even if the subtle body remains close to the physical form, that subtle form will be far away, because it would be vibrating at a frequency which is distant from physical existence.

Astral projection is important because the difference between astral projection and permanent displacement in reference to the physical form is that at death the subtle body can no longer re-enter and be unified with the physical form. At death the subtle body loses access to the physical one. If the physical system dies during an astral projection, the person will find that he cannot awaken as a physical form. He will discover himself as a permanent psychic being.

Even though generally it occurs only when the subtle body remains interspaced in the physical form, lucid dreaming may occur while the subtle body is in or out of the physical form. The stress for lucid dreaming has to do with the ability of clear recall, which means that the conscious memory is being used. This conscious memory is programmed to work fully when the physical body is involved in an activity.

Lucid dreams are about 85% reality. Rarely is it just fantasy. But it is reality on another plane of existence. It may or may not be mimicked physically at another time.

Image streaming is a form of astral projection in the sense that in image streaming one enters another dimension while the astral body remains interspaced into the physical form. Image streaming is more like what yogis do when they enter *samadhi*. In other words even though some feel that to leave the physical body one must astral project that is not true. One can astral project or switch dimensions while remaining in the physical body.

Horror in dreams

To eliminate or reduce instances of horror in dreams, one should sleep in a well ventilated room. Be sure that there is enough fresh air entering the room through a window or duct. If one has little or no ventilation of fresh air, the body will breathe polluted air. This breathing of bad air may cause the subtle body (the dreaming mind) to enter lower dimensions.

If one views a creepy movie, one may be subjected to horror dreams which replay what was seen in the video. Whatever is viewed is recorded as visual and sound media in the mind. This is stored as memory. Some is stored subconsciously, which means that even though one did not particularly make a mental note of it, it still enters the memory. It has the potency to be replayed in the mind later.

When one sees a horror video, the memory bits which are derived from the scenes, may again be replayed during sleep or even when daydreaming. These impressions even though they are mental fragments are just as frightening because on the inner landscape one's position is such that it is just as if one viewed such things physically. Imagination is a form of reality in the sense that if one is not objective to it, one will be subjected to it. It may even cause trauma to the physical body. It may cause a heart attack or arrested breathing. Even though imagination is not substantial when considered objectively it can affect the physical body. In dreams the objective self may be de-activated and the subjective self may become so prominent that fear of and belief in what is seen, takes over the psyche.

The advice is to stop viewing horror media. If horror images or sounds are viewed the mind may store derived impressions in the conscious and unconscious memories, resulting in replay at other times. Sometimes a horror scene makes such an impression on the memory, that it may replay years after it was seen. One may be unable to get it out of the mind.

Even though a horror movie may be fiction, the energy to create it is real. The persons involved in making it, the director and actors, are real. If someone writes a horror book which becomes the script for a horror media, there is some underlying horror somewhere which was the basis.

If one exposes the mind to a horror event one indirectly exposes oneself to the minds which created the horror and to actual experiences of those persons, as well as to ghastly psychic realities which exist and which are related to those people. The solution is simple. Avoid horror images.

Astral projection / Death

The difference between an astral projection and death, is the ability or disability to become conscious as the physical body. In astral projection one can and does again become conscious of the self as the physical body. In death, one does not again, ever, become conscious of that particular physical body. One is left with psychic presence only.

Brow chakra experiences (March 15, 2009)

When meditating or focusing between the eyebrows one may see a tunnel like energy moving inward and outward alternately. That is the primary activity of the brow chakra.

Focus on the center of the in and out movement. In some cases it will be like a tunnel or like a cone of energy moving from a large circle or spiral to a small one and vice versa.

Adjust the force of the focus. Test repeatedly since a super strong or very weak focus may cause this to disappear. Practice and find the right amplitude of focus which causes steadiness. When one looks into the purple light of the tunnel it may become darker but the tunnel may appear again. This may continue without the space opening during the session.

When the space of the chakra becomes clear or transparent, it may take the shape of a circle, rectangle or eye drop. In that experience one may see outside the subtle body into the world in which that subtle form has compatibility. Some objects perceived there are objects in this world. Some are of other dimensions. Sometimes one is situated far away from this transparent opening and cannot get close enough to it to see into the other environment, like being at the far end of a long corridor and not being near the window which is at the end. At other times one sees only one place, one building, one person or a group of persons. Sometimes one sees various things just as if one looked through a camera lens which was moving over a scene.

If one finds that the building, vegetation or persons seen have forms of light energy, one should know that one gained access to a world in which everything is made of light. One transferred into a body which is made of light.

It is an experience of transcendence when one peers into another dimension, a parallel world which is higher than this physical existence and far beyond the ghost lands where most of the disembodied souls go after leaving their physical bodies.

Reincarnation - ongoing

People who are deceased may or may not wait for their surviving relatives to become dead. The idea that deceased family members wait for loved ones to die is based more or less on the view in some religions that the departed family members will wait for judgment or for the savior to appear.

Reincarnation is an on-going affair, whereby anyone who passes on may or may not take a body immediately. No one waits in the hereafter for the death of a loved one necessarily. Let us say for example that one's grandfather passed ten years ago. It is hardly likely that he is still in the astral world. By now he may assume an embryo through parents, even someone who was not a family member. He may take an embryo in another country in another race, somewhere.

Wherever a deceased person finds a birth opportunity, that person is usually drawn into it. He/she takes a body, just as if someone is hungry and cannot get a meal from his relatives, he will take a meal somewhere else because of the pressing need. Rebirth is such a strong impulse that the risk is that one will take the next body wherever and with whoever one is allowed or fated.

Just as now we have difficulty controlling sex desire and if there is opportunity for it, we take it, so after losing a body one is drawn towards the sex desire of those who have physical forms. Through that attraction one become attracted in a way which causes the psyche to develop as an embryo.

The decision to return to this planet is not decisive. It is more of an instinct. Take for example the return to this body early each morning after sleeping. Does one make a decision to do that from the dream state? Do one say to oneself, "I will now return to my body?"

In the same way by an instinct for living as a physical form one is drawn into the next birth opportunity, but it is mostly involuntary. It would be nice if it was deliberately done but that is not the case. During astral projection a few persons deliberately return to the physical body but most people do so impulsively.

Subconscious energies

Much of what we do is governed by the subconscious mind. The observing self is influenced by this subconscious and may do things which defy common sense but which are enforced by the subconscious.

This is normal because the subconscious keeps energies which are released from the conscious mind. Even if the conscious mind decides to give up something or to delete it from memory, the subconscious will, more than likely, keep that as a memory which will trigger dreams and related considerations in the future. After days, weeks or years, even after lives, such a memory surfaces or a dream that is related is experienced.

There is another way to regard this. The psyche has stockpiles of unfinished relationships which it yearns to complete. It will take an opportunity to fulfill these either in the physical or dream world.

This is not restricted to just what happens in one lifetime. In fact sometimes one meets a person in a dream with whom one had a relationship in a previous life. In that dream experience one is drawn into an agreeable or disagreeable relationship based on the original circumstance.

Two persons who have a relational bond or a subconscious need to be together for one reason or the other, based on this or that attraction, are likely to meet repeatedly in dreams.

This may be done by the subconscious mind even if the conscious mind renounced or forgot the affair. Both persons have subconscious minds which may communicate even if there is no attempt to do so consciously.

A part of the psyche may transcend one's detachment. That part will meet with the other person who also has such a subconscious need.

Devastation or emotional trauma from this lifetime may reinforced a subconscious need from a previous life. This results in a strong urge to fulfill a specific desire and may cause one to be impulsive or aggressive.

Suicide aftermath

After committing suicide, one experiences confusion hereafter. Then one deals with accountability to the affected persons on the physical side. One experiences apprehensions regarding meeting persons who are investigating the cause of the suicide.

After some days the suicidist is faced with this thought:

"What should I do? I am not dead. I still exist. People can reach me mentally. Who will help me? Where should I go? What of those on the physical side whom I hurt terribly?

Afterlife reunion?

The question about whom one would meet in the afterlife is answered by reviewing the type of persons one meets in dreams, particularly lucid dreams and astral projection experiences. If one does not usually meet a certain person during dreams, it is hardly likely that one would meet that someone in the afterlife.

A person's psychology survives in the afterlife. That someone will associate in a way that is similar to what transpired in the earthly life. There are both positive and negative realities in the afterlife. As in this life, nearly everyone hopes for the best, and everyone wants to achieve wellbeing. In the afterlife there is a similar attitude.

Cataleptic trance

During dreams, immobile states of the physical body or of the astral and physical combined are mostly due to desynchronization of the astral one, where it is not fully in sync with the physical system. If this happens when other fearful circumstances or persons are present, one may feel that those unwanted incidences or people are the cause of the immobilization while in fact they are present coincidentally only. When the astral form is in a cataleptic trance it does not respond to willpower.

Cataleptic trances may occur when the astral body separates from or becomes unified with the physical form or during day dreaming. It has short duration. If you find yourself in a cataleptic trance you can recognize the condition because you will be awake in the physical body but you will have no power to move it. You may think and interrupt the breathing rhythm. The ability to control the breath is one way to break the trance; by holding the breath as long as one can and then suddenly releasing it. Sometimes that works. Sometimes it does not. In any case, the trance does not last for a long period. It usually ends of its own accord. Then one can move the body, or rather make the physical body function normally.

Sleep paralysis

Sleep paralysis is a separate condition from bad experiences during the paralysis. It is important to know that if one has a sleep paralysis where one is conscious in the physical body but cannot move it, the condition of the physical body is different to any psychic experiences one may have while in that condition.

Sleep paralysis (catalepsy) occurs when the subtle body is not synchronized into the physical one fully. When this happens one finds oneself unable to move the limbs of the physical system. One can think. One can adjust breathing to some degree. One may hear sounds made in the physical environment. It is just that one cannot move the hands or feet or cause the body to rise from its position. Usually this lasts for seconds or a few minutes. Though it rarely does it can last for a longer time.

Sometimes one can make a moaning sound and others may hear that. Someone who is active on the physical side may shake the body if that person hears a moaning sound. That shaking action may cause the subtle body to be synchronized fully into the physical system.

Holding the breath and then sudden releasing it, can cause the subtle body to be properly synchronized. Sometimes when using this method, the subtle body synchronizes for a few seconds and then resumes the cataleptic condition.

Be sure that one has ventilation while sleeping. Due to low energization stale or stagnant air may cause cataleptic trance. What is experienced during a cataleptic trance relates to the associations and mental condition at the time of the trance, but the experiences with other influences are not the trance itself.

Realize however that if one's body dies, it will be worse than a cataleptic trance. One will not find the physical body as a consciousness reference. One will not arise as that form. One would be left outside the body and will only have the psychic parts of the self and the astral environment for access.

Dream meanings

Many dreams are occurrences which happen just as life occurs here in the physical realm. If you drive five miles and have a flat tire, what does that mean?

The point is that some things occur in the dream dimensions, the astral world, just as a matter of course. These incidences may or may not correlate to what happens physically.

In a dream experience one may lack discrimination and objectivity. One may not discriminate as one would while being the physical body. In a dream one may use whatever little discrimination one has at the time. One may react instinctively rather than rationally.

Being suddenly suspended in air is natural for the subtle body, the dream form, but since one lacks objectivity one measures its performance to that of the physical form which would fall from heights. The dream body, the subtle form, is buoyant towards gravity and acts just like an astronaut would if he or she was outside the earth's gravitational field.

One awakens on this side of existence by the lifeForce mechanism which is in the physical body, as that mechanism operates to pull the dream form back into the physical form bringing the dream to an end. There are dreams however which occur while the dream body is in the sleeping physical body, but other experiences occur with the subtle form at a distance from the physical one.

Joint psyches

It is not possible to merge one's coreSelf with anyone else, no even with God. What is possible and what is before us as reality is that the psyche of one coreSelf can and does temporarily merge with the psyche of another self.

In such situations, it is like two tenants living in one apartment, rather than two tenants in two separated rentals.

We have physical experiences of this in the situation of a pregnancy. In the initial phase the mother-entity is not aware of the intrusion of the child-entity. But why should we be surprised when in fact, the entity in a body is usually unaware of many involuntary functions in the body. Functions like digestion, blood flow and air absorption happen without deliberation.

One aunt told me of her first pregnancy. Even though her abdomen was distended with the child, she did not understand it to be a pregnancy. She thought it was weight increase. It is possible for one entity's psyche to be joined into another's.

The confusion occurs because we mistake ourselves for the psyche. It is not the entity, but the entity lives in psychological compartment which is the psyche. Other entities can enter that compartment.

To assume an embryo one must enter the psyches of both parents. After birth, when the infant's psyche separates from the mother's, the infant feels dependence on the mother. It cries and fusses if it is bared from the mother. This is psyche dependence by the infant. It is not entity dependence.

One other common experience of psyche contact and interchange is sexual intercourse and related romantic exchanges. In these one feels a cross-over of energy from one's psyche to the other. Yes, it is possible to connect into the psyche of another but only temporarily. It occurs in this physical existence as we observe in pregnancies, and also in sexual experience.

A tiny planet

One of the things we need to do is to put ourselves into perspective. In spite of the fact that every human being feels special and feels that he or she requires special care for survival, still we need to keep in mind that we are on a tiny planet, in a tiny universe, out on the edge of nowhere. We are not in a central position in our galaxy. The galaxy in turn, is not in a central position as it moves in concert with other galaxies.

We could not know this in primitive life because our means of physical perception was limited to our bodies. Now we have some credible evidence by electronic instruments which show us where we are located. In such a situation our pride in ourselves and our centralized needs for ourselves will not go away but at least we can express a sense of humor and understand that our opinion of and value for ourselves is for the most part imaginary. It is not supported by the reality.

What does it mean to be God? Who is God? Where does God live? What are God's responsibilities?

Is this God aware of the fact that we are located on a small planet, out on the edge of nowhere, on a planet which is fragile and which cannot sustain itself without help from a dying sun? Do we really think that we can find the answer to the meaning of life in our ninety year lifespan?

Christianity once told us that the universe, this creation, was some five to seven thousand years old. Hinduism says it is billions of years old. Modern astronomers give about 14 billion. In consideration, are we convinced that we can discover the meaning of life in just ninety of those years?

Psychic side of life

Encounters with persons using psychic powers is normal. Because we use physical objects as the reference, we should not be spooked by psychic phenomenon. The psychic is more enduring.

We should program ourselves to understand that life transpires on many levels. The physical plane is one of many dimensions. When we find ourselves in any of the others, we usually get wonder struck because the bodies used in those other places, have powers which are impossible for the physical system.

The point is that in the psychic world, we should expect that we will assume suitable bodies with suitable abilities which from this physical perspective will seem to be fantastic.

Regarding psychic experience

Some psychic experiences occur while the self is synchronized into and is conscious of the physical body. There are other experiences when the self is displaced from the physical form.

One can have a psychic experience while one is physically conscious. In that case the mental focus shifts to the psychic mechanism which connects one to the physical body. It becomes aligned to the one which provides subtle consciousness. The value of this is that you get an idea of what it will be like when you can no longer be the physical body. At that time one can no longer switch to being a physical form. One will be left with subtle perception and will have to endure whatever is good or bad in the astral places.

The psychic side is there. Even if you contact it while conscious of the physical body it is the same reality. Generally the perception is clearer and more accurate if the subtle body separates but one can develop more clarity if one practices and notes everything which appears. As for fear of being overpowered by astral criminals, it is the same as in this world, where we have criminal and violent people. There are people on this side trying to control us, people who want to abuse us. It is the same in some other dimensions.

Astral projection repeats

It does happen that sometimes, one has one astral projection, then wakes up on the physical side, then nods out again and has a reconnect projection. This may even happen more than thrice.

It may be an unwanted experience. One may get a scary astral encounter and then one escapes from it and is drawn back into it more than once. This can happen. A yogi may try relaxing more and forgetting the desire to astral project. The desire itself may produce a tension which discourages projection.

Initially it is hardly likely that one could astral project by mere desire or will power, but one may spontaneously have an experience of the subtle body falling out of the physical one. One technique for successful astral projection is to let the system do it, and to put one's mind in the mood which is conducive to it. Silence helps and so does relaxation after the body is rested. If the body is not rested, it will more than likely enter a drowsy state. In that condition one may not be aware of the separation of the subtle body. But if the system is rested there is more likelihood of being aware of a projection.

Think of it. One astrally projects anyway. What one lacks is not astral projection but awareness of it. The subtle body separates from the physical system during sleep but one is not aware of the displacement. Naturally, the mind is focused into physical awareness. If one changes that preference consciousness of the projections may begin.

Subtle body out of sync

Even though there is much literature on astral projection the truth is that most of the techniques concern putting the self into a condition which facilitates projection and other subtle body experiences. This is like wanting to have a tornado or hurricane occur. If you live in Alaska and you wish for a hurricane, it may be possible once in every hundred years but if you live in Jamaica or Florida; it would be possible at least once per year.

Instead of thinking of causing a hurricane, one should move to a location where hurricanes frequently occur. For psychic development one should try to put the self into a condition in which the desired psychic occurrences are more likely to happen.

A question is.

Under what conditions would sleep paralysis or astral projection be likely to occur?

In my experience, sleep paralysis occurs frequently when I sleep in a room in which there is no or very little ventilation. It can happen when there is adequate ventilation but it rarely does so.

Sleep paralysis means that the subtle body is out of sync with the physical one. In that sense it is a form of coma. It is a comatose condition in which the person in the physical body is aware of that body and may even hear sounds around that body but cannot move that form.

Psychic accuracy

One should gage the accuracy of one's psychic perceptions. Develop a way of checking the validity. Is one's claircognizance 100% correct or 5% correct? To check the accuracy keep a notebook. Jot down any claircognizant, clairsentient and clairaudient experience. Check to see if it is correct. When one is consistent in this notetaking, one may develop a method of checking these experiences against reality.

The psychic abilities are operations of the subtle body just as walking on a solid surface is an ability of the physical form. When a psychic ability is perceive and used, there may be interaction in the mind with memories and prejudices. These combinations cause distortions and changes which make psychic perception inaccurate.

If one learns how to stop the memory and prejudices from interfering with incoming psychic information, one's perceptional accuracy would increase.

Physical body trance release

There are dimensions which are adjacent to the physical level but which are subtle. When in these worlds one may float about or even feel as if the subtle body is physical. It depends on the vibrational frequency of the world one enters. If one comes back into the physical body and finds that it is paralyzed, that it is in a cataleptic trance that means that the subtle body did not synchronize properly. It is not that the physical body is actually paralyzed but what occurs is that the subtle body was not in sync with the physical one and could not operate it. As soon as the subtle form becomes interspaced correctly it can again operate the physical form.

Catalepsy occurs more frequency if the physical body is in a room which is poorly ventilated or if a hallucinogenic or narcotic drug or even alcohol was consumed.

By manipulating the breath, by hold it and then suddenly releasing it, one may sometimes cause the subtle body to be jolted into sync with the physical form. In a cataleptic trance one can hear noises around the physical body. One may hold the breath but one cannot do anything else. Sometimes one can make the physical body create a groaning sound and if anyone is present in the room and hears that sound and was advised beforehand, that person can shake the body and that will cause the subtle form to come in sync, which will give the required control over the physical form.

Subtle body trauma

One should program oneself to know that in a dream the dream body (subtle form) cannot be subjected to death as the physical one can. The dream body can be subjected to shock. It can act as if it is a physical body but it cannot be killed by the means used to kill a physical form.

If it is stabbed for instance, it may act as if it is a physical form and then it will suddenly and instantaneous resume itself, as if it healed instantly from the damage. It is subjected to the intentions of others but only as a mimic action, like on a movie set where an actor is shot with blank bullets and falls as if dead and then walks away as soon as the camera is no longer focused on him.

If I am stabbed in a dream, I will survive it. It cannot be fatal. Repeated death is not a physical possibility but it is possible in the dream world because the subtle body can mimic trauma and survive all violence inflicted to it. The question is:

Why is the subtle body submitted to trauma?

The subtle form is subjected to violent psychic associations because of physical interactions. If one associates with violent people on the physical level, one will in turn do the same in the dream world. If one is careful on the physical side it will pay off by more positive less-scary associations in the dream world.

Lucid dream control

One should not think that one can get lucid dreaming or astral projection under full control. We do not have the physical body under full control. If we did it would not have disease.

If one gets a lucid or vivid dream and wakes up, one may reenter the astral experience consciously if one goes back to sleep again. My intention here is to inform that this happens only because the physical body is somewhat rested. When it is rested one is more likely to have extradimensional lucid experiences because the lifeForce can then release more energy into the subtle form and the memory in that form is then more operative and less vague.

This brings to fore the requirement of pranayama breath infusion which is the method for increasing the energy used by the lifeForce, so that it can more efficiently express energy in the subtle form.

If one sets an alarm clock for 4am with intentions to rise at 6am one can awaken, turn off the alarm, and remain reclined but awake for two hours during which one may have a lucid dream. Because of the restful condition of the physical body, it is more likely that one will have lucid experiences at this time. When the physical system is rested, it is likely that the subtle body will be more energized if it is displaced from the physical one. This is due to the increased energy available from the lifeForce for operating the psychic circuits of the subtle form.

Compost / organic produce

In some cities there is an effort to generate organic soil from household food garbage. This is a good effort but it is flawed. One cannot produce organic material from food which was produced using fertilizers, herbicides and pesticides. For organic material one has to begin with organic material. Some people feel that so long as the food waste is composted, it becomes organic but that may be untrue. If one begins with stuff which was from man-made interference in nature's process, one will get nothing else in the end.

For something to be really organic it has to be based on soil and food waste which was not interfered with at any stage by manmade stuff. It is a triple problem of fertilizers, pesticides and herbicides and now to add to this, we have genetically modified foods.

Because these bodies were produced through the evolutionary process of material nature, they are affected adversely by rash introductions. They may not adapt favorably to the molecular changes produced by the manmade chemicals which are in fertilizers, pesticides, herbicides and some of the modifications of genetic engineering.

Every food we use is affected but some are more affected because of the chemical draw of the plant. For instance citrus like lemons extract strong chemicals from soil. Some other plants take little from the soil in comparison. Since lemons, oranges and their related species take much chemicals, if they are fertilized, and treated with pesticides and herbicides their roots may absorb much of this. When eaten those chemicals will go into the human body and may damage organs.

Even the air we breathe is laced with chemicals. The water which falls from the sky as rain is laced with acids and other dangerous chemicals which come from the use of various types of fuels and chemicals. Each of us is affected. It is not possible to be exempt. In addition one does not know how much one contributed to this in previous lives of exploitation of the earth and the people on it. Scientists have found DDT in remote locations where humans never resided nor used the chemical.

DDT is proven to cause genetic changes in fish such that the fish are unable to reproduce. Now more and more we may hear about humans who want children but cannot produce any despite prolific sexual activity.

Stillborn birth

A person who left a stillborn body is apt to enter into the psyche of the same or a different parent as soon as the baby form is lost. The key to understanding this is to know that anyone who formed an embryo is in a compatible state with the would-be parents. That self can immediately re-enter into the same or into another parental form according to suitability.

What is this suitability?

It is the likelihood that the would-be parent will beget an embryo shortly. Thus if someone left a still born body and if the parent(s) do not intend to foster a new pregnancy, the astral self who was to be the child, will be forcibly drawn to other parents. It will again assume the form of a developing embryo. If that attempt is successful, it will be born as a baby.

Astral existence clarity

One should program oneself to know that in the dream existence one's subtle body cannot be damaged irreparably. Even if it assumes a damage it recovers immediately. In this world if the body is damaged, it may take weeks for healing but in the dream dimensions traumatic recovery occurs instantaneously. However since we become aware of dream dimensions with the physical reference, we assume that the dream world operates like physical reality. In many respects it does not. In the dream world things can happen suddenly. It can be illogical and inconsistent with what occurs in this world.

There may be for instance a sudden flood of tide waters in the dream world. It may last for only one minute of earth time. In that minute the ocean level may rise 100 feet and then recede the same distance. If one experiences that one may be scared if one is not conscious of the fact that the dream body cannot be killed by subtle water.

In the dream world, in an instance a new landscape can appear for no reason. Then it may suddenly disappear. In terms of time, what we experience may be experienced by someone in another dimension in a much accelerated or even decelerated way, such that one year for us may be just one minute or one year may last for one hundred years. It all depends on which phase of the subtle body we experience.

During a ghastly astral experience, one awakens on the physical side. This happens because the subtle body is rapidly retracted into the physical system. One interprets that as waking up. It is switching from a dream dimension to this physical reality.

The danger which one faces in a dream acts as a trigger to move the mind back into the physical body. When that action takes place, one finds oneself to be the physical body again.

Whenever one is in an astral projection or in a conscious or lucid dream, one is in a death state, in the sense that if the physical body dies during the experience, one will be stuck on the dream side permanently.

Lack of memory

Some people assume that after death, one will have many choices which are unavailable when one used the physical body. Such assumptions are questionable. Think of it in this way. More than likely we will not have any more choice than we had before. Even though once we are conscious of ourselves as human beings, we developed a body through which we exhibit a range of choices, still it is likely that history will repeat itself again in the sense that we may be placed again in the same configuration of not remembering previous choices except the recent ones since we became aware of ourselves in the present body.

In a book from India, in the *Bhagavad Gita*, there is a story concerning this, where the warrior prince Arjuna became worried about the death of relatives in a civil war. A person named Krishna explained that anyone who exists now, and all those who existed previously, as well as those who will exist in the future, will definitely go on existing eternally.

When the warrior questioned about this, Krishna explained that the problem was one of a lack of memory, an inability to remember past lives. That inability means that one is likely to be unobservant of many phases of existence, even one's existence. We know that we exist now. We realize that we have no memory of say something that happened a million years ago. Hence how can we conclude that this existence may not be repeated with no recall of what occured? As for becoming part of the whole again, that should be considered in reference to our ability to realize ourselves as a part. Suppose I am part of the whole before I became conscious of myself as I know myself right now, then what does that mean if we cannot remember that wholeness? Imagining what it would be like in that wholeness or what it was like in the past in that wholeness. This leads to paradox.

Communication with the departed

The rebirth situation is mentioned in the *Bhagavad Gita*.

यं यं वापि स्मरन्भावं	yaṁ yaṁ vāpi smaranbhāvaṁ
त्यजत्यन्ते कलेवरम् ।	tyajatyante kalevaram
तं तमेवैति कौन्तेय	taṁ tamevaiti kaunteya
सदा तद्भावभावितः ॥८.६॥	sadā tadbhāvabhāvitaḥ (8.6)

yaṁ yam - whatever; vāpi = va — or + api — also; moreover; smaran — recalling; bhāvam — texture of existence; tyajaty = tyajati — abandons; ante — in the end; kalevaram - the body; taṁtam - that that; evaiti = eva - indeed + eti — is projected; kaunteya - O son of Kuntī; sadā - always; tad — that + bhāva — status of life + bhāvitaḥ — being transformed

Moreover, whatever texture of existence is recalled when a person abandons his body in the end, to that same type of life, he is projected, O son of Kuntī, always being transformed into that status of life. (8.6)

Taking that statement at face value, it would mean that when a person passes from the body his/her texture of existence (psychological energy) remains intact. The existence which currently we experience only in dreams, astral projections and trances stays on the subtle plane.

The energy is mental and emotional. That implies that after leaving a body the person continues feeling and thinking as before, but he/she no longer has a physical way to relate feelings and thoughts to people on this side of existence.

If one has only partial and sporadic psychic perception one will become aware of relatives and friends who passed on by the penetration of their feelings and thoughts into one's psyche. One will find oneself speaking in the mind to them, thinking back and forth. One may even meet them in dreams for relationship and discourse.

Fear of sleep

It is natural for the mind to associate darkness and sleep with fear. If we consider the animals we will find that in the jungle at night those species which do not have good night vision, hide from the ones who do. Many big cats hunt in the daytime and the nighttime, but some prowl more at night than they do in the day. Some animals which are not predatory move around during the night under the cover of darkness due to feeling that they are safer at night than in the daytime when they could easily be seen.

One person may be fearful of sleeping, while another may be fearful of waking. One person may have a state of mind where the daytime is undesirable and the night is opportune.

The mind may be fearful when it feels it has less control when the body sleeps or it may be that it feels insecure if it is not in touch with the physical world.

Since sleep is necessary it is best to discipline the mind so that it accepts sleep as nature's method of rejuvenating the physical body, and as nature's opportunity for the mind itself to explore what is beyond the physical.

Physical reality is traumatic. The dream world is another plane of existence, or rather it is another series of such planes. There are desirable and undesirable phases in the dream world, just as there are in the physical world.

Masturbation

Masturbation may be psychologically driven or it could be based on the needs of the body. In observing animals like goats for instance, one could see that if a billy-goat is isolated, it may masturbate frequently even though there is no sexual stimulus in the environment, no pornography, nothing. In the animal's case, the urge is driven from within the body/psyche.

Once when I tended goats I noticed that if there were male goats together and if no nanny-goats were present, one male would mount another and go into sexual actions and ejaculate semen. The mounted males would not allow the horny animal to engage homosexually, but the horny ones would go into sexual frenzy nevertheless. This behavior is observed in horses as well. Sometimes fowl cocks exhibit the same behavior and bulls also.

Consider that in the elderly years the sex drive decreases. The libido reduces. One reaches a peak of sexual drive at a certain age. Then it is all downhill unless one uses artificial means. Should a man be embarrassed because his libido decreased due to the age of the body?

There is a story from the life of Mahatma Gandhi that is worth repeating this. Once he was asked about celibacy because it was known that he did not lay with his wife. The question was focused on the idea that if one does not pass semen either through masturbation or sexual intercourse, one will suffer from bad effects. Gandhi said that he had no bad effects and that his semen was absorbed into his blood stream and was being used in his body for purposes other than sexual intercourse.

Of course Gandhi was from India, where there is a belief that semen is used in the brain and therefore if one does not ejaculate it will go into the brain.

I feel that at 37 or older there should be no need to masturbate since the libido factor decreases and one is no longer pushed by sex drive, but if one keeps remembering sex, then it may be impossible to stop masturbation. The problem may be that one keeps remembering the pleasure.

Motive for meditation

Much hinges on the motive for meditation. Depending on that, one could practice regardless of moods or one may practice when one is in the mood.

One aim of meditation is mood control. Meditation itself if done consistently banishes the powerful influence of moods to such an extent that the meditator ignores the moods and persists with practice. Usually one does not realize that one is submerged in an influence by a mood. The spread of it is hardly felt until its consequences become unpleasant

It is not that one can eliminate the moods altogether. But one can develop objectivity towards the moods so that when one arises, one will remain in the psyche outside its influence.

Sharing spiritual advancement

Some of us were in spiritual societies where the idea was that you take the information from a spiritual master and pass the information on, even if one does not understand nor have integrated or verified it. This is a teaching of many of the spiritual societies which were established by teachers from India.

When I lived in one ashram, a spiritual master made a point to say that if a boy who is uneducated repeats after a math teacher that 2+2 = 4 that is a fact even though the boy himself does not understand the equation.

I do not accept the statement. It is dishonest to send someone to speak of subjects which he did not integrate. In fact there is no statement in the *Bhagavad Gita* that supports this, even though later on the India, other noted and reliable teachers established this. In the *Bhagavad Gita*, there is a statement as follows:

इदं ते नातपस्काय
नाभक्ताय कदाचन ।
न चाशुश्रूषवे वाच्यं
न च मां योऽभ्यसूयति ॥१८.६७॥

idaṁ te nātapaskāya
nābhaktāya kadācana
na cāśuśrūṣave vācyaṁ
na ca māṁ yo'bhyasūyati (18.67)

idaṁ — this; te — of you; nātapaskāya — na — not + atapaskāya — to one who does not perform austerity; nābhaktāya = na — not + abhaktāya — to one who is not devoted: kadācana — at any time; na — not; cāśuśrūṣave — ca — and + aśuśrūṣave — one who does not desire to hear; vācyaṁ — what is to be said; na — not; ca — and: mām — me; yo — yaḥ — who; 'bhyasūyati = abhyasūyati — lie is critical

This should not be told by you to anyone who does not perform austerity or is not devoted at anytime, or does not desire to hear what is said or is critical of Me. (Bhagavad Gita 18.67)

Why do I say it is dishonest?

The teacher cheats in the sense that he did not take the time to educate the student and to bring him to the experience and understanding. He used the disciple to attract followers. Why capture followers if one is unable to properly train them. If one is not going to care for them individually, why capture them?

Suppose I begin a school. I enlist six students. On the first day I gave them books. I ask them to sell the literature. They go out and convince sixty students to join. I keep doing this. Obviously I will have a large attendance but what about the teaching?

This is why I said that the teacher cheated. He did not have the time to train each student. Still he wanted more followers. He was greedy for students.

To share spiritual advancement, one should share one's advancement and realization, not mine, not the teacher's. One may use the teacher's literature but only to share what one integrated.

Love

Like currency love is a convertible energy. If you make pottery, one may try to exchange an ornate piece for a cart of groceries but the grocer may not agree. He prefers cash. Affection or love is like cash but specified affection is like the pottery. Once the love converts into specific affection, as love for a spouse, love for a child, love for a parent, or love for a friend, it assumes a moral dimension. That is where the restrictions apply.

If one insists that the grocer take the ornate piece, and if he still refuses, one may leave the pottery and confiscate the groceries, but then the grocer may call the police. One will be arrested for shoplifting, even though the pottery may be worth ten times the value of the groceries.

Love or affection is relational currency. The problem arises when one converts it inappropriately. One should weight the liabilities before one expresses it impulsively.

Science and spirituality

Eventually we will correlate science and the spiritual side. Much of what we called mysticism and psychic experience is the movement of subtle energy but it is subtle material energy, the same energy which is used to transmit media over internet and which is used by the sun for emanating light.

Eventually we will take science into account. Religious people usually think that science is hostile to religion and it is, but that hostility is based on superstitions which were imposed on society. Religion and science need to progress side by side with each giving and taking according to the evidence.

The dimensional situation is of particular interest to anyone who is serious about existing in any way other than three dimensionally in a material body. How do you transit from one dimension to the next without losing memory and identity?

Masturbation / Subtle sex

Masturbation is definitely not part of spiritual life. It is part of social life. In fact sexual intercourse is part of social life. But that does not mean that we can totally ignore the sexual needs of the body, no more than we can ignore physical eating which has to do with maintaining the body.

Whatever has to be done for the basic maintenance of the body should be done, but if one finds that it hampers spiritual life and distracts from it, one should find a way to curtail that? The body is here. It is useful even in spiritual life. A certain percentage of social life must be maintained but we should determine the amount.

If one overdoses on social life, the spiritual development will be curtailed. If one neglects social life altogether spiritual life will be hampered as well. One should strike a balance to do both aspects and still come out ahead on the spiritual side.

Each case is different. Some spiritual teachers and their establishments gave the wrong idea, that there is a one-size-fits-all in spiritual life. Nothing is further from the truth. Each person should have a tailored carefully charted course that is suited to his or her spiritual development in terms of the removal of impurities and hindrances. There is no set rule about sexual restraint or sexual permissiveness in spiritual life. One person's situation is his. Another's is another's.

A person should know what is preferred and should gradually over time implement what is ideal. If one has an overpowering sex drive and if one's mind and emotions are wired for sex because of one's psychology, one's only out is to gradually curtail it.

When the subtle sex drive is sublimated, the animalistic urges are reduced, but even then one cannot be sure that they are fully terminated. Suppose one loses the body and takes another embryo, can one say for sure that when the new body reaches sexual maturity one will not be crazy for sex all over again?

The problem is that when one no longer has the physical body, the subtle one may immediately assumes sexual interest. One will again be pulled back into a physical body for rebirth.

Sex is the loop for rebirth. Ever felt the pulling force to any of the sexual areas of any person on earth? If you have, that same pulling energy will cause you to again be birthed from another mother's body.

Subtle perception now

Even in spiritual groups there is discouragement for dream recall, where dream recall and related discussions are considered to be taboo. Some spiritual groups consider it to be hallucination or mental speculation.

This occurs because of the blur between reality and illusion in dreams. The astral reality borders on illusion. If one considers this in all seriousness one will realize that since the dream existence does border on illusion that is more reason why we should make an objective study of it.

Merely sticking to the physical side and depending on statements from scripture will not protect one from the vagueness of subtle existence. It will do absolutely nothing to provide clarity in subtle perception.

If the subtle world is a mix of reality and illusion why are we unable to sort it? In the physical world, we easily sort what is a video performance and what is reality. Why are we unable to sort the dream existence? If we are spiritual beings with divine intelligence and if we have the ability to go a spiritual world, why are our dreams not distinct so that the dreams experiences are just as distinguished as physical existence? We have to earn it. It has nothing to do with waiting until the body dies. If we do not have it now, if we cannot develop it now, the confusion of real subtle experience and imaginative subtle experience will continue after the body dies.

Both aspects must be studied, namely the imaginative powers of the mind as well as it perceptive features. If one has a camera and takes a snap of a scene, when one looks at that scene later, one knows that it is a photo. That has usefulness even though it is an impression. It is not the place but it is a photo of that place. Similarly the photo ability of the mind is useful.

Again if you take that impression of the photo and transfer it from the camera to a computer, you can use a program to change its colors. One may mix it with another photo and create a new image which has no real counterpart. However one knows one did that. But if one shows that new image to someone who does not know, the person may mistake that for the impression of a real place. In the mind there is blending where it mixes and creates new images which are not representations.

Just as we physically know that when we mix images in a computer, we should know when the mind is mixes images and creates illusions. We should know when the mind perceives subtle reality. But to think that sudden we will have this ability at the time of death is self-delusion. If one develops the ability now then it is likely to happen.

Why neglect the study of this, while telling yourself that at death you will all of a sudden have it? One uses the subtle body every time the physical body sleeps. Does one realize this? That same subtle form will permanently be disconnected from the physical body at the time of death. Be reasonable with yourself. If God does not allow you supernatural perception while you act as a physical body, it is unreasonable to think that he will do so hereafter.

Begin mystic practice now. Study the *Bhagavad Gita*. It mentions *jnanachakshu* and *jnanadipa*. That is the energized intellect which is capable of accurate subtle perception. Arjuna experienced it when he viewed the universal form. Besides that there is direct spiritual perception, which is similar to the physical perception of our present bodies. It is similar in the sense that in this body we automatically perceive physical objects, and in that body, one automatically perceives spiritual objects.

If one cannot sort between a valid subtle world experience and an imagination, one will not have higher experience later at the time of death of the body. Arjuna did not have to wait until death before he experienced the subtle world and then the dimensions which were higher than the subtle world. His perception of these were realer than physical perception.

In the *Mahabharata*, Arjuna was described as going to the Swarga subtle dimension before he went to the battle of Kurukshetra. He did that by advanced yoga practice. Later at the time of death of his body he returned to that Swarga dimension when he first left the physical body permanently. We should be attentive to subtle experiences and strive for psychic clarity before the physical form is made unavailable to us.

Why pay attention to everything else besides what is psychic, especially since the only different between the astral experiences during sleep and the astral experiences at death, is the fact that at death, one cannot awaken as the physical body? One will be stuck in the dream world with the same vague perception of subtle reality and imagination that one has now. Help the self by improving that perception now. Do not illusion oneself with ideas about God changing that suddenly at the time of death.

Survival after death

Until we can prove conclusively beyond any doubt that our mental and emotional energy will not continue to exist beyond the death of the physical body, we should remain open-minded regarding life after death. No one has proven that the mental and emotional energies completely vanish at death.

But at the same time no one can show us that force in a physical way. Thus both positions holds until proof of one can deny the other conclusively.

From the position of physics all energy has to keep on existing in one form or the other, as the physicists state nothing can be created or destroyed. Once one has something, one cannot fully convert it into nothing.

The problem is tracking the conversion from one state to another, and especially tracking mental and emotional energy when it does not have a physical body to convey or express itself into the physical world.

In dreams we experience ourselves in a mental and emotional make-up which is similar to the one we use while awake. The dream states may portend what we will experience ourselves as when the body dies.

Marijuana - hallucinogenic?

To determine if marijuana is hallucinogenic, one should acquire some marijuana flowers, only the flowers not the leaves or stems. Do the usual, which is to roll a joint or use a pipe. You only need one joint, a small joint like a cigarette not a blunt which is like a cigar.

The second issue is the definition of hallucinogenic. It should be known that one popular drug which is labeled as hallucinogenic is LSD (lysergic acid diethylamide). There is also mescaline and psilocybin. Mescaline is closer to peyote in the experiences one has after taking it, while LSD is more outlandish, because it is more concentrated.

How am I giving this information about the effect?

From personal experience with these substances.

Hallucinogenic? The word means that someone sees objects that do not exist. It implies that the person's mind creates things which are not real. However in the spiritual field the word does not mean that. It means that the persons sees things that exist in another dimension, such that he or she may or may not properly interpret what is seen and may become alarmed as a result.

Recently I discussed this with a young man who explained his marijuana usage. I told him that whatever he wanted from marijuana he could not get in full until he smoked the flowers. Someone suggested the use of hashish instead but I said that hashish is not as potent as the flowers and does not complete the experience of the plant. Hashish is all parts of the plant mixed with the plant's resin and sometimes mixed with cow dung. The resin is where you find the active ingredient in its most isolated and concentrated form; but most of that is found in the flowers.

A hint of this is given when one smokes it and there is a bursting sound from within the cigarette or the pipe, when a seed pops due to being burnt and explodes in the cigarette or pipe, then one will find that one gets an extra buzz as it is called. The seeds also carry a greater percentage of the active ingredient than the leaves but it is the flowers that have the full effect, which is similar to mild dosages of LSD.

To be clear, when these drugs are taken the person does not hallucinate, does not see what is not there but sees what is there in other dimensions. The danger for the person is the disapproval of society. If the person is unable to understand that he or she shifted to another dimension that person is traumatized.

Another factor is that the person's sense of time and priorities may change in such a way that the person will no longer care about social responsibilities. Hence people will be dissatisfied with the person's neglect of duties.

Hallucination means seeing into other dimensions, and seeing other realities which do not necessarily align with nor coordinate with, nor make sense in terms of this physical plane.

Krishna about drugs

Even though there is no mention of drugs for shifting consciousness in the *Bhagavad Gita*, in the discourse with Arjuna, Krishna mentioned it in the discourse with Uddhava.

जन्मौषधि-तपो-मन्त्रैर्
यावतीर् इह सिद्धयः ।
योगेनाप्नोति ताः सर्वा
नान्यैर् योग-गतिं व्रजेत् ॥१०.३४॥

janmauṣadhi-tapo-mantrair
yāvatīr iha siddhayaḥ
yogenāpnoti tāḥ sarvā
nānyair yoga-gatiṁ vrajet (10.34)

janmausadhi = janma — birth + ausadhi — herbs, drugs; tapo = tapah — austerities; mantrair = mantraiḥ — by special sounds; yāvatīr = yāvatīḥ — as much as; iha — in this world; siddhayaḥ — mystic skills; yogenāpnoti = yogena — by yoga practice + āpnoti — attain; tāḥ — those; sarvā = sarvāḥ — all; nānyair = nānyaiḥ = na — not + anyaiḥ — by other methods; yoga-gatim — objective of yoga; vrajet — one can achieve.

By yoga practice, one achieves all those mystic skills, which may otherwise be gained by birth, herbs or drugs, austerities, and special chants, but one cannot achieve the actual objective of yoga by those other means. (Uddhava Gita 10.34) (Bhagavatam 11.15.34)

The Sanskrit for yoga is yogena and yoga-gatim. Many commentators and speakers define what yoga is according to their particular beliefs but if you read chapter six of the *Bhagavad Gita* the details of yoga practice are given by Krishna.

Drugs are listed as a method of transiting to other dimensions but yoga is the recommendation coming from India. As far as mushrooms are concerned, some people are saying that the soma beverage used by ancient ritualists in India was mushroom derived. Up to this point there is no direct evidence to support this. The soma plant was described as growing in the Himalayan areas but nobody knows for sure what botanical genus it is.

What were the effects of Soma?

The descriptions say that persons who took it were able to see and communicate directly with persons who used celestial bodies. These are bodies used by people in higher dimensions.

Descriptions tell of drinking soma. Some researchers claim that soma was a hallucinogenic drug. Others contest that. Regardless it was hallucinogenic because if you use a physical body and you can see celestial beings and converse face to face after drinking something, it means that one transited into the world of those beings. One used a subtle body with subtle eyes and senses. That is exactly the kind of experience one has when taking hallucinogenic drugs like LSD. The persons who denies this about soma gave that opinion based on the bad publicity given to the drugs.

One should note that a particular drug or herb transits the user to a particular dimension or set of dimensions. For instance heroin takes one to pleasure yielding dimensions at first and then it takes one to lower worlds which are degrading and hellish. The particular herb or drug will take one to a particular level. It may be that Soma always took its users to higher celestial worlds and that is why it was approved. Interestingly it was only approved for priests, ascetics and people of the royal families. There is no description of it being given to the common people. Its use was secret and restrictive.

Even today in the Andes and other parts of South American, indigenous people use hallucinogenic herbs and mushrooms in religious rites. They trip to other dimensions. They gave descriptions of the beings they meet. This is done under the supervision of their priests or shamans.

But even there sometimes someone freaks out when he or she finds the self in a strange world in an experience which is beyond the capacity to interpret or accommodate.

It is well known in the developed countries that some people OD, overdose on drugs. Sometimes this is explained in a simplistic way to mean that the person took a larger quantity than the physical body could handle and was killed by a heart attack or some other organ failure due to the influence of the drug on the involuntary functions.

Actually such a physical breakdown does happen, because these drugs may cause the heart to race at break neck speeds and then fail, or the lungs may not breathe and the body is starved for air and the cells die, or the brain operates certain of its cells with too high of an electrostatic charge and that causes brain malfunction, or some other organ may become chemically altered enough to cause total failure.

But such explanations though useful in discouraging drug use, do not analyze the fact that once you transit to a higher or lower astral level, you can no longer monitor the operation of the physical form. Thus the physical body is left to its own devices as permitted by the influence of drug. While one is in a higher or lower experience, the body on this side of existence may die. One is left without a body. One is left in that higher or lower world for a short time and then one finds the self in the astral existence which is just adjacent to this world, and in need of an embryo which will not be easy to acquire.

One will not remain in the higher or lower world because the effect of the drugs on one's subtle body will diminish. One will be in the dream existence which one usually experiences when one is not under the influence of the drug.

Meaning of self

Each sect defines the self in a different way. Generally speaking there are two broad definitions. In one the self is a limited human individual. In the other it is an unlimited divine person

Besides that the self is defined as the cultural person or it may be the opposite which is the same person freed from cultural trappings.

Others attests to a self which is a soul, which survives the physical body in an unseen format. Others say the only self is the Supreme Soul or God.

Some say that in the psyche, there are two selves; one, is the limited individual spirit; the other is the Supersoul.

It depends on personal beliefs and spiritual objectives. Self is so subjective that it is not easy to define or distinguish it.

Sleep paralysis

Sometimes the astral body assumes a cataleptic state which means that it does not move. This may happen simultaneoulsly to the physical system upon reentry into it after an astral projection. It is rarely a permanent condition. If it happens upon reentry into the physical body, one should adjust it by controlling the breath rhythm or by trying to make a sudden physical movement with a hand or foot. Do not be scared of it. Know what it is as it occurs. Be confidence that it will not last. When the astral body is interspaced into the physical one, if both forms are not perfectly synchronized, there will be a mismatch. That is experienced as a cataleptic state in which one cannot operate the physical one.

One may hear supernatural sounds, see supernatural objects and feel supernaturally in one way or the other, when the astral body attempts to leave or be combined into the physical one. The vibrations and sounds may be activity of the kundalini lifeForce energy. When that is aroused, it may produce a loud sound or it may vibrate the subtle body or physical one or both. Sometimes one sees a flash of lightning in the body but none of this causes harm. One should not be afraid.

Slaves to thinking

In an indirect way, a great thinker in India, Patañjali, stated that the vibrational operations of the mind should be stopped. He listed five modes of mental operation which should be curtailed

वृत्तयः पञ्चतय्यः क्लिष्टा अक्लिष्टाः ॥५॥
vṛttayaḥ pañcatayyaḥ kliṣṭā akliṣṭāḥ

vṛttayaḥ – the vibrations in mento-emotional energy; pañcatayyaḥ – fivefold; kliṣṭākliṣṭāḥ = kliṣṭā – agonizing + akliṣṭāḥ – non-troublesome.

The vibrations in the mento-emotional energy are five-fold, being agonizing or non-troublesome. (Yoga Sutras 1.5)

प्रमाणविपर्ययविकल्पनिद्रास्मृतयः ॥६॥
pramāṇa viparyaya vikalpa nidrā smṛtayaḥ

pramāṇa – correct perception; viparyaya – incorrect perception; vikalpa – imagination; nidrā – sleep; smṛtayaḥ – memory.

They are correct perception, incorrect perception, imagination, sleep and memory. (Yoga Sutras 1.6)

Most human beings are slaves of the thinking process which is used in abstraction, visualization, ideation, tool-making and language?

The endeavor for increase self-control is individual not collective. If one cannot stop the impulses one must obey them. Whatever is impulsive is independent of one's will. It may control the self.

Body astral/physical

There are basically two types of astral projections. In one the astral body remain interspaced in the physical system. In the other, it is displaced from it.

Both types are valuable in terms of understanding the subtle world and for realizing the subtle body and how it is linked to a living physical form. It is important for one to get used to being an existence with an astral body alone because that is the hereafter situation.

Having a dream, and then arising as the physical body means that one experienced the subtle body as it was displaced from the physical one. Then one was re-established as the subtle body and the physical one.

Meditation affects association

When one meditates, especially if one recently started a practice, one will find that one develops a change in association, whereby some persons who were close seem far away. Some who were emotionally distant become friendly.

This is because intrinsic changes occur in the psyche through meditation. One may reach a deeper level of the self. Then one's surface or cultural personality changes. Others notice the change. Those who were close and who feel one's detachment, panic and act to maintain one's association in an effort to keep one near and dear.

In advanced stages of meditation this is handled by being kind to such persons even though one realizes that the relationship with them is superficial. One understands that if such persons are hurt, the pain has to be absorbed by somebody. One may maintain an association even if it is no longer of great value as it was before.

However in the beginning stages of meditation, one cannot do this proficiently. Thus one should gradually decrease the associations which seem to hamper spiritual advancement.

Meditation opens the subconscious and exposes the other you(s), the you from the most recent past life and from others. When that surfaces in the conscious mind one seems to have changed. Relatives were familiar with the surface self which was recently formatted in this life. When meditation opens the psyche and the deeper self moves into the conscious mind, it may frighten people who knew one before and were only familiar with one's recent cultural identity.

Eventually one will reach a stage in meditation where a compassion and caring interest develops, one which one can express without drawing oneself totally into the surface self which others are familiar with.

One way to conceive of this is to study how mothers do baby talk. The mother assumes a different mood which is based on a need to nurture the child. The mother assumes a fairy tale character to accommodate and relate to the infant. In advanced meditation one does a surface talk to relate to persons who have not ventured into their deeper self. Through that their anxiety over one's development goes away.

Patañjali on drugs

In Patañjali *Yoga Sutras*, drugs are listed as one of the methods of developing or experiencing mystic abilities. It is a valid method but Patañjali neither elaborated on nor recommended it.

जन्मौषधिमन्त्रतपःसमाधिजाः सिद्धयः ॥१॥

janma auṣadhi mantra tapaḥ samādhijāḥ siddhayaḥ

janma – birth, particular species; auṣadhi – drugs; mantra – special sound; tapaḥ – physical bodily austerities in haṭha yoga; samādhi – continuous effortless linkage of the attention to a higher concentration force, object or person; jāḥ – what is produced from; siddhayaḥ – mystic skills.

The mystic skills are produced by taking birth in particular species, by taking drugs, by reciting special sounds, by physical bodily austerities or by the continuous effortless linkage of the attention to a higher concentration force, object or person. (Yoga Sutras 4.1)

The word for drugs in the Sanskrit means herbs, it is *aushadhi*. Interestingly in the next verse, Patañjali wrote about switching to other dimensions. He explained how that is possible.

जात्यन्तरपरिणामः प्रकृत्यापूरात्॥२॥

jātyantara pariṇāmaḥ prakṛtyāpūrāt

jātyantara = jāti – category + antara – other, another; pariṇāmaḥ – transformation; prakṛiti – subtle material nature; āpūrāt – due to filling up or saturation.

The transformation from one category to another is by the saturation of the subtle material nature. (Yoga Sutras 4.2)

In other words when one's consciousness is shifted into another dimension due to being tilted into the vibration energy of that higher or lower level, one is transformed whereby one's perception is of that dimension.

Trust issues

Trust issues come about because of expectation. Particularly in the present culture, we have much expectations. Even in childhood one is given a set of values which cause one to project great expectation upon others. Once expectations are projected if the person does not satisfy it, one becomes disappointed and retreats into the mind to hide from the reality.

Suppose you never saw a dog but I tell you of one. I state that dogs are kind animals. I transmit this agreeable feeling into your mind. Eventually you see a dog. You approach the animal with the ideas I gave you, but that particular animal happens to be ferocious. It bites you. You can see that the problem is not the dog but the description which I gave you. The adjustment needs to be made in the reference one has in mind.

Not all dogs are ferocious. Not everyone is worthy of trust. One has to get out, form relationships and learn how to recognize the breed of dog which is friendly.

Do not expect so much from the world. Stop feeling that the world should be a place which is cushioned for you. Part of the world is agreeable. Part is not. You cannot absolutely control which portion you will be in at every moment.

Do not expect anything from anyone. If one is an insect in the jungle do not expect every plant to supply nectar, be on the lookout for those plants which will close upon you and digest you. Do not feel that the world is here only to please you.

Why should the insect feel disappointed because some plants have no nectar and some others are death traps? Everyone wants something to enjoy. In some cases a person enjoys hurting others or enjoys doing things which though not intending, result in hurting others.

One should abandon resentments and grudges. Mentally move away from the feeling that one is special and that the world should accommodate one's needs. There are different characteristics in each human being. Some are incapable of being trustworthy. It is not necessarily a fault. It may be a natural tendency like the carnivorous plants which entrap insects and digest them.

Astrology in *Bhagavad Gita*

On numerous occasions the subject of astrology was mentioned. I was asked as to whether it is a superstition and if the astrologers fleece people. I wrote three commentaries on *Bhagavad Gita*. Even if those commentaries are invalid and do not add up to much and turn out to be a nuisance to society, still the fact that there are three and not just one, is noteworthy. Why would anyone do three commentaries and not accept astrology. *Bhagavad Gita* validates astrology in chapter six where Krishna spoke of the positive and negative times for a yogi's passing from the body either under the solar or lunar influence.

Unless I want to erase the statements in the Gita about the importance of the planets in the life of a yogi, especially in relation to his passing from the body, I could not deny the value and worth of astrology.

When astral projecting and trying to reach other higher dimensions, I sometimes find that the subtle body is unable to leave the influence of the earth or the influence of the moon. That itself is evidence of the astrology. From the perspective of yoga, astrology is valid. The planets and stars exert influences. There was a famous guru who indicated that when leaving the body an advanced person does not have to worry about the sun and moon. I disagree with this. We read in the *Mahabharata* that as great a yogi devotee as Bhishma waited until the sun's influence prevailed before he left the body. In any case it is not a matter of contention because if one is advanced to that degree where the sun and moon no longer has a bearing on one's subtle body's behavior, then some power is in you and we cannot argue about it.

Astrology is for real even though an astrologer may make mistakes in the forecasting. Can the astrologer see all the angles? That depends on his level of intuition, his mystic perception and his schooling in how to create the tables or charts which are necessary for the correct plotting of the person's horoscope.

The human being is born under local and cosmic influences. There is no question of taking a body which is free of dominance. It is not possible to sidestep every influence. But there is a chance to maneuver through them and come out with a positive destiny.

Dream body synchronization

When the dream body fails to synchronize into the physical sleeping form, the physical system is experienced as being paralyzed. This immobility may be for a few minutes, after which one may again awaken as if one is the physical body with the usual command over its movements

Psychic talk

One cannot speak physically to someone who is deceased but as one speaks, one thinks. That mental process is psychic talk. A deceased person can also do such thinking. If one thinks back and forth to someone, more than likely one communicates on the psychic level.

Consider that the only difference between a dead person and the same one living is that in the dead state, the person lost his or her most efficient method of communication with people on the physical side. That method is the one of using a physical body to relate. Once one loses the physical body, the ability to communicate on this side of existence becomes limited to thinking only. That means that unless the person on the physical side is accustomed to receiving thoughts with or without the support of physical speech and physical hearing, that person will be unable to communicate with the deceased and will be doubtful that such communication could take place.

Astral projection if done in fact, and if it is not mere imagination, would be a shift over to the side of existence where a person is permanently shifted and restricted after losing the physical body. One should realize that the same astral body and the same astral world exist side by side with the living physical body. When one is awake as the physical system, one is simultaneously in the astral system, but one's astral awareness is focused into the physical world. If that focus is intense one will lose track of the astral situation. If somehow one can slacken and decrease the physical focus while using the physical body, one would become more aware of the astral dimension and would have seamless communication with those who are restricted to that side of existence.

Breath rate during astral projection

If without taking drugs one does astral projection, the breath rhythm may be reduced but it will never stop unless one is due to lose the body. If drugs are involved, one risks losing the body.

If one uses drugs, the physical body's involuntary operations risk closure because the involuntary behaviors may be interrupted by the influence of the drugs.

There is no need to feel that the body will stop breathing when an astral projection occurs to a sober body which is not under the influence of drugs. Astral projection is just the same as a dream state except that usually in a sleeping state one is not aware of the separated subtle form.

The breathing system in the body is not run by the individual who has that body. It is not true that one controls the breath, except superficially. The breath is controlled by a lifeForce mechanism in the body. This system is kundalini.

Unless someone used drugs which interferes with the lifeForce's usual operations, there is no need to be fearful of losing breath. A decrease in breathing rate is no indication that the body will die during a projection. In fact invariably there is a reduction. When the lifeForce senses that the body is not exerting energy, it reduces the breathing rate. Bears who live in the northern hemisphere go into hibernation where the heart beat and breathing rate is almost nil. The individual self has nothing to do with it; it is run by the same type of lifeForce system, which is in a human body.

When one moves into astral consciousness one may sense the astral and physical vibrations, or just the astral one alone. One may confuse one for the other. Have you ever moved a hand or foot suddenly in a dream and then wake up immediately after only to realize that the physical hand or foot did not move? That is an instance of an astral body movement which is not coordinated with a physical one. Have you ever have a sexual experience in a dream and then find that there is no emission of sexual fluids on the physical side? Have you had such an experience and then discover that sexual fluids were expelled physically?

The kundalini force can be realized in several ways but one sure way to know that it functions and that it protects both the astral and physical systems, is to be suddenly retracted into the physical body when one has a frightening or anxiety-ridden astral experience. One is drawn back as rapidly as thought. It is not that the individual draws himself back. He or she is pulled by another force. The retraction mechanism is the lifeForce.

Part 6

Naad sound

Naad sound is sometimes called the sound current. Kundalini is the psychic lifeForce in the psyche. Apart from tinnitus, which is a nuisance sound in the ear, there is a yoga practice where one focuses on the sound which is heard in the head. This is a high pitched frequency which is usually heard near the right or left ear. It is used by some mystics to transfer to other dimensions.

Drugs / God

The important thing is that after taking psycho-active drugs some people who did not believe in reincarnation and who felt that the physical body was the limit of their existence, feel definitely that their existence was more than the physical system and that it would continue beyond the body.

Is it true that the subtle body is affected by drugs? How can a material substance affect the subtle body and cause subtle perception in a person who is normally very materialistic and has no psychic confidence?

One Swami from India denied that drugs could produce any such perception. He said that drugs cannot reveal anything about God. Are the experiences with psychedelic drugs illusions and hallucinations?

Point of reference

When one drinks alcohol one may observe a shift in consciousness towards mental happiness or emotional ease or even toward depression, worries and sadness. When one gets an inspiration, intuition or supernatural vision, one can know that it is an upward or downward shift. An upward shift is an enlightenment with a minor or major realization.

The point of reference is the place from which you measure whether it is enlightenment or not. Enlightenment is highlighted by insight into a more secure existence and the connection from here to there, from sober state to that level of existence. Enlightenment means making contact with higher reality. It does not mean that such contact will cause you to prosper physically. In fact it may cause you to neglect your physical well-being.

Real experience in dreams

Lucid dreaming is a real experience in another dimension. That is different to seeing imaginative creations in the mind. If one has an idea of the city of London that is not the actual city. Just as we may imagine something about the physical world and see it in the mind in the form of deliberate or spontaneous imagination, so during psychic states one may imagine or one may in fact visit other dimensions, other realities. When one makes an actual contact with other realities and when it is not imagined by the mind it is lucid experience.

Astral projection is similar to lucid dreaming. In some experiences both astral projection and lucid dreaming may take place simultaneously. In astral projection you feel yourself to be in a subtle body. In that experience you interact in another world, in another dimension, in an astral or celestial place.

Sometimes however if one is in a dimension which is very near to this physical place in vibrational frequency, one may perceive the physical body lying in a bed or perceive a house or some other object in this world.

The idea that you can hurt someone during an astral projection is misleading because it is the same thing when you think of someone in a bad way, that thinking energy may reach the person and cause the person to become depressed or to be doubtful and to develop a bad feeling towards you. But that happens even when one is not astral projecting. It is not particular to astral occurrences. The astral form is present when you use the physical body. Its powers are expressed through the physical form at that time.

Types of psychic perception

There are essentially three ways to view a place psychically without doing an astral projection. These are:

- Through the third eye
- Through the intellect organ
- By spiritual perception

Usually the method used is the third eye. That is located between the eyebrows. In other words you find that you can see directly through the center of the eyebrows without using the two physical or subtle eyes. It is like if a window opens there. You look through the skull into an environment.

Perception using the physical or subtle eyes or using both simultaneously includes use of the intellect. However the intellect by itself can function as a vision orb, where while looking into the intellect one perceives various realities here or there. The common use of the intellect is when it is used during physical eye or astral eye perception.

When using the eyes of the astral body, the intellect is used to focus through those eyes. When using the eyes of the physical body, the intellect is used to focus simultaneously through the astral and physical eyes because at that time the astral is interspaced into the physical system.

Avoidance of providence

There was always a huge effort by individual and collective human beings to center everything on the convenience of human beings but that is a farce. It is not going to happen. We are not the center. We will not be the center for any time in the future. There is already a center to this existence, even physically. We should accept that it so happens that we are not the hub.

Modern astronomy explained that the earth or the sun is not in the center of the galaxy. Our galaxy is not the central one of the galaxies which orbits in the local star cluster.

We should not be discouraged. We should not take ourselves so seriously that we should begin regretting our situation as being incidental existences in a trivial universe, on an insignificant planet. It is better to take it as it comes and do the best with the situation.

If there is a disease in the body which is based on parental neglect, past life bad habits, genetic inclination and just plain chance, then what is the need for regret? In the story about the Avanti brahmin, a story which was told by Krishna to Uddhava there is a summary of the situation.

जनस् तु हेतुः सुख-दुःखयोश् चेत्
किम् आत्मनश् चात्र हि भौमयोस् तत् ।
जिह्वा क्वचित् सन्दशति स्व-दद्भिस्
तद्-वेदनायां कतमाय कुप्येत् ॥१८.५१॥

janas tu hetuḥ sukha-duḥkhayoś cet
kim ātmanaś cātra hi bhaumayos tat
jihvāṁ kvacit sandaśati sva-dadbhis
tad-vedanāyāṁ katamāya kupyet (18.51)

janaḥ — people; tu — but; hetuḥ — cause; sukha – happiness; duhkhayoḥ — of distress; cet — if; kim — what; ātmanaś = ātmanaḥ — for the spirit; cātra = ca — and + atra — in this; hi — indeed, for; bhaumayos = bhaumayoḥ — concerning material nature; tat — that; jihvām — tongue; kvacit — sometimes; sandaśati — bites; sva-dadbhis = sva-dadbhiḥ — with one's teeth; tad = tat — that; vedanāyām — in the agony; katamāya — by which of the factors; kupyet — one should get angry.

"But if the people are the cause of happiness and distress, then what is it to the spirit, for in this case, that concerns material nature. And if sometimes one bites the tongue with his own teeth, which of the factors should be blamed for the agony? (Uddhava Gita 18.51)

दुःखस्य हेतुर् यदि देवतास् तु
किम् आत्मनस् तत्र विकारयोस् तत् ।
यद् अङ्गम् अङ्गेन निहन्यते क्वचित्
क्रुध्येत कस्मै पुरुषः स्व-देहे ॥१८.५२॥
duḥkhasya hetur yadi devatās tu
kim ātmanas tatra vikārayos tat
yad aṅgam aṅgena nihanyate kvacit
krudhyeta kasmai puruṣaḥ sva-dehe (18.52)

duḥkhasya — of misery; hetur = hetuḥ — cause; yadi — if; devatās = devatāḥ — the mystic supervisors of sensual energy; tu — but; kim — what; ātmanas = ātmanaḥ — of the spirit; tatra — in that case; vikārayos = vikārayoḥ — relating to the two mystic supervisors who cause bodily changes; tat — that; yad = yat — which however; aṅgam — limb; aṅgena — by a limb; nihanyate — is struck; kvacit — now and then; krudhyeta — should be angry; kasmai — to whom; puruṣaḥ — the person; sva-dehe — in one's body.

"But if the mystic supervisors of sensual energy, are the cause of misery, then in that case what may be said of the spirit, since the incidence relates only to those two mystic supervisors who cause the changes? However, if now and then a limb is struck by another limb, to whom should the person be angry? (Uddhava Gita 18.52)

आत्मा यदि स्यात् सुख-दुःख-हेतुः
किम् अन्यतस् तत्र निज-स्वभावः ।
न ह्य् आत्मनो ऽन्यद् यदि तन् मृषा स्यात्
क्रुध्येत कस्मान् न सुखं न दुःखम् ॥१८.५३॥
ātmā yadi syāt sukha-duḥkha-hetuḥ
kim anyatas tatra nija-svabhāvaḥ
na hy ātmano 'nyad yadi tan mṛṣā syāt
krudhyeta kasmān na sukhaṁ na duḥkham (18.53)

ātmā — individual spirit; yadi — if; syāt — is regarded; sukha – pleasure; duḥkha — pain; hetuḥ — cause; kim — what; anyatas = anyatah — other factor; tatra — in that case; nija — his own, individual; svabhāvaḥ — inherent tendency; na — not; hy = hi — because; ātmano = ātmanaḥ — besides the soul; 'nyad = anyat — any other factor; yadi — if; tan = tat — that; mṛṣā — false; syāt — should be; krudhyeta — should be angry; kasmān = kasmat — besides whom; na — neither; sukham — happiness; na — nor; duhkham — misery.

"If the individual spirit is regarded as the cause of pleasure and pain, then what other factor is responsible? It would be reliant on the individual's inherent tendency, and there is no other factor besides the individual spirit. If there should be such a factor, it is false. Then who should one be angry with? Neither happiness nor distress is real. (Uddhava Gita 18.53)

ग्रहा निमित्तं सुख-दुःखयोश् चेत्
किम् आत्मनो ऽजस्य जनस्य ते वै ।
ग्रहैर् ग्रहस्यैव वदन्ति पीडां
क्रुध्येत कस्मै पुरुषस् ततो ऽन्यः ॥१८.५४॥
grahā nimittaṁ sukha-duḥkhayoś cet
kim ātmano 'jasya janasya te vai
grahair grahasyaiva vadanti pīḍāṁ
krudhyeta kasmai puruṣas tato 'nyaḥ (18.54)

grahā — influential planets; nimittam — cause; sukha – happiness; duḥkhayoś = duḥkhayoh — and of distress; cet — if; kim — what; ātmano = ātmanaḥ — concerning the self; 'jasya = ajasya — of that which is birthless; janasya — of what is produced; te — those; vai — indeed; grahair = grahaiḥ — by the planets; grahasyaiva = grahasya — of a planet + eva — only; vadanti — they say; pīḍām — misfortune; krudhyeta — should direct the anger; kasmai — at whom; puruṣas — person; tato = tatah — thence, from that; 'nyah = anyaḥ — separate factor.

"If the influential planets are the cause, then what concern is it to the birthless spirit, since that concerns those planets which are produced. They say however that the misfortune of one planet is caused by another. Since the person is a separate factor, to whom should one direct the anger? (Uddhava Gita 18.54)

कर्मास्तु हेतुः सुख-दुःखयोश् चेत्
किम् आत्मनस् तद् धि जडाजडत्वे ।
देहस् त्व् अचित् पुरुषो ऽय सुपर्णः
क्रुध्येत कस्मै न हि कर्म मूलम् ॥१८.५५॥
karmāstu hetuḥ sukha-duḥkhayoś cet
kim ātmanas tad dhi jaḍājaḍatve
dehas tv acit puruṣo 'yaṁ suparṇaḥ
krudhyeta kasmai na hi karma mūlam (18.55)

karmāstu = karma — cultural activity + astu — let it be assumed; hetuḥ — cause; sukha-duḥkhayoś = sukha-duhkhayoḥ — happiness and distress; cet — if; kim — what; ātmanas = ātmanaḥ — for the individual spirit; tad = tat — that; dhi = hi — factually; jaḍājaḍatve = jaḍa – inert principle, insensible principle + ajaḍatve — and the sensible principle; dehas = dehaḥ — body; tv = tu — but; acit — not conscious; puruṣo = puruṣaḥ — the person; 'yaṁ = ayam — this; suparṇaḥ — a ray of the sun, what is spiritually enlivening; krudhyeta — should be angry;

kasmai — at whom; na — cannot be; hi — since; karma — cultural activities; mūlam — the basis.

"If it is assumed that cultural activity is the cause of happiness and distress, then what does the spirit have to do with that, since surely cultural acts are involved in the insensible and sensible objects. The body itself is not the generator of its own awareness, only the spirit who uses the body is spiritually-enlivening. Thus to whom should one direct anger since the cultural activity cannot be the basis? (Uddhava Gita 18.55)

कालस् तु हेतुः सुख-दुःखयोश् चेत्
किम् आत्मनस् तत्र तद्-आत्मको ऽसौ ।
नाग्नेर् हि तापो न हिमस्य तत् स्यात्
क्रुध्येत कस्मै न परस्य द्वन्द्वम् ॥१८.५६॥
kālas tu hetuḥ sukha-duḥkhayoś cet
kim ātmanas tatra tad-ātmako 'sau
nāgner hi tāpo na himasya tat syāt
krudhyeta kasmai na parasya dvandvam (18.56)

kālas = kālaḥ — time; tu — supposing; hetuh — cause; sukha-duḥkhayos = sukha-duḥkhayoh — happiness and distress; cet — if; kim — which; ātmanas = ātmanah — for the spirit; tatra — in that case; tad = tat – that; ātmako = ātmakaḥ — being of the same nature; 'sau = asau — that; nāgner = na — not + agneḥ — from fire; hi — hence; tāpo = tāpaḥ — burning; na — not; himasya — of snow; tat — that; syāt — becomes; krudhyeta — should the anger be directed to; kasmai — at whom; na — not; parasya — concerning that which is supreme; dvandvam — duality.

"Supposing that time is assumed as the cause of happiness and distress, then what is that to the spirit? In that case, that same time has the same nature of the soul. And factually fire is not affected by burning nor snow by the cold. Thus to whom should the anger be directed, for there is no duality in that which concerns the supreme?" (Uddhava Gita 18.56)

Basically this says that there is no use in tagging anything because it is all intertwined. It is based on essential natures of the forces which are involved.

Who or what or which religion can guarantee that in the next life one's parents will have bodies which have no genetic defects, and that such persons having such bodies will not be neglectful in some way, and that the reactions which are due to one will not manifest?

There are religions both from the East and West which promise these things but will the promises be validated?

We cannot control these things absolutely. As for the dysfunctionality of parents, we live with that and take our chances for good and bad and try to do the best. Even the people who are rated as divinities, people like Jesus

Christ in the Western countries and Krishna in the Eastern system, even they were subjected to hassles and had to act or react to unfavorable situations. As a baby and infant, Jesus had to be hid here and there by his parents because the ruler of the country had a paranoia about children who would be destined to kill him. And the same was in the history of Krishna where in an effort to save him from being killed his father switched him for another child. The child who was switched was killed in fact, as the ruler who was scared to death of any infant who would be a threat to him, snatched that swopped infant and bashed it on a stone floor. Krishna's father did that to save Krishna from that fate. Imagine if you knew that your son was to be killed by somebody who had this astrological reading which said that the child would kill him. Then soon after delivery you took the infant to a hospital ward and switch it secretly for another infant. Then the threatened person came to your wife's bedside, snatched the stolen child and killed the infant.

There is no escaping these hassles. We should not try to straighten all kinks of circumstance. Some of it must be endured. There is no point in trying to find a way out of a dead ended existence which is the situation in this material world with its perpetual on-going birth, death and whatever is forced before us in-between.

Worldly possessions

There are two paths. One is drastic activity reduction, *nivritti marga*. The other is expansive social participation, *pravritti marga*. In the reduction one avoids social opportunities. In the other, the person uses these in an informed manner on the basis of understanding that everything is temporary but valuable nevertheless. In the *Bhagavad Gita*, the path of informed detached involvement is recommended to a person named Arjuna, while in another book named Uddhava Gita, the other path of complete detachment and deprivation is recommended by the same teacher to a person named Uddhava.

Deep dreamless sleep

Deep dreamless sleep is akin to what Patañjali called *chittavritti nirodhah* which is a state of mind in which the usual oscillations of the mind cease. Is this boredom? Yes and no. It is boredom if this is experienced in a lower level. It is super perception if it is experienced in a higher state of consciousness. If for instance one gains no insight in that state of thoughtlessness, then it is called *jad samadhi* which means a stilled state of mind in which there is no higher perception but only blankness. Otherwise if there is higher insight into other dimensions or into the mechanisms of consciousness, it is rewarding for the person concerned.

A total subjective state in which there is no objective feedback is to a greater extent static or passive and should be developed into an objective state. To do this, one should repeatedly go into that subjective realm with intention for recalling what takes place. It is like reading this entry after it is written using white ink on white paper. How would one read that? Our minds are so insensitive that when we are confronted with anything transcendental we identify it as void and empty.

Phones in the psychic world

There is little difference between a departed soul's status after he leaves the body and that of his status before he left the body. Once he is departed one is deprived of the physical way of reaching him but the psychic method is as before. What changed is one's orientation for communicating with the person. The shock of death is that we can no longer relate by the reliable physical means. If we condition ourselves to the psychic side, we could continue communications and relations with those who can only use the psychic side.

Do phones ring in the psychic world? They do but only in dimension which is directly adjacent to this world. In such dimensions a departed person creates an environment which suits his or her needs which is based on the circumstance of the most recently life in a material body.

Usually a person creates a house, just like the one he or she lived in before passing from the body, and usually the person's sickness which was endured at death of the last body, persists for a time in the astral world as well.

Damaged astral body

How does a blind man, a deaf man or a maimed man astral project?

Such persons astral project using the same subtle body, the body used in actual dreams. First of all we should realize that the physical body is created in the body of the mother on the basis of the subtle one.

A blind material body does not imply a blind subtle one. The same goes for a deaf or maimed one. In fact persons who lose limbs usually speak of phantom limbs which gave pain and movement. The lost member is there as a psychic reality. The pain is psychological. When a physical limb is lost, the subtle counterpart remains even though it may be damaged. Thus the injured person may feel that limb from time to time. This is corroborated where sometimes in a dream one moves a hand or foot and then finds that the physical member did not move. It means that the subtle limb moved independently of the physical counterpart.

Loss of physical sight is not loss of subtle sight. Whatever subtle sight was there before may continue. In some cases the subtle sight will be lost for a time. But even then it is usually for a short time.

The astral body is sometimes affected by physical injury but for short periods of time. The astral form heals quickly. Just as the physical body has a healing system of its own which is independent of one's willpower and in fact is even independent of one's objectivity, so the astral body has a healing system which is faster than the one we experience physically.

Sometimes in astral experiences one is attacked by someone who stabs the subtle body with a knife, but even though a wound appears, it instantly heals. Would there be pain? Yes and No. There is pain if the person had a legitimate gripe, otherwise even though a wound may appear; it disappears faster than it was created.

If someone with dementia departs from the body after a short period of say about 6 months for the most, that person's subtle body will not retain the psychological effects of the disease, but if it is for a longer period, the person may have that forgetfulness and lack of reference in the subtle body and would, more than likely, take a new body with an absentminded demeanor in infancy and youth.

If a person was on morphine or any other narcotic the subtle body may retain an addiction to those drugs. In the next body in childhood, the person even though forgetting the last body and its history, may manifest a desire to have such drugs.

The subtle body retains the psychological habits. Whatever lifestyle one has is retained and carried in the subtle body, which contains the mental and emotional energies.

Thought control

A yogi should cease lead-on thinking. Once a thought arises in the mind there is a hypnotic energy which forces the person to see the idea to the end of its development.

As it develops, memories of related occurrences arise and mix with the original lead-on energy. For this to happen one has to be attached to the thought as the involved viewer in the mind. If one is involved in a thought and if one can cease interest in it, one should terminate the curiosity. This will close the thought pattern even though the mind may divert to another sequence of ideas.

Once one finds the self to be hypnotized by a thought, one should become objective to it, then reduce interest or curiosity about it. If one maintains even a bit of curiosity, that interest causes one to be hypnotized. It disables one's command over the mind.

Silver cord

The physical body has an aura when it is alive. It loses that when it dies. However when the astral body is separated from the physical one during astral projection, the physical system experiences a reduction in energy. Its aura shrinks. During astral projection, a portion of psychic force remains with the physical body to carry on digestion, cell repair and nerve management, but much of the self's energy goes with the astral form for psychic operations.

A psychic may see the silver cord which connects the physical body and the separated astral one but only if the psychic is focused on the level of vibration of the cord. It is not always seen because the psychic perception of a person is not always on the same level as the vibration of the energy transmission between the two bodies. Even though it is called a silver cord, it can be seen in other colors like cream or white, grey or even orange. It depends on the health of the person. Even though it is described as a cord it is a stream of energy. At death of the physical form, the lifeForce permanently leaves the physical body and remains with the subtle one only, at least until another physical form is developed.

Astral disability

It does happen in the astral world that one finds oneself to be in a scary dimension where violence of some type is applied to the astral body. In many such situations, the body heals immediately if the violence is accepted by it. Sometimes when someone or an animal attempts to inflict violence it does not penetrate the astral form but on occasion it does.

In some astral dimensions however, in hellish ones, violence does last for a time. It does not necessarily disappear as suddenly as it is inflicted but that is due to some consequence which is due to someone because of a previous action which was inflicted on the psychological plane and which was not resolved in destiny prior.

There are astral tigers. In fact even some extinct species of tiger like the saber tooth can be seen in some dimensions in the astral world. Even though they have no physical access to this planet, their astral forms still exist in adjacent dimensions. Their predatory instinct endures.

When one is attacked by a tiger in this world, one is unable to outrun or disappear physically because the tiger body has more running ability than the human one and a physical form cannot make itself disappear. The astral body is different. It may disappear from an astral level. If one is chased by a tiger one will find that one's body vanishes suddenly from the astral dimension where the tiger was seen. The tiger will be unable to follow one into that other dimension because there are thousands of such dimensions. The subtle body will go into one in which the tiger cannot trace it. This happens by psychic instinct.

Some persons are born with physical disabilities. We can assume that some people have astral handicaps. The astral body is not being born. It is not dying as the physical one does. It is continuously energized and de-energized life after life. It is the same body that is being used to be the basis for a series of physical forms.

The astral body is easily understood if one views it as the container for one's mental and emotional energies. These energies persist after the death. The surviving subtle body pursues another physical form because it has an instinct for functioning through physical energy.

The astral body does carry in it the desirable and undesirable psychological energies which were not resolved in destiny. Unless a person is 100% good, his/her subtle body will have defects. It is nice to posit that everyone is an angel but the reality is different. Even angels are sometimes found wanting. In so far as the psychological energies are corrupt, the subtle body will be flawed.

Defects in the subtle form do manifest in the physical embryo, but added to that are genetic defects inherited from the parents. A person may have a defect which results from his or her psychological faults or from parental genetics or from a combination of both.

Spirit going away

When a non-mystic person passes from the body, he/she has no idea of what will occur on the psychic side of life. There is much information about what happens to a person after the death of the physical body. Most of it is speculation. Much of it relates to the fact that we want to hear positive things about the hereafter. When someone passes he/she goes to an astral existence which is the same or is similar to the astral dream existence experienced during the life of the body. Most people do not go to the heaven promised by their religion. They do not see guiding angels. Only a hand full of people may have such experiences. Of those few transit to a higher dimension permanently. Most experiences occur in death just as they do in life, in a flash and then it is over and one finds oneself in the astral world as a wandering spirit or ghost, trying to figure the missing physical existence.

Just as one was not in control of the overall circumstance of physical life when one used a living physical body, so after that form becomes inaccessible one will not be in control of the astral form. One will have to make do at that time with pleasant or unpleasant circumstances.

The idea that just after death one somehow becomes knowledgeable and has a clear view of reality and of the possibilities of the future, is a hopeful concept but it does not apply in most cases of people who pass on.

Most deceased spirits go to an adjacent astral world and remain there for a time until they again enter into the body of would-be parents and again become an infant of a mother on this side.

They go to the same astral world we all go to during realistic dreams, lucid dreaming and astral projection. The different between going there while the physical body is alive and going there once it is dead, is that while the body is alive one awakens and makes use of this side. When the body is dead one can no longer directly access this side. Until one becomes transformed into an embryo, one must permanently remain on the other side. Some persons go to a heavenly world or even to a hellish undesirable place, but most people stay in an adjacent astral place.

Dvaita / advaita

Dvaita is Sanskrit for two things.

Usually Advaita Vedanta is the philosophy of not having two aspects, especially as having the one aspect of an Absolute Truth, where there is no plurality of souls or spirits but only one sum total super existence or energy.

Advaita means one or it means not-two or non-duality. Dvaita indicates duality. However it depends on the particular philosopher or sect which uses these terms.

In the *Bhagavad Gita* there is also the aspect of non-duality but it is explained differently as not having a different response to happiness and distress, or to heat and cold, having the same mood towards these, even to pleasure and pain.

जितात्मनः प्रशान्तस्य
परमात्मा समाहितः ।
शीतोष्णसुखदुःखेषु
तथा मानावमानयोः ॥६.७॥

jitātmanaḥ praśāntasya
paramātmā samāhitaḥ
śītoṣṇasukhaduḥkheṣu
tathā mānāvamānayoḥ (6.7)

jitātmanaḥ — of the self-controlled person; praśāntasya — of the person who is peaceful; paramātmā — the directive part of the self; samāhitaḥ — composed; śītoṣṇasukhaduḥkheṣu = śīta — cold + uṣṇa — heat + sukha — pleasure + duḥkheṣu — in pain; tathā — also; mānāvamānayoḥ = māna — honor + avamānayoḥ — in dishonor

The directive part of a self-controlled, peaceful person remains composed in the cold, heat, pleasure, pain, and also in honor and dishonor. (Bhagavad Gita 6.7)

It means that one should be nondual or impartial towards the weather, the sensations in the body and the status one is allowed on any occasion.

As I wrote above the meaning of Advaita Vedanta depends on the particular philosopher because *Bhagavad Gita* is also rated as Vedanta, even though it does not advocate every definition given for advaita.

Failure of celibate efforts

In so far as this physical world is the reference and in so far as physical objects are the objective, the self is part of a dream. If one works from this level and use this level as the standard, anything which is subtle is dreamy. Conversely if one takes the subtle as the standard, then anything which is physical would be dense and would have less value.

In physics there is an idea that subtle matter, particles, are the reality and that the solid substances which we perceive are part of a grand illusion. Alternately, in physics there is the converse where the physical substances are the reality and the particles are illusory and shifty.

While the physical body lives one should do meditation and dedicate oneself to finding the truth by exploring other dimensions. Do not wait to do this at the time of the death or after. Read the *Bhagavad Gita* about other dimensions.

Moon travel

Yearly, millions of dollars are spent to accomplish the conquest of other planets, even though practically speaking this is a dead end. Why do we persist at this? Obviously it is a recurring desire of mankind.

Bhagavad Gita proposes space travel to the moon or the sun for yogis who are interested but it says that those who reach the moon will have to circle back to the earth, while those who reach the sun may go beyond that. Krishna discussed space travel using the subtle body not the physical one. That is the least expensive method, especially considering that even if it gets to the moon the physical body will soon die.

In fact the evidence is that if it gets to the moon the body will perish faster because it will have to live in a manmade insolated environment continually because it cannot tolerate the moon environment. Since it is genetically designed for a stronger gravitational force a physical body will suffer on the moon because of the reduced gravity. One great Swami denied that man could reach the moon in a space ship but man accomplished that anyway.

Krishna does not deny that man can reach the moon either physically or astrally. I have never seen any statement of his in the Sanskrit which denies moon access. But Krishna did not in anything I read, recommend physical presence on the moon only astral presence. There are also stories about Krishna going into outer space on several occasions. Once he went to the Swarga place which is a type of paradise but in the Sanskrit it does not say that he went there physically. However some commentators seem to think that he went there with the body which was visible to physical beings of this world.

In relation to the moon, my proposal is for astral journeys there. I suggest that one make the journey now and not to wait to do so at the time of death. It is always a good idea to go to a place one may relocate to beforehand; just to be sure it is what one desires.

Here is some of what Krishna said about yogis going to the moon or sun. Remember that this concerns the subtle body not the physical one. No space ship is used. Only expertise at astral projection is required.

यत्र काले त्वनावृत्तिम्
आवृत्तिं चैव योगिनः ।
प्रयाता यान्ति तं कालं
वक्ष्यामि भरतर्षभ ॥८.२३॥

yatra kāle tvanāvṛttim
āvṛttiṁ caiva yoginaḥ
prayātā yānti taṁ kālaṁ
vakṣyāmi bharatarṣabha (8.23)

yatra — where; kāle — in time; tv = tu — but; anāvṛttim — not return; āvṛttim — return; caiva = ca — and + eva — indeed; yoginaḥ — yogis; prayātā — departing; yānti — go; tam — this; kālam — time; vakṣyāmi — I will tell; bharatarṣabha — O bullish man of the Bharata family

O bullish man of the Bharata family, I will tell you of the departure for the yogis who do or do not return. (Bhagavad Gita 8.23)

अग्निर्ज्योतिरहः शुक्लः
षण्मासा उत्तरायणम् ।
तत्र प्रयाता गच्छन्ति
ब्रह्म ब्रह्मविदो जनाः ॥८.२४॥

agnirjyotirahaḥ śuklaḥ
ṣaṇmāsā uttarāyaṇam
tatra prayātā gacchanti
brahma brahmavido janāḥ (8.24)

agnir = agniḥ — summer season; jyotir = jyotiḥ — bright atmosphere; ahaḥ — daytime; śuklaḥ — bright moonlight; saṇmāsā — six months; uttarāyaṇam — the time when the sun appears to move north; tatra — at that time; prayātā — departing; gacchanti — they go; brahma — to the spiritual location; brahmavido = brahmavidaḥ — knowers of the spiritual dimension; janāḥ — people

The summer season, the bright atmosphere, the daytime, the bright moonlight, the six months when the sun appears to move north; if at that time, they depart the body, those people who know the spiritual dimension, go to the spiritual location. (Bhagavad Gita 8.24)

धूमो रात्रिस्तथा कृष्णः
षण्मासा दक्षिणायनम् ।
तत्र चान्द्रमसं ज्योतिर्
योगी प्राप्य निवर्तते ॥८.२५॥

dhūmo rātristathā kṛṣṇaḥ
ṣaṇmāsā dakṣiṇāyanam
tatra cāndramasaṁ jyotir
yogī prāpya nivartate (8.25)

dhūmo = dhūmaḥ — smoky, misty or hazy season; rātris — night time; tathā — as well as; kṛṣṇaḥ — the dark moon time; saṇmāsā — six months; dakṣiṇāyanam — the time when the sun appears to move south; tatra — at that time; cāndramasam — moon; jyotir = jyotiḥ — light; yogī — yogi; prāpya — attaining; nivartate — is born again

The smoky, misty or hazy season, as well as in the night-time, the dark-moon time, the six months when the sun appears to move south; if the yogi departs at that time, he attains moonlight, after which he is born again. (Bhagavad Gita 8.25)

शुक्लकृष्णे गती ह्येते
जगतः शाश्वते मते ।
एकया यात्यनावृत्तिम्
अन्ययावर्तते पुनः ॥८.२६॥

śuklakṛṣṇe gatī hyete
jagataḥ śāśvate mate
ekayā yātyanāvṛttim
anyayāvartate punaḥ (8.26)

śuklakṛṣṇe — light and dark; gatī — two paths; hyete = hy (hi) — indeed + ete — these two; jagataḥ — of the universe; śāśvate — perpetual; mate — is considered; ekayā — by one; yāty = yāti — goes away; anāvṛttim — not return; anyayāvartate = anyayā — by other + āvartate — comes back; punaḥ = punar — again

The light and the dark times are two paths which are considered to be perpetually available for the universe. It is considered so by the authorities. By one, a person goes away not to return; by the other he comes back again. (Bhagavad Gita 8.26)

नैते सृती पार्थ जानन्
योगी मुह्यति कश्चन ।
तस्मात्सर्वेषु कालेषु
योगयुक्तो भवार्जुन ॥८.२७॥

naite sṛtī pārtha jānan
yogī muhyati kaścana
tasmātsarveṣu kāleṣu
yogayukto bhavārjuna (8.27)

naite = na — not + ete — these two; sṛtī — two paths; pārtha — O son of Pṛthā; jānan — knowing; yogī — yogi; muhyati — is confused; kaścana — at all; tasmāt — therefore; sarveṣu — in all; kāleṣu — in times; yogayukto = yogayuktaḥ — disciplined in yoga practice; bhavārjuna = bhava — be + arjuna — Arjuna

Knowing these two paths, O son of Pṛthā, the yogi is not confused at all. Therefore at all times, be disciplined in yoga practice, O Arjuna. (Bhagavad Gita 8.27)

Meditation defined

Meditation methods were developed in India, China and Japan for the most part. In Japan it came to be known as Zen which is a word which is traceable to the Sanskrit word *dhyana*. There is speculation that when the Japanese used to pronounce *dhyana*, they said zyan (zi-an) which evolved into Zen.

In China the Taoist sages developed meditation practices. Some did it independently without contact with India. Later when Buddhism spread from India to China, meditation as taught by Buddha was practiced.

In India meditation was defined by Patañjali in his book *Yoga Sutras*. According to him, meditation consist of the highest three stages of a practice called yoga which has a total of eight parts (*ashtanga* yoga). Those three states are *dharana*, *dhyana* and *samadhi*. Taken together Patañjali called this *samyama*, which means the complete (*sam*) restraint (*yama*) of the automatic operations in the mind.

I will give a brief explanation of the three stages but bear in mind that if you practice them, they usually evolve into or devolve into each other. In other words if you begin with dharana it may spontaneously develop into *dhyana* which may convert into *samadhi*. The converse is true where if one is in *samadhi*, it may devolve or degrade into *dhyana* which may degrade into dharana.

Dharana is when one shifts the attention from this level to any other higher plane of consciousness. In doing so you would link into that plane of existence or to a person or object in that dimension. A question arises as to the shift method used. For details please read Patañjali's *Yoga Sutras*. There is more than one method of shifting. Patañjali even mentions drugs as a method even though he did not recommend that. His recommendation was the yoga process of which the first five preliminary steps were explained by him. *Dharana*, *dhyana* and *samadhi* are the final three steps, making a total of eight procedures.

Dhyana is when the attention is shifted from this level of existence to any other higher plane of consciousness even momentarily. In that practice it happens spontaneously without deliberation and mental exertion.

In the first method, *dharana*, one makes an endeavor to shift focus. One should hold the attention there or one may find that it reconnects with a previous preoccupation or begins a new unwanted display. In the second method, *dhyana*, one does not make an endeavor. It happens involuntarily without the mental exertion which is required in *dharana*.

In the third method, *samadhi*, one's attention is shifted from this level of existence to any other higher plane of consciousness for more than a moment, for an extended period, say for 15 minutes or more. In that practice this is done spontaneously without deliberation and mental exertion. It persists for a time unlike *dhyana* which happens spontaneously for a moment or two only.

Bond of mutual attraction

The agreement to live as man and wife, either being formally married or not, has within it a natural lubricant in the initial stages when nature provides interest and attraction. The force of attraction is the social adhesive. It keeps two people in harmony no matter what.

The problem however is that nature does not maintain that bond forever. When nature stops supporting it either temporality or permanently, the couple must hedge themselves. If there are children, the couple could focus on child care. The children then become an adhesive.

Siddhi mystic powers

In the yoga system there is a statement regarding the use and development of psychic abilities. This is from the Yoga Sutras.

ते समाधावुपसर्गा व्युत्थाने सिद्धयः ॥३८॥
te samādhau upasargāḥ vyutthāne siddhayaḥ

te – they, those abilities; samādhau – in samādhi continues effortless linkage of the attention to a higher concentration force, object or person; upasargāḥ – impediments; vyutthāne – in expressing, going outwards, rising up; siddhayaḥ – mystic perfectional skills.

Those divination skills are obstacles in the practice of continuous effortless linkage of the attention to a higher concentration force, object or person. But in expressing, they are considered as mystic perfectional skills. (Yoga Sutras 3.38)

Patañjali claimed that using the psychic powers creates obstacles to *samadhi* which is deep meditation practice, but he wrote of yogis who develop mystic abilities through yoga.

One related topic is the calibration of psychic abilities, which means that the psychic should figure the degree of accuracy. For instance on the physical side we have eyeglasses which are designed to compensate for vision deficiency. An ophthalmologist checks the vision and determines its deficiency. Then calibrated lenses are created. If the psychic knows the degree of distortion of an ability, he or she, taking that into consideration, can better advice clients

Prolonging life

Each person has his or her way of looking at life, according the childhood background, the teenaged experience, the adult years and the resulting philosophy which one develops and relies on for a position or perspective.

Some assume that God is responsible for one's wellbeing. Whether it is God, nature or providence there is an ultimate force under which we function. If we act or do not act, that force will prevail. It will eventually deprive one of the physical body.

One may act in a limited way to prolong the life of the body. If for instance one has a terminal disease and one is told by a doctor that one's life may be prolonged for one year if one agrees to take a narcotic drug, one should consider if the drug will negatively impact the subtle body and thus cause suffering hereafter.

Meditative states

Meditative states may come about spontaneously or deliberately. Once you get a spontaneous blessing in the form of an advanced meditative state, the next step is to develop a practice through which you can induce the condition deliberately. Some persons, a few, continue to have meditative states regardless of not developing a deliberate practice. They are mystics.

Consequential energy

The force behind a specific consequential reaction may require that one be inconvenienced or facilitated. This reminds me of a child who was the son of a wealthy man. In the past life the child did humanitarian services. The consequence was such that he took birth in a wealthy family, born with a buttery silver spoon in his mouth. The problem was that the positive benefits were delivered in the infant stage of his life at a time when he could neither appreciate nor properly utilize the wealth. That is tragic. If I have money coming to me from pious acts in a past life, I prefer to have it during the adult years. Why should providence award it in childhood when I cannot best enjoy it? That is another hitch about consequential energy, where it may not surface when one can best enjoy it.

Something like that happened in my experience. When my body was about 16 years of age, it was in Trinidad where my father had a job that put him in the category of the well-to-do. He lived in a palatial house. I stayed there for about two years for the most. Because my father lost the job, the privilege was terminated. Since then I did not lived in a palatial building again.

Some years after around 1974, a friend of mine toured the United States. I went with him. We stopped in Atlanta where his parents lived in the suburbs. There we met a young woman who lived in a castle house on the outskirts of the city. I wrote poetry then. This young woman met me there and we did poetry readings. Her father was a wealthy doctor who had several opulent homes. The one in Atlanta was her residence.

While I was there I thought, "This rendering of positive and negative returns from previous lives is inexplicable. This lady lives here like a goddess while others live in the slums. I lived in an opulent place before but the opportunity was squashed because my father was an alcoholic. These renderings of fate are jokes on a living being."

Popularity

Popularity affects one even after leaving a body. Unless one reforms the self beforehand and unless that reforming action is effective, any good or bad character traits will continue after leaving the body.

Attraction to popularity is such that it supersedes one's good qualities and makes itself the priority. On the psychic plane popularity is a virus. If one becomes more popular that one should be, it causes ruination. Each person is important as an agent of a divinity, but it is possible to expand that importance artificially. When one does this or when one comes under influences which do this, ruination is the result.

Complex destinies

There has to be different types of destiny, because even on the physical level which we endure presently, we see that there is disparity. Some are helplessly victimized.

Recently there was a plane crash where the only survivor was a 13 year old girl. More than one hundred other persons lost bodies. Fate is complicated. Why did the girl survive? What collective destiny was forced on the others? Were they killed, to emphasis the lone survivor?

Some reactions are based on the individual's action in this or a past life (*adhyatmic*) Some are based on the reactions of other limited beings (*adhibhautic*). Some are based on supernatural agency (*adhidaivic*).

Some are due to a combination of the three in varying proportions. We can assume that we are subjected to reactions which were caused by the actions of other limited beings as well as by supernatural agency, and also by willful or nonwilful activity.

Regularity of meditation

To get consistent results from meditation, one should do it daily. It must be a habit. Daily practice is likely to give consistent results. Sporadic meditation also gives results, except that it does not allow one to consolidate the progress.

Paradise hereafter

Nearly every religious system has paradise as the promise of salvation for the followers. If one is born in a Catholic family and is indoctrinated accordingly, one will have a belief in a certain paradise. It will suit the culture in which the belief surfaced. For instance in a Catholic-described heaven one will not find angels wearing saris and dhotis.

If someone else, say Mr. Chaudouri was born in India and was indoctrinated as a Hindu, he would believe in a heaven which fits neatly with Indian culture. The angels in that paradise would not be illustrated wearing robes.

Progress made in previous births

Spiritual practice through the yoga system or any other method is not limited to what we get from India. It is not limited to the Vedic system or to the Vedic deities.

If anyone researches, it will be discovered for example that spiritual practices which are authentic were developed in other parts of the world, notably China, Japan and some parts of Western Europe. Other societies and cultures also developed systems even though many were not noted in writing.

One should begin spiritual inquiry with a system which seems to be compatible to one's cultural orientation or to one past life. It so happens that we are culturally bound. Thus initially it is best to make use of that limitation.

Each system from the East or West focuses on and stresses a particular aspect of spiritual development. One should check the systems to see which would be most useful.

Even though I wrote books based on the Eastern approach of yoga, still I studied some Western systems. I studied the Hermetic system, Gurdjief, Aleister Crowley, Rosicrucian, Apollonius of Tyana, Madame Blavatsky, Theosophy, Aquarian Gospel, Urantia and many other systems developed in the Western societies, some of which were independent of or affiliated with the Eastern approach.

One has nothing to lose by checking these systems. In the 1960's and 1970's I took help from Colin Wilson's books like *Mind Parasites*, Herman Hesse's books like *Glass Bead Game* and *Siddhartha*, Albert Camus's books like *The Stranger*, H.P. Lovecraft's pioneering works like *Dunwich Horror*, Kahlil Gibran's books like *The Prophet* and many other texts. One should go wherever one will to make spiritual progress, taking help from others.

I took many births and lived in many cultures. Each is suitable depending on what I developed in a particular birth at a particular time and place. Checking these systems is one method of reviewing what was done in previous births, to reintegrate the progress made in those locations under the auspices of those cultures.

Alternate realities

After sleep when one becomes aware of the physical body, it may not be operate as usual. It may not allow one to arouse the body. This is called cataleptic trance. It means that the dream body did not properly synchronize into the physical system, where the physical nervous system does not respond to one's willpower. One method of causing the synchronization to occur is to manipulate the breath. This may cause the physical body to become responsive. In some experiences, the forms synchronize for moments and then desynchronizes again, resuming the paralysis of the physical one.

When that happens one should again manipulate the breath to cause the systems to synchronize. Sometimes one finds that a force pulls one back into a particular dimension or dream. Remain objective about this. There are many astral dimensions which the subtle body may slip into. These are alternate realities or parallel dimensions which are adjacent to the physical world. There are many such locations.

Astral projection control

There are many books and articles which advocate astral projection and lucid dreaming as something that could be totally under control. Perhaps those who write that experienced it in that way. Perhaps some persons write that to commercialize their literature. My conclusion from over thirty-five years of astral projection and lucid dreaming with detailed notes and studies from others who were expert, is that it is not always under one's control. For that matter most people astral project nightly during sleep. They have so little control that they do not remember that it occurred.

The idea that one may have absolute control is fallacious. That defies nature and logic. There are so many things over which we have no control. I mean natural things. Has your skin ever been cut? How did it heal? Next time you are cut, sit and compel it to heal.

Psychic perception in children

A time may come when we develop psychic clarity. One is and was always in contact with deceased persons but the awareness of that is mostly subjective. One may struggle to objectify it. One is in touch with persons who are in the astral world awaiting rebirth and who were related to one in this or a recent past life.

The mere idea that departed souls get rebirth through souls who use physical bodies, indicates that those departed people are in touch with the living, otherwise how could they become developed embryos in the wombs of females who use living bodies. The contact is there. It is ongoing but it is not objective, because one is insensitive to the psychic level and is sensitive to the physical plane.

When the sensitivity increases on the subtle plane, there will be objective perception just as there is on the physical plane. Would it be possible that collectively we would reduce the physical focus and suddenly develop the mystic one or have both operating efficiently?

Who will bring this about? Which divine being?

The implication is that the divine person would have to exert that influence forever from then onwards, otherwise we would resume this level as soon as the divine infusement relaxed.

Early on a child has psychic perception but it is discouraged in infancy. It is not approved in most societies. Nowadays people are more accommodating to psychic perception and do not discourage children as before.

Dream interpretation

To get into the true meaning of a dream one should sort between what actually happens in the astral world and what is imagined. One should know when imagination mixes with actual psychic occurrences and appears in the mind or through the mind as one reality. A composite experience which is a combination of real psychic happenings and imagined mental constructions cannot be interpreted correctly unless it is sorted.

To sort these, a person must either be proficient in meditative and trance states or be a mystic who just happens to have an accurate intuition. Interpretation of dreams also needs to take into account the dreamer's cultural background and present jargon. Seeing a black cat for instance, may mean the opposite for a person from a different culture.

Usually our physical judgments and assessments serve as reference when we enter astral dimensions. We put the same emphasis from the physical world there. That should be changed because the laws of nature in the astral dimensions vary from that in this physical reality.

Astral occurrences do not necessarily correspond with physical ones. Some astral features are not connected to physical history. Hence one should not assume that an astral act necessarily has a physical completion or corresponding situation.

Reaction in which future life?

Even though we have some control over how we act currently, we have little or no control over when a reaction will be played out. When will destiny hurl at me a reaction from a past life? Will I know that it is a reaction? Or will I naively regard it as a fresh action?

Will destiny be gracious to me where I am aware of the previous act which is the foundation of what currently happens?

Regarding if the link of an action will go into immediate or distant effect, Krishna provided information when he listed five factors for accomplishment.

पञ्चैतानि महाबाहो
कारणानि निबोध मे ।
सांख्ये कृतान्ते प्रोक्तानि
सिद्धये सर्वकर्मणाम् ॥१८.१३॥

pañcaitāni mahābāho
kāraṇāni nibodha me
sāṁkhye kṛtānte proktāni
siddhaye sarvakarmaṇām (18.13)

pañcaitāni — pañca — five + tāni — these; mahābāho — O mighty-armed man; kāraṇāni — factors; nibodha — learn; me — from me; sāṁkhye — in Sāṁkhya philosophy; krtānte — in conclusion, in doctrīne; proktāni — declared; siddhaye — in accomplishment; sarvakarmaṇām — of all actions

Learn from Me, O mighty-armed man, of the five factors declared in the Sāṁkhya doctrine for the accomplishment of all actions. (Bhagavad Gita 18.13)

अधिष्ठानं तथा कर्ता
करणं च पृथग्विधम् ।
विविधाश्च पृथक्चेष्टा
दैवं चैवात्र पञ्चमम् ॥१८.१४॥

adhiṣṭhānaṁ tathā kartā
karaṇaṁ ca pṛthagvidham
vividhāśca pṛthakceṣṭā
daivaṁ caivātra pañcama (18.14)

adhiṣṭhānaṁ — location; tathā — as well as; kartā — the agent; karaṇaṁ — the instrument; ca — and; prthagvidham — various kinds; vividhāśca = vividhāḥ — various + ca — and; pṛthakceṣṭa — movements; daivam — destiny; caivātra — ca — and + eva — indeed + atra — here in this case; pañcamam — the fifth

The location, the agent, the various instruments, the various movements, and destiny, the fifth factor. (Bhagavad Gita 18.14)

Unless the factors are present a reaction cannot manifest. However if it cannot manifest what happens? Is the energy dissipated? It does not. It goes into dormancy, into a non-reactive state and remains in that condition until the five conditions are in place. As soon as the five aspects are present it becomes manifest regardless of whether the target is ready for the challenge or not.

Residue of past births

Usually one may find some residue in the psyche which may correspond to certain habits, lifestyle, likes and dislikes from a past life, but one will not usually find all residues from all past lives, especially from lives which were compressed in the subconscious mind. As a kid I always had a fascination for the cultures of India and China, but not much for the European countries, but that cannot mean that I did not take birth in Europe. Currently many people who took birth in Asian nations migrate to European countries.

Arjuna was shocked when Krishna claimed memory of a particular past life when Krishna said he explained the idea of karma yoga to Vivasvan, a legendary god in the Vedic pantheon of deities. Arjuna did not think such recall was possible

Recently when I visited the Czech Republic, the humans were similar to other humans elsewhere on the planet. They had two feet, two eyes and had similar needs like humans elsewhere. I could easily relocate there. I could take a parent there. I could adopt the cultural and social habits there if I took a body there. Somebody there could be my mother or father. I could be sexual with a woman there.

At one place off in the countryside where we stopped to use bathrooms, there was a lady who collected fees for bathroom use. It was about 75 cents in Euro currency. Even though her body was over 50 years and perhaps she was never near a black body, she examined me as if she wanted me to stay and get intimate with her.

Buddha, when he sat for meditation and was successful in piercing the causal plane, saw past births, millions of them. Some he said were even in aquatic species.

One does however and it is natural, hold prejudices towards certain preferred births. Those are the ones, one is likely to remember or to have an intuition about.

Value of old age

To benefit from materialistic life and from having this material body type, one must forego the advantages of youthful life in terms of sensual fulfillments. As it is, the system is geared only to the peak of youth and nearly everyone wants to remain in a youthful material body.

If one passes from the present body, one will more than likely need another one. To get that one will be attracted to two people who can have sexual intercourse to beget the embryo. If one remains in this world in an old body one will also be attracted to those who have youthful bodies, for the very reason that it is through such bodies that one will get the next form. If one is in infancy one will also be attracted to youthful bodies, especially to female ones because they breastfeed infants.

The scope of this existence has to do with youthful bodies. If we are attracted to these for sensual fulfillment, we will get into trouble because we will not calculate the responsibilities.

Fulfillments carry with them a package of responsibilities. If that is neglected it converts into inconvenient liabilities in this or in a future life. The system of action and reaction is so thorough that a person cannot escape from the repercussions of his or her activities.

The lifeForce in the body is unhappy about the deterioration of the body but it cannot stop that. It struggles against that and tries to adjust for that, but it is unable to do anything about that. The iSelf in the body also tries to adjust for that.

Apart from youth, there is infancy and elderly years. If it is used only for fulfillments youth is useless for spiritual purposes. If in youth one forgets to consider the infancy and to regard impending old age, one fails to make spiritual advancement.

If one considers the helplessness of youth and the ignorance one has when in it, and if one reviews the incapacity and insecurity of elderly years, there is a chance that one will make a bid for spiritual life. But if one focuses on youth why should one care?

The elderly years are more valuable than infancy because in maturity one develops discrimination and can assess the gamut of material existence and get serious with the self about pursuing spiritual life. In that sense old age is congenial.

In the life of Gautama Buddha, one of the things which jolted him out of the youthful sensual life was the sight of a person with an old wrinkled body. After seeing that and seeing a dead human form, and an ascetic who neglected material existence, Buddha struck out for spiritual realization.

He was in the prime of youth when he did this, He was a wealthy prince with a wife, concubines and a son.

He questioned himself, "What is this? Why the old age? Why death? Why the austerities to detach from this? How long will youth last? Will sensual fulfillment become displeasure?"

Clairvoyance

Anyone who is clairvoyant without practicing meditation or using other methods to become psychically perceptive, will usually retain the ability. Sometimes however a person who was clairvoyant in childhood loses the ability in the adult years. But it is more likely that the ability will be retained.

Clairvoyance also represents the responsibility for its usage. Say for example that you perceive something and inform a person about it. Then based on that information the person acts in a specific way, you would share in the responsibility of that action.

Suppose one's clairvoyance was muddled at the time or that it was inaccurate, or suppose that you misinterpreted a correct psychic perception, then who is liability if you share the information with someone and that person acts on the basis of what you perceived?

To better manage clairvoyance, one should calibrate it. This is something that many psychics fail to do because they are not aware that they can fine tune the ability.

Just as one may not have 20/20 vision, so the clairvoyant ability may not be completely accurate, but if one measures the accuracy one can learn how to regulate the offset. The other aspect to monitor is how one interprets what one perceives by clairvoyance. That can also be a source of inaccuracy if one does not upgrade that by purifying the psyche.

Did the body exist before the self-awareness?

The individual awareness was there before the formation of the embryo. It served as the psychic core around which the body was produced. However the individual awareness was subjective at the time. It was subjective to itself. It developed objectivity after the brain was somewhat developed in the embryo.

In love

There is a parody about love where a king discovered that the queen was in love with their charioteer, who was in love with their cook, who in turn was in love with another man besides her husband.

The king himself was in love with one of the queen's servants, who though married was in loved with a peasant, who though married was in love with a woman besides his wife.

What then is love?

Part 7

Understanding evolution

While many spiritual teachers condemn science and some are so set against it that they immediately reject anything science presents, and sometimes do this with good reason, it is not in our interest to have that attitude.

As we transmigrate we endeavor to adjust the undesirable features in the type of body we become. This adjustment business was noticed by Charles Darwin who said that the various species are related in a chain of development and that there were cases of which one species evolved into another over short or long periods of time. This idea was vehemently rejected by some spiritual teachers both in Christianity and in Vedic systems. But what Darwin said is factual and what those spiritual teachers said about creative prototypes is to an extent true as well. Both views have validity. We should ignore neither of them.

There were initial species or prototypes of creature forms. Those prototypes were capable of adjustment and evolutionary adaptation, which is Darwin's idea which is backed solidly by fossil evidence and also by some observations in living species like lizards which change skin color and some other queer adjustments which are made even in the human species, like people who migrate from one country to another, change diet and develop certain diseases, skin tone and other barely observable features, which were unknown in their native land.

When I lived in Trinidad in 1966, my body was a teenager. With some friends I used to dress in a fashionable way. One of the attractive garments was turtle neck sweaters. A friend of mine always wore such sweaters to parties. They were expensive but he wanted to be in a certain class. He adopted this from movies and magazines. Teenaged girls were attracted to him because he was stylish and had expensive turtle neck cardigans. Trinidad has a tropical climate. Those sweaters were developed for use in cold areas where the air had freezing temperatures.

My friend became attracted to sweaters without understand why they were developed. We had not experienced cold climates in our bodies. We were ignorant of the fact that people in Canada and elsewhere wore such clothing in the winter season, primarily because it kept their necks insulated from cold air. Such an attraction even though it seems trivial could cause this same friend to take birth in a country like Canada or Russian, where one has to wear such garments several months of the year to protect the body from winter climates.

Merely by adapting to something which one is attracted to in another species may cause one to switch to that lifeform. We may even change or cause adjustment in the species we are in without understanding where that change may lead. Right now many humans who migrated from the underdeveloped countries into the developed ones find that their cultural orientation changes in undesirable ways because of new influences. We find that inside the cultural forms of our children there are drastic changes which are reminiscent of Darwin's idea of species adaptation and change.

Do our children look different? They certainly do. It is a small and subtle change but it there nevertheless. Darwin's idea is not far fletched. The biggest changes in our children is not physical. It is psychological and emotional. Darwin's idea which he pushed as a biological fact, is even more sensationally verified on the psychological plane.

Cat and mouse

In a game of cat and mouse, a starving cat had to hide himself under a rug since all remaining mice were too scared to show their faces.

Believing that the cat was no longer in the building, the mice who were themselves starving and who wanted to get out and play, silently and suspiciously came out. At first they could not believe that the deadly cat who killed their parents and siblings was gone but when they saw no sign of the menace, they began playing happily again. They ate whatever snippets they could find in the building.

Unknown to them, the cat was silently listening.

It did not want to scare them away. It bore on with hunger, waiting for the moment when the majority of them were away from their safe hole which they bored in a corner. "Hum!" it began thinking, "It is worth waiting. This will be a nice dinner."

Choice about death?

Considering that there are individual and collective effects, it is not sensible to think that someone's pick of death departure is absolute. There are so many other factors which could come into play, and which could either support the desired time or rupture that.

The idea of picking a day to die is relative and highly dependent on how the end of life plays out. Unless providence facilitates one's pick-a-day hopes may be frustrated.

One should not be disheartened over the inability to control time and circumstance. We are tiny in contrast to the scope of the galaxies. We are composite infinitesimal parts of an infinite reality.

Dimensional experience of a yogi

There is a story in the Puranas about Markandeya, a yogi, who lived inside the deity Krishna. Markandeya spent eons inside the body of that deity and experienced many lives there. Then he was belched from the deity into a cosmic environment which he lived in many cosmic cycles prior.

The yogin said that there were universes in the body of the deity. He lived on several planets here and there within the body of that cosmic person. This story is narrated by Markandeya to Yudhishthira in the *Mahabharata*.

Reading peoples' minds

Some people after hearing about yoga and mystic powers get this idea that a yogi can and does read minds. They feel however that they should observe how the yogi does this. That is a silly game because in yoga the purpose of telepathy, clairvoyance and related mystic powers is to give the yogi access to other levels of existence from which he can absolve upcoming complications of destiny and exit from this mire of the material world. It is not for reading minds and such curiosities and adventures.

Mystic powers are a serious part of a yogi's development since without that ability he could not sidestep obstacles which are thrown before him by destiny and which would otherwise set him on a course of haphazard transmigrations.

It has nothing to do with reading minds. Even if a yogi knows what is in someone's mind that does not mean that the yogi can abuse the information without consequence.

A yogi does on occasion become aware of someone's thoughts but if he is interested in advancement that information cannot be used by him exploitatively.

Submission and yoga practice

Willingness to practice yoga is directly connected to the willingness to be a small-time nobody. For the practice of yoga, it is necessary to submit to someone who is advanced. It is not that the teacher needs honor. The process of learning with or without a teacher, requires submission. Even in cases where a person discovered yoga techniques without the presence of a physical teacher, that person submits to a revelation or inspiration.

For genuine submission one must be willing to take a student's posture and it does not end at some point in the future, since as one advances one has to submit for higher instructions either from the same teacher or from others. Many who come to study yoga do not want to submit. They have the notion that yoga is a process which is free from the need for student submission.

Subtle sex solutions

It is possible to relieve some sexual attractions through meditation but some relations cannot be solved in that way. One can tell by the way the energy moves in meditation. More or less sexual energy is a recurring force. It does not take an absolute no for an answer. It resurfaces repeatedly and may override resistance at another time.

Regardless, one should make the effort to resolve sexual encounters. That is the least a yogi can do. Knowing that every instance cannot be solved is no excuse for not endeavoring with the ones that may be terminated. In addition some which cannot be solved can be reduced if one confronts the energy and deals with it head on. There is no hard and fast rule. All fires cannot be extinguished with water. Some expand if one applies water. Each relationship require personal attention and care to see what one can do to terminate it.

It may be that some females are perpetually connected to a specific yogi. As such he cannot renounce those persons. He should not try to do so. He should instead try to monitor the relationships.

The idea that everything is linear and equal is hogwash. Everywhere one goes one will find disparities. In sex it is the same in that there will be a stronger attraction to specific females. Or in the case of heterosexual women, varied attraction to specific males.

Something to consider however is that such attraction may or may not be an indication of a deeper relationship. For instance, I had a strong irresistible attraction to Jane Goodlooking in a previous life. When I met her in this life, she used an elderly body. My body was a teenaged one. I felt some attraction but it was not as strong as my attraction to Rosie Thicklip, who currently used a teenaged body and who was my grandmother in a past life.

Why the change in attraction?

It is due to the fact that the sex appeal of a person, though an eternal attribute is supported or squelched by the condition of the material body. Ancestral energy is involved. One may become attracted to a not-so-sexy female, if the ancestors possess that person's sexual energy. Some get married in a huff and puff, and then about 4 or 5 years after they are at a loss to explain why the marriage took place.

Some muse, "Why did I do this? What did I see in that person to whom I now have a commitment? I will divorce. I was not in my right mind when I did this."

Kundalini burst without sex charge

Sometimes one finds that the kundalini lacks a sex charge due to the sex energy being dissipated in a physical or astral sexual encounter. Then one should still make an effort to raise kundalini. Sexual activity may hamper kundalini arousal, while celibacy may boost it. For the most part celibacy is regarded as positive towards kundalini arousal but it may suffocate kundalini if it is done to thwart the rebirth effort of ancestors.

Kundalini always has a sex charge but it does not always have a full charge. It derives a sex charge from the nutrients taken into the physical body as well as the psychic energy taken into the subtle form.

The basic kundalini is a survival mechanism, like a most basic organism which tries to survive, like a virus for instance. Its main business is to survive. Initially it is not concerned with anything else. Later when it is feels safe the reproductive urge develops.

At first the child's kundalini is in the father's body. It desires to survive. It finds however that it can survive and do nothing else in father's form. It experiences itself as an urge to move into the mother's form. This allows further development for a more sophisticated means of survival.

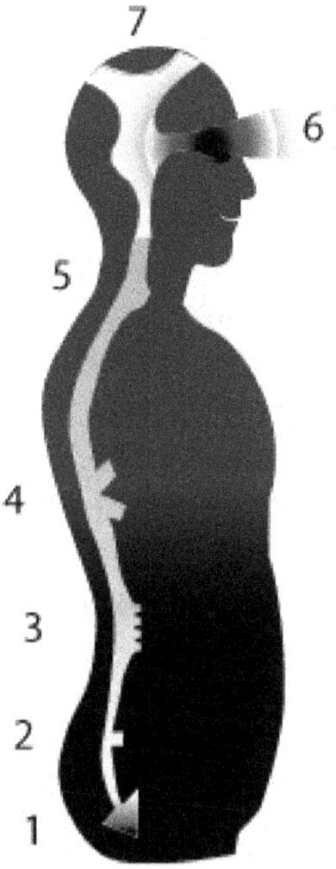

In an adult body kundalini maintains the primal survival urge but it also gets interested in reproduction. For that is takes help from the second chakra. As kundalini develops itself it moves from mere survival to reproduction, then it moves to expanded nutrition, then It moves to distribution of energy at the fourth chakra, then it moves to expression at the fifth chakra, then it moves to refined perception at the sixth chakra, then it moves further to cosmic sensual detection at the seventh chakra.

Kundalini is influenced by and influences in turn each chakra. It is not a matter of needing a sex charge. It has to have that as it develops from the survival impulse. That is the way it develops. Suppose I say that a hibiscus plant gets a charge of energy from its flowers. If someone ask of the necessity for flowers, that would not be a good question. We understand that at a certain stage the plant produces flowers as a matter of course. In the same way kundalini carries a sex change as a matter of course. In one sense the plant feeds its flowers and in another sense the flower supports the plant. Sex urge feeds kundalini. Kundalini feeds on the sex urge.

There is a special practice where the yogi tries the utmost to raise kundalini without drawing energy from the sex area. Usually in kundalini yoga, sex energy is the main way of charging kundalini but in some special methods, one avoids that energy and raises kundalini without it.

There are also occasions when for one reason or the other, the yogi finds that the body has no sex charge. When that happens he or she may have to work harder and longer in the exercises to arouse kundalini. Then when it is aroused in this way, the yogi should take note of the nature of the energy just to understand what sex energy does to kundalini when it infuses kundalini as the main cause of its rising.

These observations are required if one is to advance into higher states. For instance, suppose a yogi gets addicted to raising kundalini with infusion of sex energy, what does that mean for him as far as where he will go when the physical body dies?

Will he go where great yogis who have eliminated the sex charge in their psyches reside?

Can a yogi be satisfied in a dimension where the sex charge is absent?

Celibacy in kundalini yoga

Patañjali listed celibacy as one of the required practices. So did Krishna and other masters of the masters of yoga, but still unless one reaches a stage where one can notice what sexual expression does to one's progression, there is no breach.

In kriya yoga there is no one standing over the student telling him to do this and do that or not to do this or that. The most the teacher will do is bring it to one's attention that perhaps a certain lifestyle is counterproductive to one's aims. Yoga as Patañjali defined it is not for people who need to be propped by peer pressure.

It is like a school affair and less like a guru-savior process. The student should study the instruction, apply it and get checked by the teacher to see if he or she assumes the correct process.

Some people object to the academic approach. They are not suited to Patañjali yoga. He was a bookish practical yogi. He left instructions in written form about yoga and its accomplishment.

Breach of celibacy means that I observed what sexual expression does to my practice. I do not like the effects. I decided to attain celibacy. Due to that my practice accelerated. My teachers were appreciative of the advancement made. Soon after the sexual urge asserted itself again. As expected, as per my conclusions, my practice suffered. There was a lag in advancement. I checked my psyche and realized that it was due to the breach of celibacy.

On the other hand, we should not be fanatical about celibacy. We should not command people to cease all sexual expression. It would be easier to stop the Milky Way from spinning, than it would be to stop sexual expression. One man or one woman in millions may do it but not the others.

Kundalini / Sex charge

Kundalini always has potential for survival, acquiring nutrition and then using the stored nutritional energies for reproduction. Reproduction means sex charge. What we do in yoga is train kundalini to use the energy for promoting increased clarity in psychic perception.

Since kundalini's basic outlay is survival and reproduction, that potential will always remain intact though a yogi may alter the system. Kundalini has no concern with celibacy. That is unnatural for it.

Our existence as we know it came about after the sexual cosmic charge *(sutram)* was initiated by the Supreme Being. It will not be possible for us to upset it at any stage.

A yogi may ask the Supreme Being for an exemption from the influence of the cosmic sexuality but it is hardly likely that it would be granted to him. Great yogis do sometimes get an exemption where their highly purified subtle bodies maintain neutrality towards sexual influence. But that is rare.

More or less, so long as one is in these material worlds and their adjacent subtle places, one will not be absolutely celibate. Still a yogi should strive for that nevertheless but he or she must be reasonable and accept the restrictions which are imposed by fate.

The trick is to locate loop-holes in the sexual and reproduction system and use those but it must be something legitimate which is approved by the Supreme Being or it will result in abject frustration.

A yogi passed from his physical body long ago, sometime in the 1963. He stayed in the astral world. Recently just last week in 2010, he transferred to the Brahma world which is out of the influence of the sutram cosmic sexual force. Until one reaches that place one cannot be totally exempt from sexual interplay.

Because kundalini is innately attached to sexuality, one must exert a discipline to thwart it from sexual interest. If one relaxes kundalini will resume its normal behavior which is full time sexual interest.

Unfortunately, there is no cure-all or savior like in fundamentalist systems. It has to be worked out painstakingly by the individual. It is complex.

It involves relationships from many past lives. In the final analysis each person must maneuver the exit in a gradual way over a long period of time.

There is no quick fix. Kundalini grafted itself into the psyche of the individual. It lives alongside the coreSelf which is like a good wife or husband. It is near impossible for the core to divorce the kundalini. One should keep striving. One of these days, perhaps in another universe, some trillions of creative cycles down the road, one may achieve freedom.

In the meantime one should support and endorse righteous lifestyle and service sexual responsibilities when they are established by fate.

Kundalini up-the-front movement

Kundalini up-the-front movement by itself without arousal through the spinal chakras is a rare way. It does occur spontaneously when doing kundalini yoga.

This experience is denoted by a bliss energy moving from the groin through the front part of the subtle body but usually it stops at the neck and does not extend into the head. This practice reveals the frontal nadi passages. It reacts with and eliminates stagnant used energies which are lodged in the front trunk of the subtle body.

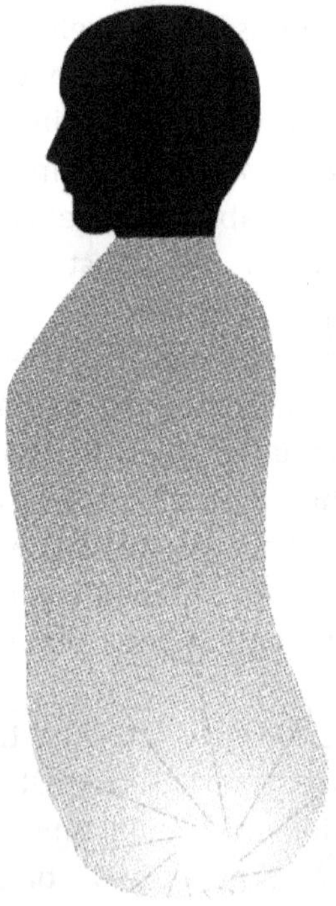

Infancy without a nurturing mother

I was at the home of parents who have a two year old child. The mother works full time. The father works fulltime but from his home computer. A lady of Spanish ethnicity cares for the child during the day. This child dislikes the nanny. He feels that his mother should render all care.

Because he took a long time to speak, someone said that the child was retarded. I feel that his body is not retarded. His mental situation is great even though his physical body is short by American standards.

It may be that he was in a state of emotional shock due to the absence of the mother. That may cause the late-start for talking.

Does anyone think of the next body?

Does anyone feel that he/she will go to heaven or will not exist or that it does not matter since one will not remember the previous identity if there is another life or any other state hereafter?

Imagination orb locator

Yogeshwarananda gave a reply to a recent question about the practicality of finding the imagination orb (intellect) which is an invisible psychic adjunct in the head of the subtle body.

He replied to something inquired by Sir Paul Castagna about how to know for sure that the orb exists.

Early this morning while meditating Yogesh showed a procedure.

- Do an intense session of rapid breathing. When you feel that kundalini stirred and moved through the spine sufficiently, sit to meditate.
- Check to see where kundalini is located and how its energy flows. Resituate focus in the iSelf's default location in the central head.
- Focus forward but not outside the head. Keep the focus in the head but forward. As soon as there is an image, idea, picture or any such thing, note the location.
- As soon as the thought vanishes and there is silence and no image or idea, make a soft non-forceful contact with the location, try to hold the focus as if the location was a floating cloud which was barely visible.
- In a short time another image or idea will pop up. It will do so at the same location. Again note the place. Again hold the attention as if you hold something like mist or fog.
- Keep the soft focus.

A person's attention is an auxiliary power supply for the imagination faculty. The attention goes to the imagination faculty (intellect) automatically. Normally it is not controlled by the person.

The imagination faculty also takes power from the kundalini life force. It is more submissive to that than it is to the iSelf.

If someone is successful at focusing on in and out breaths, then anytime that focus slackens, the attention energy will take its default route which is to give energy to the imagination faculty. That will cause thoughts, ideas and images to arise spontaneously.

Since that is the default configuration of the system, a meditator has to expect that this will happen. One should accept it as the natural operation. Patañjali instructed yogis. In fact, it is his order that yogis change the natural way of mental operations. Buddha also instructed his followers to upset the system. However as soon as one relaxes one's hold, the system will resume the default behavior.

This is why it is necessary to transit to other dimensions where the default is set up in a different way, in the way which Patañjali and Buddha suggested.

If in any meditation one finds that one can stop the emerging thoughts and images, it means that one is in a leverage position. There are three ways of knowing that one is there:

- Thoughts come in slow motion.
- Thoughts are absent. There is a blank mind only. The place where the thoughts usually arise is void.
- There are no thoughts. One is absorbed in bliss energy or a powerful up-pull energy which pulls the coreSelf into the top of the head.

Help from gurus

One should have confidence in yoga teachers. Without that one will not get far in meditation. Even Buddha, who excelled the teachers, had full confidence in them and used their systems to the max until he acquired the benefits of their particular practices.

The tendency for confidence in teachers never ends. It continues onwards into the advanced stage. People who have no confidence and who specialize in criticizing and resisting can only get so far. To go higher one must be pulled up by someone.

A person on this level of existence cannot get to the spiritual plane with tools from this side of existence alone. Even if such a person gets to a high level he or she will not remain there unless there is an affinity and relationship with someone on the higher plane who is a permanent resident there.

About a month ago, Yogeshwarananda gave some mystic procedures which I should master. He said that I would reach the plane of existence which is above the astral heavens. After that, his teacher, Atmananda, came. He gave a process which he said would allow me to go to a place which is called Satyaloka in the Indian yoga books.

In both cases, I took assistance. It is not that I could not discover these methods. I could. Still I take help and follow instructions.

When Atmananda gave the techniques it was like handing a person a package. He said, "Hold this for a while. Use it to follow me to that place later. I will send a message when you should to give this to others.

There was a time some years ago when Yogeshwarananda came into my subtle head in a miniature form. He showed the intellect organ. It looked like a jelly-fish with a milky yellow-white color.

But I saw this before that and after without his assistance. Why do I have to deal with him? Do I need him? Yogeshwarananda is one of the persons in the Indian yoga books who is titled as the Vedas Personified. These are super-people, supernatural beings.

Many people go to Buddhism because they do not want to take anyone as an authority. The idea is to follow Buddha who discovered everything by himself. When I visited a temple in South Korea some years ago, a lady said that she wanted to establish her Buddha nature. She said that since we are potential buddhas no teacher or god is required for assistance.

Some persons are agnostics. They are averse to submission. Still Buddha himself submitted and went further after he extracted the potential benefits of the systems of his initial teachers.

Furthermore if one reads the life of Buddha one will see that he maintained a strict system of discipleship once he was established as a master. For that matter he made it clear that there would not be a buddha like him for thousands of years in the future.

Everyone can be buddha?

Well not in the sense of Gautama's accomplishments.

I associate with Gautama Buddha from time to time. I inform that I never saw anyone near him who did not have a disciple attitude. If one does not see him as God then one is unlucky. In my relationship with him, I am like a son. It is similar to my relationship with Shiva.

With Buddha though, I am like a son of concubine. That means a low status son. Does he give me meditation procedures?

No. The relationship is that I should stand in a corner and wait.

He had never once said, "Come here. Do this meditation." He does not care if I meditate. He does not want to be bothered. I am not important. I am insignificant

The lady I spoke to in South Korea prayed to Buddha for help to become enlightened. When I was there I went into the temple and a super-large murti icon of Buddha instructed me to teach her. He said, "Get her started. She should be given the preliminary instructions about transmigrations and the continuity of the person after death."

When I spoke to the lady, she already had this idea that she was like Buddha. Because of her attitude I could not instruct her.

There are different grades of coreSelves. One of a certain grade even in the enlightened state of itself cannot become another grade. Gautama Buddha is a certain grade. Bhaktivedanta Swami did us a great favor by using the terms Personality of Godhead, Personalities of Godhead, and Supreme Personality of Godhead. He did not coin those English phrases. They were established by his guru who was Bhaktisiddhanta Sarasvati. Still since Bhaktivedanta brought those terms into common usage in English he is accredited.

Remember that the Jewish authorities, Abraham and Moses, gave the gift of one Supreme God rather than the older pagan system of multiple deities, but that gift though an improvement is terribly flawed. Bhaktivedanta will be accredited as having broadcast the information about Personalities of Godhead without conflict in the Godhead.

These divine beings like Gautama Buddha has a mass of responsibility for many resistant entities. In one sense no one in his or her right mind would want to swap positions with any of them. Do you want to be Jesus Christ where the people whom one is assigned to rescue take it upon themselves to kill one's body. Being God or God's agent is no fun.

The other side, the bliss energy side, is there but only if such beings are in the bliss world alone. As soon as they make contact with the massive ignorance which is humanity, the bliss vanishes, even for them. It is for that reason perhaps that they are reluctant to manifest in a world like this one.

There is no question of approaching Buddha as a buddha. Nobody among his disciples when he was alive did that successfully. No one does that now in the astral existence where he can be reached. If one desires his assistance one must take a subordinate position and not because he is divine which he certainly is, but due to that being one's actual position.

When publication of my books were stalled when a friend put them into computer files, I did not care about it. Sir Paul Castagna pressed the issue for publication. As it turned out I realized that I should get involved. At the time I visited a Buddha deity in China Town, Manhattan, NYC. That deity was very irritable about the lack of publishing but he avoided expressing anything about it.

I took a liberty and peered into his mind. I realized that he wanted to talk to me but he was occupied with issues in the East, political concerns which was upsetting the practice of Buddhism for many people in places like Thailand, India, Burma and China, and Tibet. Seeing that he was occupied I withdrew the desire for an interview.

That was a mental intrusion on my part but some of that is permitted. I did that to find what I should do about the books because a decision was to be made. He did not take his attention away from other concerns to advice about it. I either had to stay in the USA and publish, or return to Guyana and continue my austerities which were suspended.

In any case after I left the temple, he sent energy which was a message saying that I should be particular about who edits the publications

When I got that message energy, I check on it by returning a loop energy. Then I saw that he did not want anyone who procrastinated in practice to be involved in publishing the work. Buddha did not want that negative energy in the books. He felt that the books would fail if that energy was present since that energy would affect the enthusiasm of readers.

The other part of this is that Buddha was concerned only with his parts of my writings which have to do with what I wrote in the *sex you!* book which is a continuation of the Bardo Thodol (Tibetan Book of the Dead), a set of verses which I co-authored in Tibet in a past life.

At the time the *sex you!* book was not yet composed but some of its information was in the books which were already produced in manuscript form. Buddha wanted that Bardo Thodol work continued with relevance to modern times.

The reason why he does not care if I get any of this done, is this: It was assigned to me from many past lives and is an ongoing duty that stretches over many lives. If I do not do it, that is my problem because I alone will face the consequences of not getting it completed. If I do not care about myself in association with the divine people, they do not care either way. I will be the one who will slide down.

He has no use for me because I am like a servant who was sent on a mission thousands of years ago. If I do not complete it, there is no need for me to return home. If you send someone on a mission and the person returns home before completing it, one is not mindful of the little fool.

If I wish to return I should be enthusiastic and get the work done with or without the assistance of others. For one reason or the other many people refused to assist me during this life and in previous lives. As it is one becomes stymied in material existence by the social entanglements of each life. It is just the way it is. One gets confused and dreams up silly projects. One avoids the real duty which is assigned by the superior beings.

Worse still is when one gets this idea that there is no God or there is no Personal Deity, there is no accountability and that one is God. Down here nonsense enters the mind. One takes spiritually-suicidal liberties.

Kundalini arousal before meditation

With meditation I recommend a pre-session of some type of pranayama breath infusion. It is a procedure of ashtanga yoga that there be a session of pranayama before a yogi sits to meditate. It is not compulsory but it facilitates sensual energy withdrawal *(pratyahar)* and meditation *(samyama)*. If the subtle body is not surcharged that will limit its access to higher states during meditation.

Before meditation each yogi needs to have an effective way of surcharging the subtle body and raising kundalini. I inform that raising kundalini before meditation is preferred. If done it results in more progress in the effort to shift the mind to a higher level or to an agreeable state.

A yogi should use a method for raising kundalini through the spine into the head. That means he should feel it rise with a definite sensation and go into the head. Once it ascends meditate.

If, however, one can command kundalini to be aroused mentally and if it responds as desired, then one need not do breath infusion but should issue the command and then meditate.

It does not matter to me which pranayama or mantra method a person uses to raise kundalini. The point is that it should be aroused before meditating. If someone can drink a glass of water and raise kundalini, I am for it. But I feel that unless kundalini is aroused the meditation is low quality.

Each yogi should use a method of raising kundalini at least once, if not twice per day and then meditate. It is absolutely essential in my view. For that matter kundalini refuses to stay up. Therefore one should make a repeated daily effort to get it to enter the head. Once it is there one should meditate before it subsides again to muladhara chakra. One should take advantage of the increased psychic and spiritual consciousness which is made available because kundalini rushed into the head and became directly linked with the intellect organ there.

Some masters like Ramana Maharshi entered high states of meditation without doing pranayama. We can assume that these yogis have a log of meditation practice in past lives. If one can raise kundalini by a willpower command, one does not need to do pranayama practice but the system of yoga as defined by Patañjali includes pranayama before doing introspection *(pratyahar)* which is before transcendental absorption *(samyama).*

In my psyche, the idea of kundalini remaining in the head or moving into the head by virtue of a willpower command or by visualization is a farce. This does not mean that it does not do so in the psyche of others. My experience in this present psyche is that it does not stay up or move up unless it is forced to do so by pranayama.

In my case after years of practice, it moves up much quicker than before but the effort must be made. I learnt how to infuse it quickly because of doing certain asanas postures which cause the nadi subtle channels to be more receptive to the infused breath energy.

I could sit and meditate without doing breath infusion. The question is why do I infuse, when I can sit to meditate without that? Why make the effort to raise kundalini? It is because I find that I reach a much higher plane with kundalini raised.

Yogeshwarananda instructed that I should do the practice until this body drops dead or is incapacitated. The person who taught me an effective bhastrika pranayama is Yogi Bhajan. He expects that I will continue the practice. In addition in the astral world, there are great yoga masters who still do the practices in their subtle bodies.

Kundalini in an iron basket

Kundalini is involved in survival and sexual reproduction. That is its game. It is not concerned with spiritual aims. It has no plan to cooperate for spiritual realization. It knows that the priority is to acquire a material body and sexually indulge to reproduce the species. Transmigrating through various material forms in the biological worlds is the aim.

Kundalini does not have to take the coreSelf seriously because no matter what the core does, if it fails to rope-in and hog-tie kundalini and force it out of *muladhar* chakra, it is doomed to rebirth. It will continue to be tagged with social responsibilities in the sex-crazed worlds.

A yogi must use an effective plan to thwart kundalini and make it do as desired. It will still resist the yogi. It may still have a negative attitude towards spiritual disciplines. Even so the yogi should keep kundalini like a cobra in an iron basket.

Neglect to rope-in kundalini is a fatal flaw for a yogi. Kundalini has no interest in any high and mighty idea besides survival and sex interplay. If one has other views about it and thinks that it will cooperate to get one out of material existence; that is a mistake.

Components of consciousness

The components of consciousness which must be objectified and realized in meditation, are as follows, in order from the easiest to realize to the most abstract.

- lifeForce
- sensual energy
- intellect
- memory
- sense of identity
- coreSelf

English	Sanskrit	Details
lifeForce	*kundalini*	chakra energy channels
sensual energy	*indriyani*	senses and feelings
intellect	*buddhi*	reasoning and imagination faculty
memory	*smrti*	memory/instinct
sense of identity	*ahankara*	application of identity
coreSelf	*atma*	bare individual core awareness

Sense of identity is the most abstract adjunct and is near impossible to realize because its frequency is near to that of the coreSelf.

The hereafter man

A friend who recently passed away paid a visit. He discussed his existence in the astral world. At first I asked him if he was ready to take another body as somebody's child. He replied in the negative.

I inquired, "Do you like it on the astral side. Do you feel the need to be physical?"

He replied, "I would not say that I like it but it seems that it is where I should stay for a while."

I pushed for more explanation. I said, "How is it? Where do you stay? Whom are you living with?"

He replied, "That is what is weird about it. I do not understand how it is like this because that was not explained to me when I was on the physical side. I only exist when I think of people who are on the physical side. Like if I think about my brother for example, I find myself exactly where he is except that I can see him but he cannot see me.

"Physical people cannot see on this side, except perhaps for you. When I was alive you could have explained this to me but I was not in a mood for hearing of it. Now I see what you did by trying to give information about this.

"The thing that is funny about the astral existence is that it seems that I only exist when I think of someone on the physical side. Then I immediately appear in the presence of that person in an instant, like now, and then they do not see me but I see them. I know their thoughts which are like an echo coming out of their heads as replies to whatever I think of them.

"But where do I go from here? I have no idea. I do not feel to be someone's child. That is the furthest thought in my mind. But you may tell me how to do that. I have no idea of it. I do not see children in the astral world. I meet adults from the physical side. In fact I have not seen a baby since I came to this side."

After saying that he drifted away. His subtle body faded. He was pulled to someone who thought of him from the physical side.

Begin with Patañjali

To comply with Patañjali's second sutra about stopping the mento-emotional fluctuations and presentations one should locate the main utility used to construct thoughts. Then one should make the effort to cease the displays.

If one cannot locate something one cannot stop its operations. Thus it is important to identify the psychic utility which causes the impulsive mental and emotional operations.

Outsmarting and manipulating material nature

A yogi should constantly review his behavior in terms of outsmarting and manipulating material nature. There is a pleasure in outwiting the laws of nature which place limitations on the forms we use.

A yogi should review habits and try to curtail if not eliminate totally the tendency to outwit nature. The part of the psyche why sneers at and which enjoys when a yogi does something to circumvent the laws of nature, should be squelched.

Most of the modern scientific discoveries, even the simple ones like the washing machine, and the internal combustion engine, are feats of humanity which challenge the restrictions which material nature placed on human beings for millions of years.

At least within the past 200 years, humanity leaped away from many inconveniences but the tendency to snicker at nature and to enjoy these aspects may well hurt the advancement of a yogi, and cause nature to upset his progress by causing him to become attracted to a lower species of life in another birth. In such a lower species, how will the yogi gain the upper hand? Will he languish in disappointment because the form of another species has little potential for conquest?

Is it that the washing machine and the internal combustion engine give more time for spiritual practice?

Are there more successful yogis on the planet today because of the time saving technological gadgets?

Nature

Nature sponsors technological development, for that matter everything which we create scientifically is done in imitation to nature. There is not one invention which was not patterned after something we observed conscious or unconsciously in nature. It has imprinted itself permanently in the mento-emotional energy. There is no escaping its influence if we are in touch with it even in the slightest-possible most-detached way.

That is more the reason why we should not try to enjoy the manipulation of nature. In the end the laugh will be on us. The trick is to do whatever you must but do not be proud of it. Be sure not to take credit for it. Superficially one should and must take credit on occasion but deep inside one should tamp the quest for credit.

For instance I write books but it crosses my mind as to the proprietorship of the publications. Sometimes I get a feeling that something is taking me away from being the proprietor. The proper attitude in that case is merely to observe the confiscation of those rights and go on without the ownership energy, like a man whose bank balance was taken by the government. Usually you expect a tax law would only take a fractional percentage but in some cases, the government takes everything and then threatens to arrest the citizen if he or she does not pay interest. From the perspective of yoga, the citizen should hustle and generate energy to pay the interest.

There is a verse in the Gita, where Krishna says more or less that the supreme reality develops and devours everything. How is that? Am I not the developer of my books? How it is that reality claims to be the developer?

Providence

The use of the computer in my case is an imposition on my normal way of doing things. For me it is a force activity which was enforced by destiny and time. In such situations, one should comply with the force but that does not mean that one should think that it is under one's control. It is not. Many people think that Internet and computers are beneficial and is here as a convenience. In some cases, one identities positively with an enforcement. At other times, one identifies negatively with it.

That was like the guy who was arrested on an outstanding warrant and who smiled when the judge said that his sentence was 10 years. Usually people regret a jail term but this fellow was happy over it. He thought it was his good luck because his gangster friends wanted to kill him at the time of the arrest. He felt that he would be safer in prison.

This type of thing has to be avoided by a yogi. He should observe indifferently the facilities and blockages put down by nature. If one enjoys the computer and if one becomes reliant on it, then one will enter into a depression when one is deprived of its use. It is providence's facility. Providence is designed to humble the limited entities. It has this idea that its duty is to put into disarray the plans of mice and men.

A yogi should be respectful to providence because otherwise he or she will run into serious problems when providence decides to bite back. But even while respecting providence one has to keep it at arm's length by not getting into the habit of enjoying it and by not thinking that it is here for one's convenience.

Providence is contrary and paradoxical. No sane person would trust it to serve his interest on every occasion. At any moment it may elevate a person as the greatest human being. At the next moment fate could ruin the person. Recognizing this one should not feel at any stage that this creation is centered on one's interest or that this creation is in need of a master and one could be that individual. The main thing is to save oneself from being dumped by providence.

Working for liberation is a direct assault on fate. It should be done carefully so as to reduce providence's resistance. Only if the slave cooperates and follows instructions is the slave useful to the master. The master will never say, "You are free. You can go away." That will not happen. The slave should act in such a way as to encourage the master to release him even though the master is forever disinclined.

Computers are being used by me but not because it is what I want, nor because it is a facility, nor because of this or that, but only because providence made it a necessity.

Not using them would be offensive to providence. In compliance with fate, I use it but I know that it is based on the desire of the providence (the master) and not on my desire (the slave). Thus when it is no longer in use by me, I would have lost nothing, nor would I have gained anything even though providence which is like a python will surely enjoy, digest and excrete the history of the utility.

Patañjali put it in a nice way when he said that in terms of the liberation of a living entity, nature is more like a farmer, which is a superficial agent of the sprouting of seeds. The farmer is not the seed. It will never get the growing impulse from the farmer. The farmer does help facilitate its development, but he is not the source of the seed. He surely has no interest in crazy ideas about the seed being in absolute control of itself.

If a seed wants freedom, it has to find the motive and intelligence for that from within itself. There is no point in hoping that the farmer will tell the seed that it is okay to grow in the wild, where the farmer cannot reap the fruit which develops from the seed.

Nature does want us to blossom and produce fruits but not for ourselves, only in order to further its interest. We are captives being held bound in chains of cultural activities. We should strive for liberation quietly without allowing the master to divine our intentions.

When my subtle body is at last freed from having to use this physical form, I have no intentions of going where there are computers. The people I hope to stay with have no computers, nor is any idea like Internet in their minds. It would do me well to remain detached from technology and to know that it is not mine and was not invented for my convenience.

Déjà vu (September 2010)

The feeling of having experienced a place, event or person before even though within the conscious memory there is no familiarity with that place, event or person, is a complex psychic mechanism.

Once while talking to a woman, she told me that she had this feeling that she was married and had children previously. She said, "I am so familiar with domestic life that sometimes I feel that I did this and mastered this many times before."

In that case the feeling of déjà vu has to do with the predominance of a developed instinct from many past lives. Instinct is one of the forms of subconscious memory which could either handicap or give someone an advantage.

When déjà vu is actually a flash back of something that happened before, the subtle body suddenly and without explanation, transferred itself either into a memory of the previous event, or into the place where the previous event took place.

When it is a memory of a previous event, the subtle experience may be so intense and real, that the person thinks that the event took place. On a particular mental plane, it is reenacted by energies on that plane. Just as on this level one can see a Broadway play and see the near-identical performance night after night in a theatre, there are astral levels where the same experience can be replayed in exactly the same way repeatedly.

There is also déjà vu which is an experience of someone or a group of persons and a place which is stuck in time. During the years from 1969 through 1975, I used to go back to Tibet as it was in the 1800's. Physically those places changed, but on the astral side, those are stuck-in-time dimensions where I used to meet old acquaintances and teachers.

In the astral world some dimensions remain as they are for thousands of years. People live there and carry on in a primitive way just as it was some years or some thousands of years ago on the physical side. If one has an experience of those places, one wakes up on this side of existence with the feeling that one experienced a past life.

Déjà vu in higher yoga

In higher yoga the incidence of déjà vu becomes a trouble for the yogi. He should learn from advanced teachers how to deal with it so that it does not promote complex complicated equations of destiny.

Fate is not too particular about protecting any limited entity from repetition and from cultural entanglement which would leads to more haphazard births. A yogin should learned how to properly interpret and also quell déjà vu experiences.

Some time back when I worked at someone's house, I had a flash of a previous life when I was the son of the lady of the home. I became terribly frightened because I did not want the lady to know it of it neither on the conscious or subconscious levels. For me the information about the previous birth as her son, was open to my conscious mind but to her it was sealed deeply in the subconscious. I hoped that it remain sealed for her, since if it came into her conscious mind it would motivate her to reestablish her authority as a parent.

She was a directive female. I did not want to activate that. I carefully squelched the information in my psyche and did not look at it again until I left that place and was out of psychic range.

In higher yoga, the realization of the psychic abilities of the subtle body brings with it responsibilities. A yogi may shy away from using the mystic powers, except to advance spiritually.

Once years ago, during the early 1970's, when Sir Paul Castagna and I used to be in Denver, I met a lady whom I was in sexual relationship in more than one previous life. The lady recognized me. Because she used psychedelic drugs and meditated, she realized that we had the relationship before. I also realized it. She said to me, "I feel I knew you before. Perhaps fate crossed our paths again for a reason."

In turn I denied it. I emphatically replied, "You are terribly mistaken. I never had a relationship with you. Too much meditation and drugs led to massive incorrect intuitions on your part. Why would I have a relationship with a person like you?" She became angry about that and renounced me.

In advanced yoga the intuitional information should be carefully regarded so as not to trigger fresh karmic equations and complications. A yogi will if he is sincere and steady in meditation practice advance. The psychic powers and skills in his subtle body will increase day by day. If he is smart, if he wants to avoid haphazard reincarnation, he should not expose himself. Others should not know of his mystic insight. As advised by Patañjali he should use it only to control the mento-emotional energies.

One may use the déjà vu experiences to advance into the knowledge of what one did in the past and to make moves which simplify the consequential fated circumstances. Patañjali ordered yogis to sidestep all potential trouble spots of destiny since if something has the potential for distress in the future, and if the yogi gets a premonition of it, he should be smart enough to avoid it:

परिणामतापसंस्कारदुःखैर्गुणवृत्तिविरोधाच्च दुःखमेव सर्वं विवेकिनः ॥१५॥

pariṇāma tāpa saṁskāra duḥkaiḥ guṇavṛtti
virodhāt ca duḥkham eva sarvaṁ vivekinaḥ

pariṇāma – circumstantial change; tāpa – strenuous endeavor; saṁskāra – impulsive motivations; duḥkhaiḥ – with distress; guṇa – quality, features of material nature; vṛtti – vibrational mode of the mento-emotional energy; virodhāt – resulting from confrontation or clashing aspects; ca – and; duḥkham – distress; eva – indeed; sarvaṁ – all; vivekinaḥ – the discriminating person.

The discriminating person knows that all conditions are distressful because of circumstantial changes, strenuous endeavor, impulsive motivations, clashing aspects and the vibrational modes of the mento-emotional energy. (Yoga Sutras 2.15)

हेयं दुःखमनागतम्॥१६॥

heyaṁ duḥkham anāgatam

heyaṁ – that which is to be avoided; duḥkham – distress; anāgatam – what has not manifested.

Distress which is not manifested is to be avoided. (Yoga Sutras 2.16)

द्रष्टृदृश्ययोः संयोगो हेयहेतुः॥१७॥

draṣṭṛdṛśyayoḥ saṁyogo heyahetuḥ

draṣṭṛ – the observer; dṛśyayoḥ – of what is perceived; saṁyogo – the indiscriminate association; heya – that which is to be avoided; hetuḥ – the cause.

The cause which is to be avoided is the indiscriminate association of the observer and what is perceived. (Yoga Sutras 2.17)

Regarding the lady in Denver, someone may inquire about why I misled and outright lied to her.

One should understand karmic complications of destiny. One should do whatever is necessary to simplify these. Social providence does not care about me. Why should I care about it? If a yogi sees a way to side step social involvements which would result in haphazard rebirths, he would be a fool not to implement it.

One should do the best to escape potential liabilities. One should understanding clearly that providence is not interested in freeing one from cultural complications. Being nice is not always in one's long-ranged interest.

Mind-reading technology

Science is on the brink of telepathic communication. Mystics may lose the monopoly.

One advantage however is that if science can read a person's thoughts and if a human being can do the same that proves that some human minds may collect and correctly interpret subtle brain wave broadcasts. That would indirectly verify that there are psychic organs in the subtle body.

Psilocybin: LSD's little sister

Psilocybin, a hallucinogenic drug which is milder than LSD and which was first found in mushrooms, is being given the thumbs up for adjusting depression.

Unlike LSD and Speed which accelerate the subtle body's frequency and race a person down strange *Alice in Wonderland* dimensional pathways, psilocybin gives the person a mild ride in slow motion.

Psilocybin may however cause acute vomiting when it is derived from magic mushrooms. It may cause impulse for vomiting when it is created through chemical means.

There was a claim that these mushrooms were used in India as the soma plant which is mentioned in early Vedic rites when brahmin priests used to see the deva people from the celestial world, but many pundits in India say that soma is not hallucinogenic. However, if someone sees the celestial world and its angelic beings that is a hallucination.

Psilocybin takes the subtle body into the world of the fairies but if the dose is strong enough it will take the subtle body into the world of the astral heavens, where the Indra deity exists. Perhaps that is why some psychedelic gurus considered it to be soma.

Kundalini route

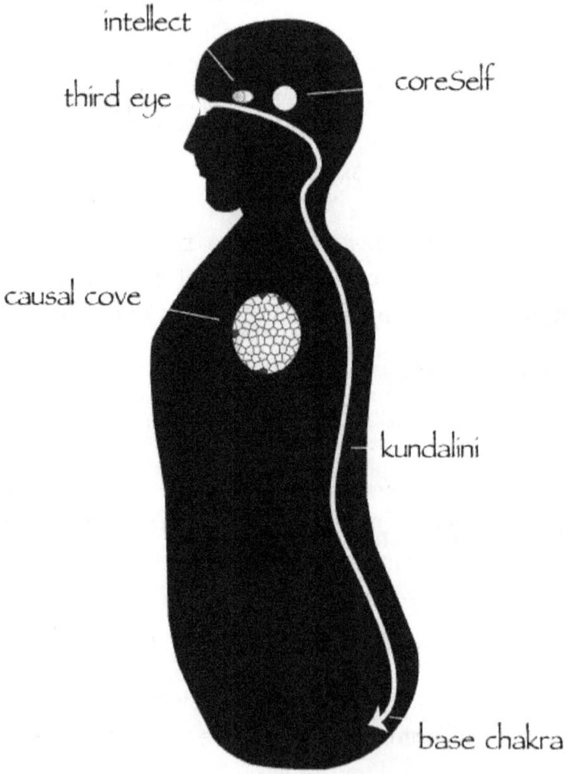

In the diagram, kundalini reached through the neck into the head and then changed direction toward the third eye. It bypasses other components in the subtle head. It bypasses the causal cove which is located in the chest of the subtle body.

The coreSelf may or may not be aware of kundalini's passage. In some cases, where a yogi is sensitive, he or she can sense the rise of kundalini from the base of the spine but otherwise some yogis do not realize kundalini until it has struck the brow chakra or third eye.

This comes as an experience of sensations at the third eye. It forcibly attracts the attention to that area of the subtle head. Kundalini may or may not pierce through the third eye, but it will usually spread through the nadi out-rays in a spatial way.

What are the components which kundalini bypasses?

They are the coreSelf and the intellect. The coreSelf and sense of identity are in a deep affair like two love birds who cannot be separated and who are fused. They are not one but for the time being, the core cannot distinguish itself from the sense of identity.

The intellect is also fused to the coreSelf but indirectly only, through the sense of identity which surrounds the core spherically like the skin of a watermelon which covers the pulp. Thus it is not such a difficult feat for a yogi to segregate the core/sense-of-identity fusion from the intellect.

As soon as kundalini strikes the third eye chakra, the intellect becomes aware of it and instantly alerts the coreSelf/sense-of-identity fused combination. This alert causes the core to become aware of the strike of kundalini upon the third eye.

One can get some idea about the nadi out-rays by squeezing down the eye lids on the eye in a dark room, and then using the fingertips of each corresponding hand to put a gentle push-in pressure on the eyeballs. As one does this one will notice lights on the inside of the head and after a time, these lights will form into a round or doughnut shape. That is the depiction of the chakra energy.

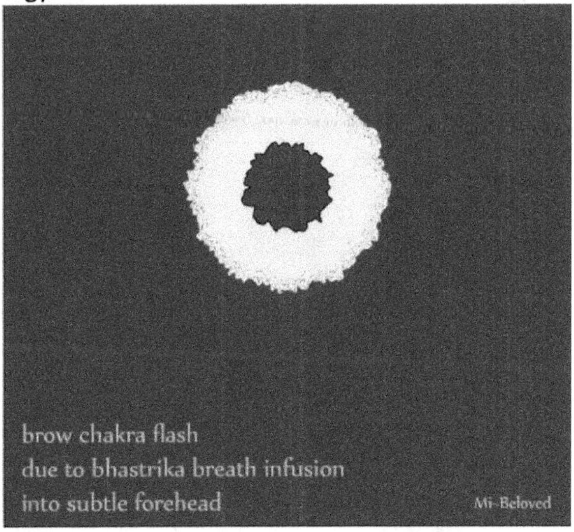

When kundalini strikes the third eye chakra it runs through the nadi out-rays just as when one engages the ignition of a car, electric power from the battery surges through the wires into the starter. Then a specific distribution of power is initiated. In a car it is not haphazard. In the subtle and physical bodies it is defined by nadis and nerves respectively.

One can see the nadis on occasion but usually one feels them. That is something like in the physical body where you feel a nerve pulsating or hurting as in the case of a tooth ache. It does have a visual value but you cannot see it except through an image technology.

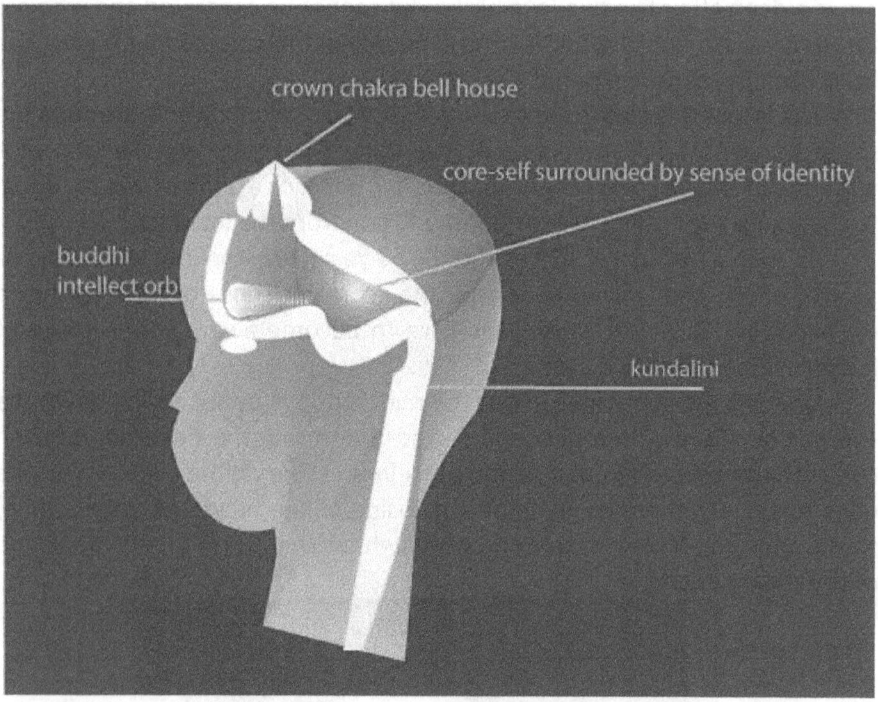

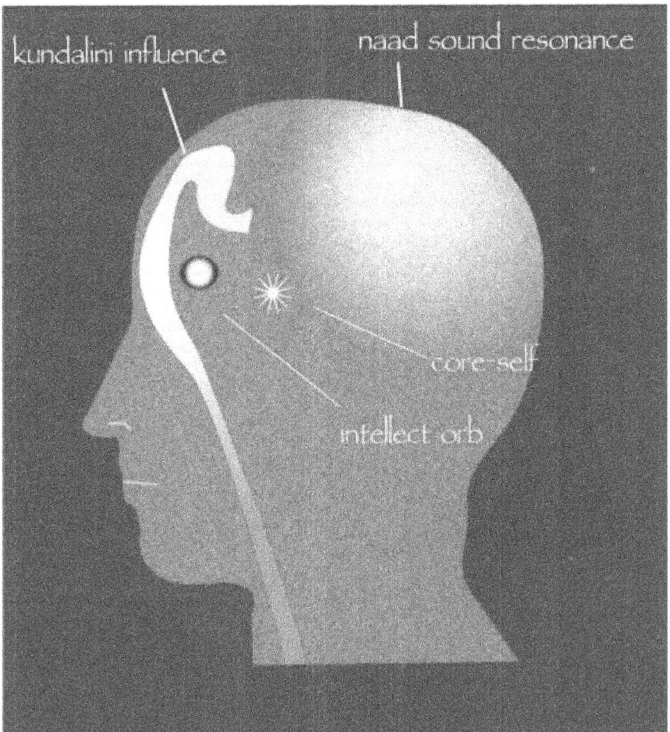

influence of kundalini in frontal lobe

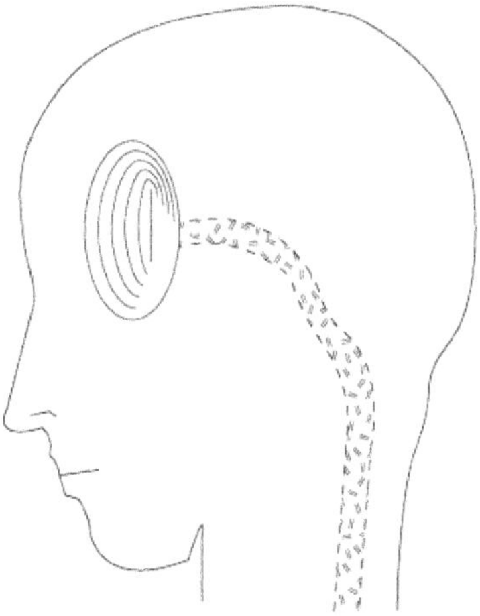

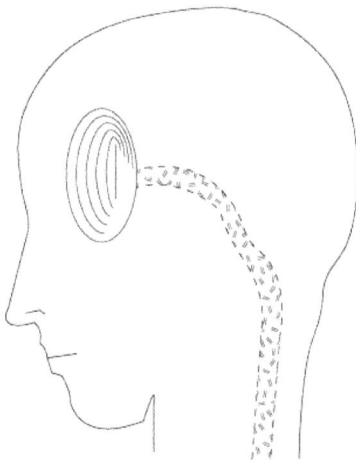

kundalini to intellect

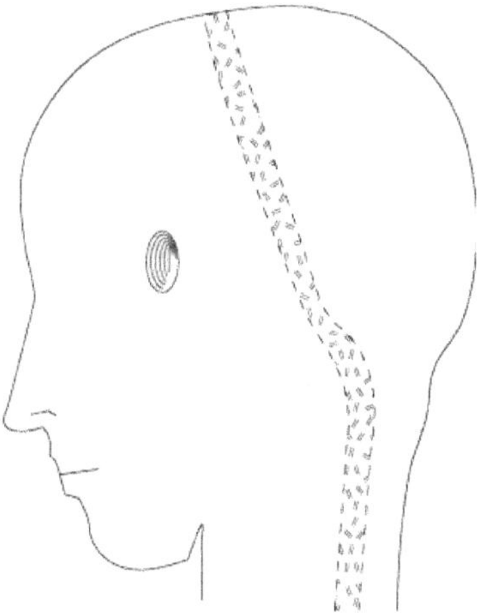

kundalini avoids intellect

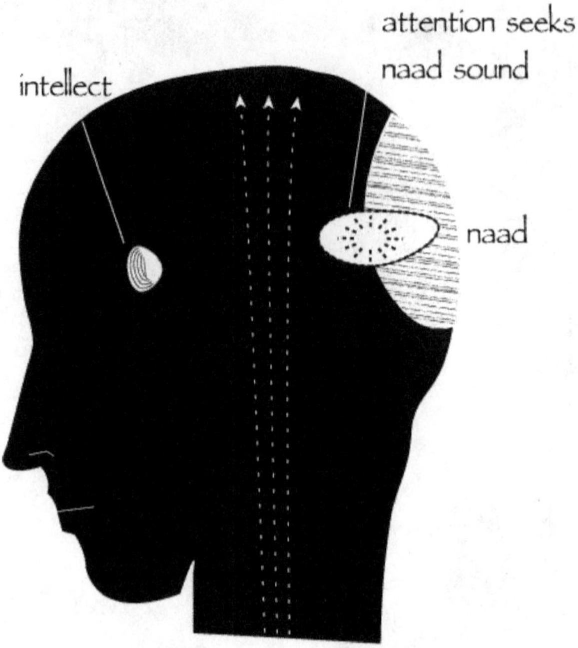

kundalini passes through head
does not strike intellect

Mind recording

The location of the self in reference to the other components of the mind is important if the self is to gain the upper hand in the mind. Location is also related to vibrational frequency such that if other components of the mind begin to move or vibrate at a greater frequency the observing self may panic if it is on a lower frequency.

This may happen on a drug experience or during meditation, or even during astral projection. In a *samadhi* absorption experience one may reach a level where the thoughts come in slow-motion like balls coming to batsman at a very slow pace, where he can hit them precisely as he desires or even stop them in midair by mental commands or even cause them to reverse into the hands of bowlers or not arise even. Patañjali instructed that we reach a stage where thought constructions are terminated during meditation.

The more one has an interest in the ideas of the mind, the least control one will have to terminate the unwanted activity. The mistake is the interest in the thought-content. If one has no interest in the content one gets control.

It is not easy to lose interest in thoughts. One must practice in meditation for some time to develop the tendency of not being interested. There is a pleasure in viewing the content. It is not easy to ignore that.

One may have a desire to control the rapidity of thoughts but it is best to control the interest in thoughts and by that disempower the mento-emotional operations. One should control the attention which pursues things outside the mind as well as things or ideas which form in the mind.

In a singing experience, the intellect in the subtle head is compelled to sing a song which was recorded in the mind. If the intellect is disconnected from the memory recording, the song stops immediately. The observing self must do as suggested or induced by the intellect. If the self can differentiate itself it can resist this influence. That differentiation does not normally happen. What occurs is that the observing self usually experiences itself as being the same as the intellect. The self feels that the constructions in the intellect are the self's creations. inSelf Yoga™ is designed to disband the seamless alliance between the intellect and the observing self.

There is however another important component in the psyche. That is the memory chamber. This has an automatic transmission system which causes it to spew ideas which were recorded. When these ideas are spewed, the intellect is victimized by the illustrations, and the observing self in turn is forced to accommodate the illustrations.

The question is how to sort these components. Sir Paul Castagna declared that the effort to sort this borders on the hopeless because it is so subtle that the observing self gets frustrated trying to find these invisible mental and emotional components.

In inSelf Yoga™, the sorting begins in earnest. The yogi stands and faces these invisible enemies. He makes efforts to defeat them.

Let me review what happens when there is spontaneous singing of a song in the mind. The initial exposure of the mind is the cause of the mind having the idea in the first place. A certain sensual entrance allowed the melody to enter the mind. The mind is a container and the observing self lives in that space, except that the container has openings or orifices. If there is exposure to an environment, the mind will absorb things that benefit or degrade it. One must therefore control what enters the mind. If one enters an environment and if the orifices are open, they will absorb sensations.

First one is in an environment either because one went there by desire or because an agency placed one there. Entry there causes exposure. This results in the recording of incidences. These impressions are retained in the mind and are replayed at a later date.

When they replay one may or may not resist according to the original emphasis with which the incidences were played. It is very similar to what happens in an industrial meat grinder. Once one puts a hand in it, one cannot withdraw without pain and without the hand being severed.

The solution is to not be exposed in the first place. The withdrawal of one's attention from a singing song or any other type of recurring incidence in the mind is a painful operation but one should learn to tolerate it.

A yogi should study how the mind records and replays incidences and how the self gets involved in this. Then one can take steps to curb the mind from recording unfavorable incidences.

Drugs or yoga

Both Krishna and Patañjali mentioned the use of herbs (aushadi - Sanskrit) as being one of the methods of attaining transcendence or enlightenment through altered states of consciousness. Neither authority recommended the use of herbs.

In the history of Krishna from the *Bhagavata Purana (Srimad Bhagavatam)*, it is said that Krishna and Balarama learned of the effects on consciousness of drugs when they were tutored by Sandipani Muni. It was part of their education.

Krishna also studied under Upamanyu Rishi and was taught the various yogic methods of reaching parallel and divine worlds. These are *samadhi* transcendence practices which used the methods of lifeForce arrest.

In the literature of Krishna's instruction there is no advice about taking drugs. I conclude that for the record and to admit all possibility Krishna mentioned the use of herbs as a method.

inSelf Yoga™ has no use for drugs. inSelf concerns using the components of the psyche to realize the supernatural. No other item is used. The reason for this is that when one is evicted from a body, one must leave the environment which that body existed in. One is deprived of the facilities of that environment. A yogi should depend on something reliable, something that will be available even when he/she is deprived of access to the materials in this existence. The yogi learns how to use those parts of the psyche which will be available beyond death.

Marijuana / yoga

Marijuana and yoga were mixed for centuries in India, especially in North India. Some yoga sects regard Shiva as the deity of ganja. They worship by smoking pot. I do not recommend it, since eventually if one's subtle body becomes addicted to it, one will go to a cross world in which the people there live on ganja. Some of them reach a stage where the subtle form becomes grafted into ganja plants permanently. That is also a form of consciousness.

In the *Srimad Bhagavatam* there is a description of a parallel world in which men are kept in addiction to smoking ganja and are used as sex slaves by the females who run the planet.

If however one feels that one must smoke ganja, my advice is to graduate as quick as possible to the flowers only, because then one would experience the full potential of the drug and one can make up one's mind if one wants to achieve anything further.

As for Shiva, there are many of them. The one who is the master of yoga, does not use ganja. But there is a Shiva who is the patron deity of the ganja plant. He is a supernatural being.

Kundalini to crown chakra

When kundalini attacks the seventh chakra, the crown or brahmrandra, it may do so from various angles. If it is a direct attack, kundalini will bypass any other energy gyrating center (chakra) in the subtle head and reach the crown directly. This will put the intellect out of commission. The coreSelf will find itself in a bright golden light or in a shimmering energy, being pushed upwards by a mystic force.

coreSelf relies on dense subtle energy for objectivity. When it finds itself in the shimmering energy of kundalini at the seventh chakra, it may lose objectivity to such an extent that it cannot differentiate itself or anything else.

Some persons marked this as an advanced stage, as oneness with the Absolute. Some yogis however who transcended the need for dense subtle energy, retain objectivity at this advanced level.

Part 8

Meditation tip

Check on the time you rest. Rising early to meditate before daybreak hinges on the time you rest. The early morning meditation begins when one retires for the day. Be your watchman to be sure that you rest early enough to make it convenient and pleasant to rise early for meditation.

Not motivated?

That is problematic.

Fix that by making a commitment to a yoga teacher and reporting regularly on one's efforts. If it hinges on you it is reliant on your self-control. Analyze that and come to a decision about self-discipline.

I meditated consistently in this life for over forty years. In all cases I reported to teachers. There were times when I pushed myself on the basis of past life advancement which I tried to recover. Mostly, I relied on a connection to a teacher.

Is a teacher necessary?

No! But if you cannot motivate yourself it is wise to adopt one. You are a person, pretending that one does not believe in a superior person is insensible. A person-self needs to be in relation to other person-selves.

Meditation posture

The concept of sitting in lotus which is given in major yoga texts from India means full lotus. It means partial lotus for those who are not comfortable in the full posture.

Still, to have persons with a western body sit in lotus is unreasonable because their limbs are not that flexible. It is best to allow people who regularly sit on couches to use a couch when meditating. In that way their minds are not stressed over the aches and pains of postures.

Reclining is great for people who are pained when sitting. When I first entered Yogi Bhajan's ashram in Denver in 1973, the ashram senior would instruct us to do various postures with rapid breathing (breath-of-fire). This was done for about 30 minutes to 40 minutes. It was very intense. There was no let up. One went from one posture to the next and in each one did breathing. In some one did breathing as one said the Sikh mantra *Sat Nam*. By the time one got to the last posture kundalini would rise. For beginners that meant that their bodies dropped to the floor.

Those who were advanced could control the risen kundalini and keep going. As soon as the exercises stopped, one was told to lie on one's back with palms up.

The ashram leader would hit a large gong at intervals. Its sound would cause the astral body to separate from the physical one. The astral form was highly charged by the postures and rapid breathing. The ashram leader would sit in lotus giving the instructions but all others would recline during the meditation. This was done at about 5am each morning.

Using the lotus posture while meditating, if that posture is painful or unnatural, is counterproductive. Generally speaking a Western body cannot do the lotus without pain and stress. I did yoga around 1966 by intuition alone. In 1969 in the Philippines I began doing it under the instruction of Arthur Beverford, who was trained by Rishi Singh Gherwal. I could not do lotus posture at that time. I forced my body into it. I sat in a military locker hidden away from other airmen who were unfamiliar with yoga. I forced myself to stay in the posture for 20 minutes. It was 20 minutes of sheer pain and cramps.

Later I invented exercises which loosed the ligaments and muscles which needed to be stretched for lotus sitting. In addition I adopted a vegetarian diet. That helped considerably.

Something happened that relates to this. Recently I travelled and was not sitting in lotus to meditate. For that matter for about 5 years prior, I relaxed the disciplines for lotus sitting. I sat in easy pose or on a couch depending on where I was located. Three months ago, after Swami Atmananda give me a technique to reach him on what is called the brahman level of existence, Yogeshwarananda appear astrally. He was annoyed.

I did not know the reason but I could sense something was amiss. I got the feeling that he wanted to say that at the rate I practiced, I would not get to the brahma level when I leave this body.

However he said nothing. I did not ask because usually with such teachers, one does not question them. One wrong question and that is the end of the connection. However, about a week after he released an energy. In it there was a warning like this:

"If you do not sit in lotus, do not consider yourself to be a disciple. A yogi has to practice brahmrandra meditation in lotus. There is no exception and no exemption for this. This is the last time that I will tell you this."

But still I would not recommend it to someone who cannot sit in it without aches and pains. I did yoga for many lives. For me there is no excuse. For me it is required. For others, it may cause them not to meditate since their minds may dwell on the aches and pains.

Founder of yoga?

This is not a good question because it presumes that there is just one purpose given for yoga. This is not true. There are several definitions.

From the ancient texts however there is a consensus. We can go to Patañjali for a definition. We can use the *Bhagavad Gita*. Patañjali gave a definition which has a total of three major parts with the aim of the final part being the reunification of the coreSelf with its purified highly energized psychic perception.

In the first part, Patañjali suggest there be no mental modifications for prolonged periods in meditation. That brings about a distinction between the coreSelf and its perception equipment. When this distinction is gained, the core is instructed to remain separate from the equipment. This separation or segregation is called kaivalyam.

The objective of yoga for Patañjali is kaivalyam, either as coreSelf being separated from the faulty perception equipment or as the coreSelf being unified with the purified perception equipment

Krishna on the other hand lists the purpose of yoga as being atma-vishuddha or the purification of the coreSelf and its psychology. This amounts to the same as Patañjali, except that Patañjali gave more details.

Traditionally Shiva is said to be the founder of yoga. His wife Durga is listed as the first student. It is said that the Siddha Matsyendranāth learned yoga from Shiva only because Devi (Durga) was instructed by Shiva. In a lake Matsyendranāth who used a fish body, listened by the shore as Shiva discussed it with Devi.

Brahma, a creator-god who is known as Hiranyagarbha, is also attributed as the founder of yoga. This is because initially he was perturbed by environmental hazards. When he appealed for help, someone whispered that he should do yoga austerities. Without training he complied and the climatic threats ceased. However Krishna is also recognized as a founder of yoga. In the *Bhagavad Gita* he claimed to be the originator of karma yoga.

In terms of yoga Shiva is regarded as the ultimate practitioner. In fact there is a story in the Puranas which goes like this:

When the supernatural people were first descended to this planet, they wanted to cause the manifestation of the ordinary human beings. Shiva was the leader of the supernatural people. They looked to him for a signal to begin producing human species.

Shiva told them to wait since he would practise yoga austerities. They agreed. Shiva entered a cave in Himalayas and Devi was with him even though she did not do the austerities. Shiva sat in lotus posture and entered an absorption state in which he was focused for thousands of years.

The supernatural people came again and again to the cave to inquire if Shiva resumed external consciousness but Devi repeatedly told them that his body was still alive but he was in absorption. Eventually the supernatural people got anxious because thousands of years went by and still Shiva did not awaken to direct them in how to produce human bodies.

They decided to begin the human creation which they did. After some years, Shiva resumed external consciousness. He realized that the creation of humans was in full swing. He dismembered his genitals and threw it away. He said, "I have no need for this. The purpose for this was already fulfilled."

When to meditate

I suggest a minimum of twice per day: Once soon after rising and once just before resting. Consider the second period to be a mind format for the first early morning session.

Mind format is part of the preparation for meditation but it is not meditation. At the end of the day, or at the end of the work period, it is difficult to assume a state of deep meditation but one should take time to catalog the impressions in the mind and set those in order.

For example something that could be done before resting should be completed. Something that must be postponed for the next day should be laid in a corner of the mind to be silenced for the time being or to become inactive until the next day. Something that should be considered before resting should be resolved immediately. In this way the mind will be de-stressed before resting, for relaxing from daily hassles and obligations.

As soon as one retires one should check to see if the mind is quieted or if some ideas persist and engage the attention. If it happens that one is compulsively focused on anxiety-producing pictures and ideas, one should retreat to the back of the head.

If one is successful in becoming relocated to the back of the head, the mind will cease its ideas and picture slideshow. Yet again, the mind will attempt to resume the slide slow. Thus, one will again be relocated into the frontal part of the head to see the mind's video.

Eventually one will drift into sleep but one may find oneself awake from time to time in dreams. When one first rises in the morning, one should do so gradually while trying to recall dreams. Make a note of the memories.

One should do yoga postures and breath infusion. Then sit to meditate. If one does not have a yoga exercise procedure, just sit to meditate. Do not remain lying in bed because one may drift to sleep. Sit up to meditate.

Motivation for early morning meditation

If the motivation for rising early for meditation is missing, that is a serious problem. If one is a person who is dependent on competition for motivation, then if one is not living in an ashram setting, it will be near impossible to induce meditation.

In an ashram with others rising early at a specific time under rules of residency, one can get that competitive kick, which will motivate one to rise and be with others. But if that competitive atmosphere is missing what will one do?

So much of what we do in the name of willful acts is done under a subtle influence. If that influence is suspended we are at a loss for motivation.

This however is a self-revelation in that it tells us that what we are after is not meditation but the energy derived from competition. There are many psychologists who studied the effects of competition. Some suggested means of eliminating it. Some said that it is a positive attribute. Sports function through competition. Even scientists are motivated to invent and discover on the basis of competitive moods in reference to their colleagues.

Unfortunately higher yoga does not prosper on the basis of competition. Krishna listed disgust as the impetus for higher yoga. That means a self and its relationship with nature reaches a crisis in which disgust permeates the psyche which strives for quarantine from nature's negative influences.

Patañjali clarified that spiritual ignorance is the cause of the affiliation with nature. He said that affiliation affords us experience. When the experience ran its course, we strive to be segregated from nature. That is called kaivalyam or aloneness of the coreSelf.

For higher yoga, it is not what other yogis do or how they compete, but how nature influences the psyche and what the core wants to do to terminate that influence. The self realizes that it is tagged for the activities which nature conducts with its energies.

Why awaken early to meditate if one is not disgusted with nature? Obviously there is no pressing reason to do so otherwise.

Five obstructions

Patañjali listed five obstructions which prevent a yogi from doing higher meditation.

वृत्तयः पञ्चतय्यः क्लिष्टा अक्लिष्टाः ॥५॥

vṛttayaḥ pañcatayyaḥ kliṣṭā akliṣṭāḥ

vṛttayaḥ – the vibrations in mento-emotional energy; pañcatayyaḥ – fivefold; kliṣṭākliṣṭāḥ = kliṣṭā – agonizing + akliṣṭāḥ – non-troublesome.

The vibrations in the mento-emotional energy are five-fold, being agonizing or non-troublesome. (Yoga Sutras 1.5)

प्रमाणविपर्ययविकल्पनिद्रास्मृतयः ॥६॥

pramāṇa viparyaya vikalpa nidrā smṛtayaḥ

pramāṇa – correct perception; viparyaya – incorrect perception; vikalpa – imagination; nidrā – sleep; smṛtayaḥ – memory.

They are correct perception, incorrect perception, imagination, sleep and memory. (Yoga Sutras 1.6)

To understand this, we may consider an automobile. Usually a consumer is interesting in driving the vehicle and wants it to be in a good condition with an automatic transmission.

Patañjali's proposal may be compared to what is under the hood which is not of interest to the consumer.

Like the human body, we may posit that a car has five sensing mechanisms:

- lights instead of eyes
- carburetor and exhaust instead of nostrils
- metallic outer body instead of skin for touching
- rare view mirror instead of ears for hearing
- combustion cylinder instead of mouth and tongue for tasting.

Patañjali is interested in what is under the hood. He claims that under the hood there are five types of operations which the car performs. Let us consider vehicles with a manual gear system.

There may be four forward and one reverse gear. The reverse is memory.

The forward gears are correct perception, incorrect perception, imagination and sleep. But Patañjali request that the driver find the neutral gear and remain in idle there.

Coma / cataleptic trance

The subtle body must stay with the physical one until the physical system dies. There is no choice in the matter. In a coma the self is usually unaware. In rare cases, it becomes aware and experiences life the way a person would who is in a cataleptic trance. Catalepsy is also known as sleep paralysis.

Coma means that because of some damage to the nervous system the life force cannot operate the body. So long as the life force remains with the body, the coreSelf must remain with the body. They are inexplicable connected. The only way a person in a coma can become free from the unconscious state is either by repair of the damage to the body or by the death of it.

When the body dies, the subtle body is instantly released making the final exit. I say final because the life force conducts an astral projection from the physical body every time the physical body sleeps, except that it returns the astral form to the physical body and the physical one awakens. At death the life force loses the ability to synchronize the astral form into the physical system.

To contact someone in a coma one does not need to be in proximity with the physical body. One should be in proximity with the astral form which is used in dreams. One can reach that body from any place. The easiest way is to speak to the person mentally and then wait for a thought flash in the mind. The flash is a mental reply from the person.

However that is only viable if the person is not in an astral coma. In which case, one may wait until that astral coma is relieved. It will terminate either by the death of the physical body or by the nervous system repair process which will result in the person becoming awake physically.

Back support / meditation

Sitting up to meditate can be a chore. It can be uncomfortable or painful. Many teachers advocate an erect spine. That is ideal. However one should work with one's spine and negotiate its curvature.

According to ethnicity spines vary. No amount of yoga will change that. Still, one can come to an agreement with a faulty spine by learning how and where to brace it during meditation.

In the diagrams below I try to show a method for bracing the lower and upper spine. Both areas may need support. When the upper back is comfortably against a wall, the lower back is usually not touching the wall. Since the chest cavity, the head and neck bear on the lower back, it needs support.

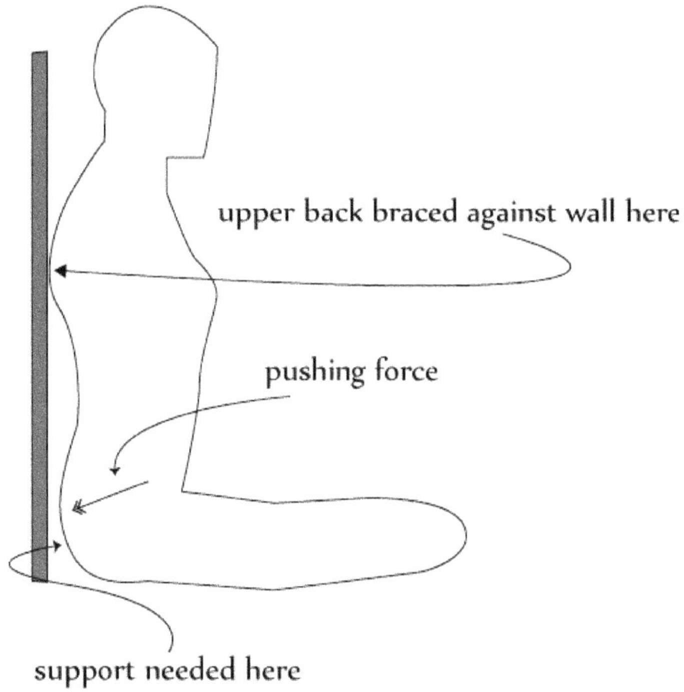
upper back braced against wall here
pushing force
support needed here

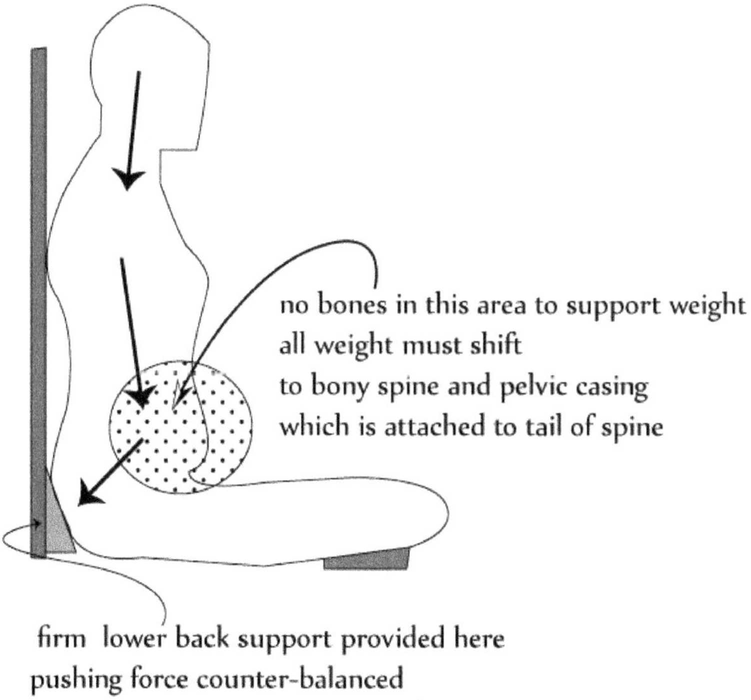
no bones in this area to support weight
all weight must shift
to bony spine and pelvic casing
which is attached to tail of spine
firm lower back support provided here
pushing force counter-balanced

The spine is naturally kinked or curved. The weight which bears down is transferred to the lower wall. To help nature in this effort one should use some type of wedge support which prevents the spine from curving backwards.

If one sits in lotus usually at least one knee will float above the ground. If this knee is not supported at the onset of meditation, it will cause the mind to be distracted. Thus I show a knee support.

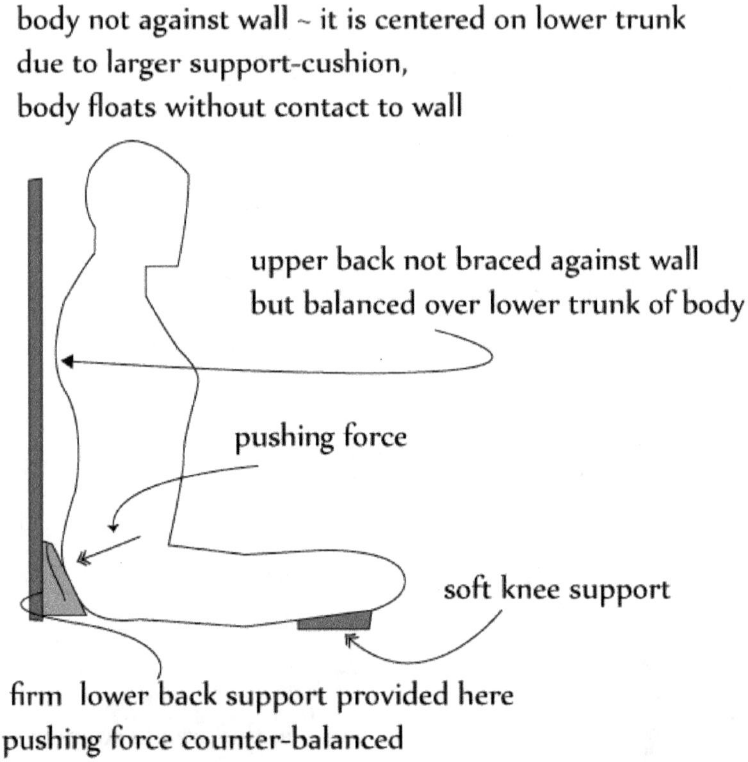

The concept of having an absolutely perpendicular spine which has no curvature is impractical because nature designed the spine with curves. What one may achieve is balance of the weight of the back, not straightness. To make it straight and to keep it in that form would require tremendous concentration which would circumvent the meditation as the mind would remain focused on keeping it in that position.

Mind locations

One meditation habit I introduced is the location-situation move. This is when a person finds himself or herself fighting with the mind and getting nowhere, stalled as it were in the chaos of the mind and not being able to silence it to enter a meditative stage.

This method consists of taking refuge in a location in which the mind is unable to dominate the coreSelf. It seems however that this method is not very practical for some persons. However I insist that all meditators seriously consider adapting this method in their routine.

First one should discover if there is any part of the mind in which thoughts and images do not occur. One should observe in which parts of the mind thoughts and images do occur. Lastly, one should know in which parts thought and images may or may not occur.

This is listed:

- locations where thoughts do not occur
- locations where thoughts always occur
- locations where thoughts may or may not occur

By knowing this one can relocate to a no-thought zone when one is helplessly besieged by images and thoughts. One can also enter a location where there may or may not be thoughts. There one may observe how one's control of the mind fluctuates according to the force and rapidity of thinking.

If one can map the thought and no-thought locations, one may easily adjust one's relationship with thoughts by moving to the thought-free location.

Sound for meditation

Ultimately all props used in meditation must be abandoned. Sound can be used to induce a meditative state or to change the stubborn attitude of the mind. We find that if a person is sad, listening to certain music lifts the person out of depression. The person may even assume happiness which is the flip of a sad mood. Thus sound can aid in meditative states.

The chanting of Om is popular. It is a valid method. If done correctly, it can take one to a spiritual plane either where there is no distinguishing sense perception or where there is that. In the past yogis used Om sound chanting extensively. By it some are reported to reach the Supreme.

However, in the final analysis one has to get the mind under control and also get the kundalini lifeForce to be cooperative and obedient to the coreSelf.

In higher yoga, the Om sound which resonates spontaneously is used. This is better since the yogi is not required to use energy to generate a sound. He or she can focus on naad fully and reach a spiritual plane.

If one practiced extensively, one can locate naad and listen to it even in a humbug city but still that is not the same as hearing it in a quiet environment. Noisy areas are not as conducive to meditation practice.

Posture / breath infusion

This morning while meditating, Yogesh came to observe my process. At the end when he was to leave, he uttered in disgust, the following words, "They want full success without mastering the preliminary stages. They do not want to do asanas. They do not want to do pranayamas. They request help with the higher stages of meditation. How is that possible? Everything has its preliminary stage, even ordinary education."

He made that remark because it is not possible to raise kundalini consistently without doing the asana postures and the breath infusion methods. Kundalini remains unresponsive to a person's imagination and willpower unless it is energized to a higher energy level. In its dense survival condition, it has no interest in higher yoga. If one does not infuse kundalini, one will make little progress.

Relationship with a yoga guru

This is an example of how one may have a relationship with a yoga guru. For about one year now, Yogesh restricted my relationship. It used to be that he would come frequently or infrequently and did not make stipulations. He would offer advice and show techniques.

About a year ago this stopped. The relationship changed where it was hinged on my reaching a certain level before he would appear. For this I must raise kundalini before seeing him.

Since kundalini is disinclined from remaining at the crown chakra, and always makes successful efforts to fall back to the base chakra after it is raised, I am now compelled to raise it daily if I want to get his association. Our relation hinges on my reaching a certain level. If I fail to get there, the relationship is nil.

When I was in the Hare Krishna Movement, there was a requirement for 1728 (16 X 108) rounds of chanting the Hare Krishna Mahamantra. If one failed to do so or even if one did so but did not associate in the group in a certain way, one was severely criticized. They said that everything hinged on association with them.

In yoga practice however everything hinges on practice. It is not group thing like the Hare Krishna Movement. There are only three factors to take into consideration:

- oneself
- one's practice
- association with advanced teachers for direction and higher instruction

Yogis are required to use the kundalini-elevator method when leaving the body for good but they cannot be successful at this if they have not mastered it while using the body, before the body's death. While in traditional religious process, the follower hopes to go to heaven or to a spiritual world to meet the cherished deity; in yoga the idea is the move up the kundalini elevator shaft in the subtle body and escape through the brow or crown chakra to a higher world.

Thus yoga gurus give senior students, methods for routing kundalini to the crown chakra long before the time of death, such that kundalini knows that passage, is familiar with it and is inclined to using it.

Folly of youth

The big illusion about youth is the lack of memory of life in old age in previous bodies. Due to that absence of past life experiences, one feels as if one will have an eternal youthful material body, which of course is a grand delusion.

The uniqueness of Gautama Buddha is that he saw the scope of many lives in many bodies. He turned away from the grand delusion.

Third eye focus

Arthur Beverford asked me to explain a third eye focus procedure which he explained to Sir Paul Castagna and myself in the early 1973. One sits to meditate and focuses on the center of the eyebrows. Beverford got this method from Rishi Singh Gherwal. I adapted the practice and discovered methods of improving on it. Beverford gave this update:

- While meditating on third eye, slowly locate the optic energy. Retract that into the coreSelf.

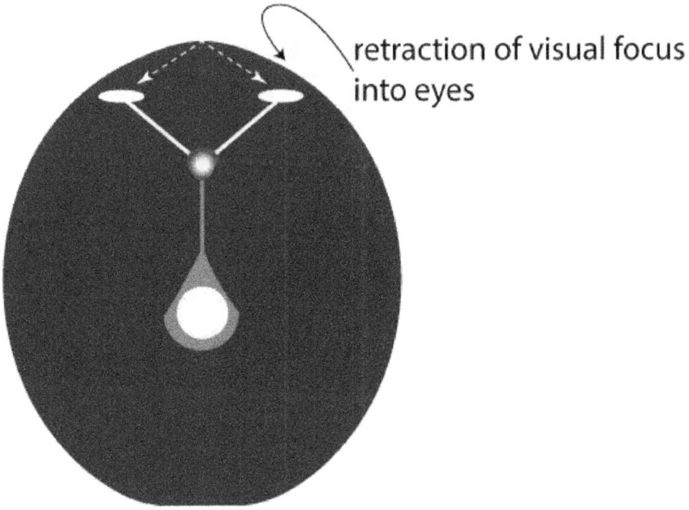

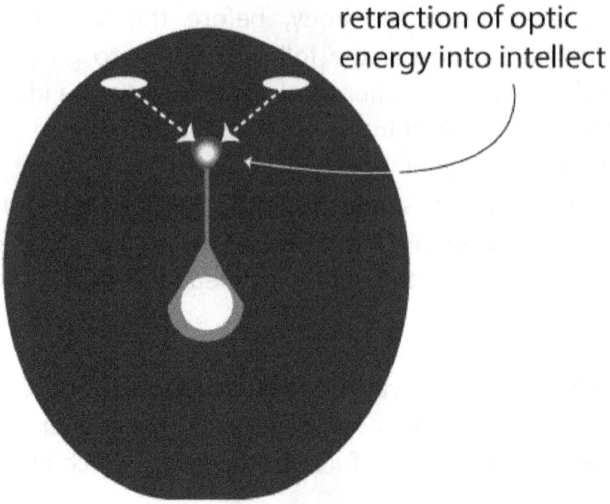

If there is an increase in thoughts and ideas because of the increased focus in the frontal part of the brain that problem is solved by retracting the optic energy while doing the focus. The optic energy is the main trigger which activates impulsive thinking during third eye meditation focus.

Reverse-pull third eye meditation

In this process one should be situated a little to the back of the head from the usual centralized position of the coreSelf. Once one is attune to naad sound. Naad is a sure footing for advanced meditators but without it one can make the effort just as well.

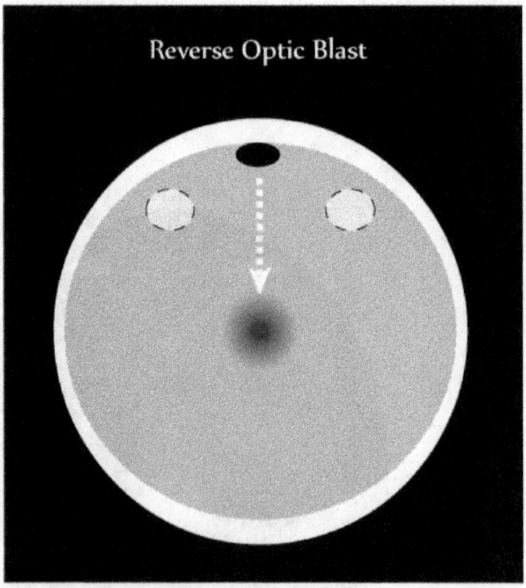

Usually in third eye meditation, one focuses forward towards the center of the eyebrows but in this procedure, one does not focus forward but pulls the energy which is between the third eye and the coreSelf into the core-self. This is a reversal pull which is vital.

This is for training the upswing kundalini energy to remain in the psyche close to the coreSelf and to commit to a complete sensual energy withdrawal *(pratyahar)*.

Many persons do yoga meditation and either pretend that they have mastered *pratyahar* sensual energy withdrawal or push on with haphazard leakage of the attention. These persons need to turn about and again do *pratyahar* to proficiency.

Sometimes one has to stop and realize that one knows very little about meditation, at least in so far as it is taught by Patañjali. Then one can make a renewed effort to gain proficiency.

In this practice begin by focusing forward into the third eye space which is between the eyebrows. As soon as you feel you accomplished that to some degree, remain still and begin to pull the energy in reverse. It is the same energy. It should feel as if it is constantly retracting into the coreSelf.

Mobility split-energy retraction

In brahma yoga practice, there is a stage where one is required to retract the mobility split-energy. This is another mystery of yoga. It is based on the evolutionary development of mobility in creature forms. At first most of the unicellular forms remain in one place. As they evolve there arises a need to change location. This occurs due to the need to feed at leisure.

If one remains in one location, one must wait for food sources to develop at that place or to drift to that place. Therefore the unicellular organisms develop mobility at first as a way of getting food at leisure by moving to the location of food sources.

Spirits who enter the material creation and who take unicellular forms get stuck in such forms until they realize that they can develop mobility. At first this comes about by forms which can use ingestion and expulsion of liquids because the first forms are in water.

Later, other types of propulsion mechanism like fins in fish and limbs in tortoises develop. However in brahma yoga our concern about this is its root cause which is the need for nutrition.

The key issue is that it originates from an internal energy. The concern is to locate that energy and curb it. This internal energy begins in the causal body which is out of reach but when it surfaces in the subtle body, it takes a two part configuration, one which produces the limbs for mobility and one which extends feelers for locating the food sources. The energy which is one in the causal body develops or evolves into two rays in the subtle form. One causes suitable limbs. The other develops eyes or feelers.

Once one gets on the move to find food. One needs a way to see what it is or to feel what it is. Then one can eat and survive.

Advance meditation is not easy because it entails the complete withdrawal of the evolutionary interest which developed while transmigrating for millions of years.

Asana postures helps to locate some of the primeval urges and bring them under control. In this case when doing stretches which concern the thigh and leg, a yogi can locate the ray energy which came out of the coreSelf for developing survival mobility. He can recall it. As this is done he will find that a vision energy is also retracted. This is the other part of the energy which came out to provide sight or feeler capacity to recognize primitive food sources.

A thigh stretch can cause the yogi to recognize a causal energy which operates mobility. Then the yogi can retract this energy. As he or she does this, a vision-feeler energy in the frontal part of the brain will feel retracted.

Clarity of mind

वितर्कविचारानन्दास्मितारूपानुगमात्सम्प्रज्ञातः ॥१७॥

vitarka vicāra ānanda asmitārūpa
anugamāt saṁprajñātaḥ

vitarka – analysis; vicāra – deliberation, reflection; ānanda – introspective happiness; asmitārūpa – I-ness self-consciousness; anugamāt – by accompaniment, occurring with; saṁprajñātaḥ – the observational linkage of the attention to a higher concentration force.

The observational linkage of the attention to a higher concentration force occurs with analysis, reflection and introspective happiness or with focus on self-consciousness. (Yoga Sutras 1.17)

The Yoga Sutras of Patañjali stress the importance of understanding the true self and to become detached from distractions. In the verse Patañjali explains the art of directing the mind on an object in order to prevent distractions.

The object is gradually understood in totality. At first this understanding is on a superficial level. In time, comprehension becomes deeper. Finally it is total. There is pure joy in reaching such a depth of understanding. For then, the individual is so much in unity with the object that he is oblivious to the surroundings.

The practice of clearing the mind of all obstacles and distractions leads the practitioner further into an understanding of what comprises the mind and makeup of the individual. If one reads further into the *Yoga Sutras* one will find that Patañjali instructs about full clarity of mind. By practicing these procedures one develops from a confused mind to a state of clarity awareness.

I am

Please review the same verse:

वितर्कविचारानन्दास्मितारूपानुगमात्सम्प्रज्ञातः ॥१७॥

vitarka vicāra ānanda asmitārūpa
anugamāt saṁprajñātaḥ

vitarka – analysis; vicāra – deliberation, reflection; ānanda – introspective happiness; asmitārūpa – I-ness self-consciousness; anugamāt – by accompaniment, occurring with; saṁprajñātaḥ – the observational linkage of the attention to a higher concentration force.

The observational linkage of the attention to a higher concentration force occurs with analysis, reflection and introspective happiness or with focus on self-consciousness. (Yoga Sutras 1.17)

The Sanskrit word *rūpa* means form, shape, recognizable appearance of an object. *Asmitā* comes from a verb form which indicates I. *Asmi* is the Sanskrit for *I am*.

For instance there is a famous mantra: *Ahaṁ Brahmāsmi* अहं ब्रह्मास्मि)

That is three words.

- aham - I (pronoun)
- brahma - exclusive spiritual existence
- asmi - am (1st. person of the verb to be)

This sentence means that *I am exclusive spiritual existence*.

Adi Shankaracharya is the one who made that phrase popular. It is a major mantra for sannyasis of his lineage. It originated in the *Brihadaranyaka Upanishad* of the *Shukla Yajurveda*.

If the individuality can be eliminated that mantra has no meaning and the Vedic rishis who established it were joking. In the *Bhagavad Gita* Krishna asserted individuality as being permanent even though he explained that its degraded forms are worthless in the ultimate sense.

Patañjali in the verse above makes an alert that when one begins the practice of fusing one's consciousness into higher realities, one will do so with flaws.

Asmitā means that when one first achieves fusion into higher dimensions or when one achieves fusion association with divine beings, one may still be aware of the old cultural I-ness which one was accustomed to in this existence.

One has to do much meditation before one can completely shed that social identity and develop or experience the self free of those associations. It is important to distinguish the spiritually pure identity from the socially formatted one that we currently use. Banishing identity is not a real thing. It cannot happen permanently. Identity is eternal and so is individuality. The dis-application of identity to temporary phenomena is the objective not the elimination of identity.

There is not a single liberated person like Buddha for instance or Shuka or Narad or Shankara or in modern history Paramhamsa Ramakrishna, whose liberations was the liberation of anyone else but these persons themselves. They existed as individual living entities distinct from others after their liberated conditions occurred.

A bothersome flawed identity does not in any way mean that identity can be banished forever. It is in existence eternally despite the numerous misapplications.

Mergence? (October 2010)

There are higher experiences with divine persons. There is the story in the *Mahabharata* where Markandeya told Yudhishthira how he (Markandeya) was lost in Krishna's Cosmic Body for eons. Then he was thrown out into another atmosphere in which that Cosmic Body resided. Even though it may be said that he merged, Markandeya, as a great yogi and devotee of Krishna, was aware during the transit in that body that the Cosmic Person was distinct from himself.

Has a fetus merged with the entity who is the mother? In a way the fetus is merged and in a way it is distinct.

Spiritual sense perception, I can testify, is a reality but normally we do not develop it. When one enters into spiritual zones of consciousness one experiences that as mergence with no distinct sense perception. But that is the beginning of the spiritual journey.

A yogi travels

Recently during travels, I got the opportunity to realize that if I took another body, it would be compliance again in terms of confirming to someone else's methods.

As an adult with a residence one does whatever one desires. One arranges things for one's convenience. This may amount to total chaos or fanatical organization. In either case one sets an environment in the way that is natural for oneself. A person who is innately disordered will in quick time demolish the most neatly organized place. Someone who is ordered will bring the most chaotic place into order.

As a child one must acquire the approval of parents. One is circumstantially limited in how much one can do to set a place in an ordered or disordered way. A disordered child will catch hell if it is born in the home of ordered parents. An ordered child will be uncomfortable in a disordered parental environment.

As a visitor it is similar since one must confirm to the likes and dislikes of the host. This guest position is reminiscent of and is a precursor of what one will face if one has to take another body. As an infant one is little more than a pet animal in the house of one's parents. A little dog in one of the homes where I visited was locked in a pen at certain times. It was restricted in where it could urinate and defecate. Its barking was quelled with strict objections. The little guy was kept indoors most of the time.

Its food was limited to whatever the owner provided. Even though it could eat to its heart's content, it was on a limited diet of hard pellets manufactured by a dog food company.

In terms of the temperature, it may be said that the little dog had it made in the shade, living all day in an air-conditioned building which many human beings in emerging countries cannot enjoy. But that advantage was offset by the disadvantage of having no choice in the matter.

In the next life, as an infant, what will be my lot?

Who will be the mother or father? How large will be the crib?

How long will I be cooped in a temperature controlled building? What food will I be served?

Fate and location

The results of previous cultural activities, especially those committed in a previous life, can only be realized in specific locations. Even if one wants to cash in on a certain cultural activity, one may be unable to because of being in the wrong place. Take for instance someone who is a recent past life was in Bolivia, and who did much pious activity there. He or she may take a body with parents who migrate from Bolivia to the United States.

In the new location that person may not cash in on the results of that Bolivian life and may become frustrated. It is like saving money in a bank in Russia and then traveling to Morocco and then realizing that one cannot withdraw the funds in another country. Subsequently, one becomes poverty stricken in that other place, even though if one remained in Russia, one would be well-to-do.

Recently a few friends were circumstantially force to relocate their daughter to the country of their birth. They migrated to the USA but their daughter's rights to a decent education were not activated there. As a result the girl went through school for many years and was found to be lacking in a basic education.

Providence is cruel to say the least. It is not concerned merely with fulfillment of one's desires. People say that we should attend to the moment, the now. We should not ponder the past or future. Unfortunately no one can convince providence to deal with us in that hopeful and bright way. Providence will agree to reciprocate for previous pious activities if one is located in a certain place only.

Take for example my books. If I was in Guyana which is my birth location, I could not publish in the way I did. At the same time, even though I achieved this, I cannot make a living in this country. I am poverty stricken. Now and again when it pleases providence, someone sends me a buck or two and I survive another day.

If I get crazy and relocate to Guyana my yoga practice would make a big jump but my book publication may be reduced. But if I go to Guyana then I will lose some of the things that I do here in a developed country. Location is the key factor into how providence will service one's fate.

In the case of my friends and their daughter, the girl has pious activity in their native country and not in the USA. When she was being raised in the USA she could not realize her pious activity results?

The point is that beneficial social actions (karma) or the positive consequences from a past life can only be realized if one is situated in the right place. Let us take the example of a person who had some money in the bank in Russia. That money was worth about 100,000 US currency. When he got to Morocco, he went into a bank and asked them to allow him to withdraw the money, the teller said that it was not possible but that he should check back on the following day when the bank manager would be available.

The man returned the following day. The bank manager told him that under special agreement with the Russian embassy, it was possible for the money to be transferred to Morocco but there would be a fee. When he asked about the percentage of the fee he was told that it would amount to 85% of the sum he had in Russia.

The man was shocked. He said, "Eighty-five percent is unfair. What are you saying? Are you crazy?"

With that he stormed out of the bank.

If providence even allows one to reap any of the results of a previous pious act in the new life in an odd place, then providence may levy a high percentage which will result in a reduction of the pay.

O yes, providence is calculative.

I will cite a case. When I was in Trinidad in 1967, I was due to go to a university in South Hampton, UK. My uncle was in England having stowed away on a ship from South America some years prior. I passed several exams which qualified me to study navigation in South Hampton. Everything was set but then as providence would have it my father was fired from his job. His income sunk. He left the island. For me I had to leave either to go to Guyana or the USA.

I got to the USA but in that location my education ditched. The education I would have received in the UK could not be acquired in the USA because I had no karmic rights to that education in this other location. These things are hard to understand and hard to accept because we like to feel that this existence will service our desires.

Currently I am like a homeless person in a way. Providence feels that it does not need for me to be in the world. I have pious credits from past lives in many places but providence refuses to return those favors. With me it has a tight purse and gives the least possible amount.

My attitude is one of acceptance. Providence cannot be relied on to give one an easy time in life. It will hardly cause one to be born with a silver spoon in one's mouth. However, having a bad attitude towards providence makes matters worse for the self.

Last night in the astral world, I explained these truths to a friend. His wife cried. Crying about what providence does to ruin situations is okay but we should review providence as a mathematically force which operates reactions to our actions and which is unfriendly at times.

The present emerges from the past. The future is rooted in the present. When seen from the causal plane the present is like a mushy substance which is squeezed between two jaws of a vice. One jaw is the past and the other jaw is the future. As the present tries to escape from the pressure which bears down upon it from those two jaws, it bulges in this way or that way. We experience the present as this moment. But it is not that in every moment I am located in a good place. Sometimes I am disadvantaged.

Religion within

This is about religion within the psyche. This is about the self objectifying its inner environment and leaving that inner psyche to go into dimensions which are external to that psyche.

Let us go back to the physical condition. In the physical condition, the self lives in a particular physical body, which in turns lives in a particular physical location on a planet called earth? This self ventures into that physical environment but only through moving the physical body. That is similar to a man who uses a submarine to go into the sea. The man is in the sea but he is not in direct contact with the water. He resides in a submarine which has a surface which is in direct contact.

In this meditation, the self must first realize that it has a consciousness membrane and within that membrane there is consciousness floating about like air in the submarine. Within that consciousness membrane there are objects like the engine in the submarine.

The meditator knows that he/she is not the entire submarine but only is a particular spiritual object in the craft, just as the submariner is a particular object in the submarine. The submariner may as he desires, go out of the submarine and venture into the marine world using a wet-suit and appropriate gear.

These dimensions are not himself or herself. They are environments just as this earthly planet and its atmosphere is an environment.

In meditation, the meditator goes outside of the psyche into other environments and when he or she does that, the person uses a higher psyche, one with the appropriate higher sensual perception. If there is no sensual perception, the meditator must interpret the environment as a mere level of consciousness with certain feelings of pervasiveness or bliss consciousness.

Spiritual relationships

The social relationships which develop for this body are not necessarily spiritual connections. In fact many social roles are inconsistent with the spiritual roles which would be if two persons, for instance, were instantly transferred into a spiritual environment.

What is a spiritual environment? That is where you live in an environment which is indestructible and which is free from deterioration.

Last night in the astral world, I was in a dimension where I met an old subtle form of a relative from this life who is now deceased but who assumed a new body and lives in the United States. The person's astral form even though it uses a young adult body, assumed a look like the person's old age body from the past life.

Even though that person has a new body which looks different from the old one left behind, still the subtle form of the person assumed a look like the old body which died about sixty-five years of age. This person, who was my social senior in her past life, made demands on the basis of our past relationship.

Somehow at the time, we both found ourselves in a hellish astral place, where there were men scattered about with crushed limbs. Sometimes even though one has not done enough criminal or anti-social activities to spend some time in a hellish place, one did enough to warrant a visit to such places to see the ghastly conditions of those who reside there. It is like having to visit a maximum security prison or a war hospital on this planet.

In any case, we did not stay in that place for long. Soon after the elderly relative badgered me about continuing the social relationship from the past life. I began to explain that the previous social role was temporary and was not my priority. I assumed this body to fulfill other purposes.

The physical body influences the subtle one to feel that all beneficial relationships formed should continue forever, but that is not possible. A yogin should facilitate the social relationships formed in each life and also fulfill his or her mission for spiritual purposes.

If we adhere only to social relationships which depend on having a certain body in a certain place and time, we will restrict ourselves to a struggle against time in the effort to keep those relationships over a span of many lives. Of course time will not honor the request which will result in disappointment and anguish.

This was one of the principles which Gautama Buddha explained to his attached relatives. Material nature is flexible and with it, I may have a father-to-son relationship with an entity in one life and then a grandson-to-grandfather relationship with the same entity in another life. Which is which?

From the spiritual angle, am I the person's father or grandson?

One way to look at this is to consider all relationships as being flexible and to feel that there is a potential for different relationships. One may surmise that the relationship energy is adaptable. However even though that assumption may work in the physical social world, it will not in the spiritual social situations.

Crown chakra

When the coreSelf is caught off-guard or is unable to direct or influence the flow of the aroused kundalini, the core floats in the consciousness energy or it loses objectivity and enters a subjective state. In that it is not aware of itself as an individual self but it is anyway. Sometimes the core remains partially objective. Then it experiences itself in sheer white or golden light or as a bliss energy, a bliss sheath.

These experiences must be mastered so one can advance to higher yoga and also get an experience of entering a spiritual dimension. It is important when doing the breath infusion that one is attentive to how the energy is moving within. One should learn how to apply the locks. It is the locks which kundalini responds to. Kundalini does not usually respond to willpower but it will respond to brute force which is the various bodily locks.

Even though yoga books usually give the third eye mind-focus lock, the draw-in-the-chin neck lock, the pull-up-under-the-rib-cage abdomen lock, the pubio-coccyx sex lock and the anal muscles pull-up lock, there are many more compressions and contractions in the body. One is taught these or is inspired to practice these as one advances.

Always remember that Michael Beloved said that kundalini does not care to respond to anyone's willpower. It will have to be forced to change habits. If the coreSelf is to be liberated there will be a power struggle between it and the kundalini. Those who do not raise kundalini and who cannot bring it under control cannot attain liberation.

This has nothing to do with the method of raising kundalini. If you could dance and raise kundalini and control it, I am for that method.

Once kundalini reaches the crown chakra, one is lifted into silence. One is completely surrounded by sublime energy. If Kundalini strikes the crown either of the five things listed below will happen. Please note that these things do not happen unless it strikes the crown. Other things happen when it strikes the other chakras. Location is important. There is nothing here that is a void or is a nothingness or anything like that.

Here are the experiences which occur due to kundalini striking the crown.

- Loss of objective consciousness with no memory after the experience
- Loss of objective consciousness with memory after the experience
- Split-second loss of objective consciousness with memory of what happen before and after
- Ascension to the spiritual level with full consciousness
- Ascension to the causal zone which is just below the spiritual level with hearing perception or visual perception of miniature people or people using bodies of light who give one an instruction regarding the practice.

Self-critique

Each yogi has the duty to discover whatever sensual hang-ups he or she may have. One should work with psychological disciplines to curb the sensual vice. Some are addicted to flavors more than anything else, some to sound, some to colors and so on. Each person needs an individual prescription for sensual conquest. Yoga practice cannot be successful without sensual restraint.

One's sensual orbs are biased to one or more mediums than to anything else. One should meditate, struggle in the psyche to control the various sensual addictions. One should locate the various vices. One should subdue them.

One has to be ruthless in meditation and not allow any sense to rule the psyche. This does not mean that one should not use a particular sense in meditation but it means that one should not be ruled by a sense unless it facilitates the objective of meditation.

Eating flesh

Regardless of beliefs about the various species and their relative or absolute values, my intention is to make spiritual progression, to increase in psychic perception. I find that is facilitated more with a vegetarian diet.

My senses work in such a way that if I see a chicken thigh in a grocery it appears to me to be similar to a human thigh. If I saw one fried at a restaurant it seems to me that they may as well have used a bigger fryer to cook a human thigh. Since I am see that sensually, I cannot proceed with eating parts of a chicken.

As for fish, I bought live fish, gut them and fried them as a duty when I was a juvenile in South America. In the family situation I was in, that was my duty. Later however a change occurred. I began to see that fish suffocated when taken out of the water. Once I gutted a pregnant fish. Hundreds of eggs came out. Once I gutted a chicken which I was instructed to kill. I saw hundreds of eggs all in different sizes from large in a soft white shell to pin size which were without shell. This caused me not to proceed with eating poultry.

Paramhansa Yogananda went to visit Luther Burbank a famous botanist who provided evidence to prove that plants have feelings. They react to violence or kindness. However Yogananda convinced Gandhi that it was okay to eat eggs if they were not fertilized. I do not accept that idea. I do not see a difference between a human egg in a woman's ovary and a chicken egg in a chicken body. Both are forms of liquid flesh. Before I eat an egg, I have to think about whether I would eat human menses because I see both as being liquid flesh.

The other thing is astral consciousness of how the various species seem when one is passed on and look back into this world and see emotional relationships. In that perception one can hardly distinguish between human or animal emotions.

If someone is serious about advanced meditation and ask me for advice, I would suggest forgoing all food which has meat, fish, eggs or any sort of animal flesh. But in the case of cows you can take milk as you would from your mother but not eat the cow just as you would not eat your mother's body.

Ultimately we make adjustments for what we wish to achieve. If eating animals accelerate spiritual consciousness, then go on with it. Personally, I experienced the contrary.

There is another part to this which is resentment. Anyone who does advanced meditation should know that resentment is a big minus in spiritual life. This applies both to the yogi's resentment of others and to the resentment the yogi receives, or is targeted for, from others. When it comes to eating animals and fish, a yogi, in the advanced stage is scared about the resentment of these creatures for being killed for the purpose of eating their bodies.

The cycle of this life always involved violence with the hawk eating the mouse which ate the grasshopper. It is true that such resentment is a part and parcel of this world. That is more reason why a yogi should reduce participation in that to the minimum.

Index

D

Q, R

S

About the Author

Michael Beloved (Yogi *Madhvāchārya)* took his current body in 1951 in Guyana. In 1965, while living in Trinidad, he instinctively began doing yoga postures and tried to make sense of the supernatural side of life.

Later in 1970, in the Philippines, he approached a Martial Arts Master named Arthur Beverford. He explained to the teacher that he was seeking a yoga instructor. Mr. Beverford identified himself as an advanced disciple of *Śrī* Rishi Singh Gherwal, an Ashtanga Yoga master.

Beverford taught the traditional Ashtanga Yoga with stress on postures, attentive breathing and brow chakra centering meditation. In 1972, Michael entered the Denver, Colorado Ashram of *kundalini* yoga Master *Śrī* Harbhajan Singh. There he took instruction in bhastrika pranayama and its application to yoga postures. He was supervised mostly by Yogi Bhajan's disciple named Prem Kaur.

In 1979 Michael formally entered the disciplic succession of the Brahmā - Madhava-Gaudiya Sampradaya through *Swāmī* Kirtanananda, who was a prominent sannyasi disciple of the Great Vaishnava Authority *Śrī Swāmī* Bhaktivedanta Prabhupada, the exponent of devotion to Sri Krishna.

However, yoga has a mystic side to it, thus Michael took training and teaching empowerment from several spiritual masters of different aspects of spiritual development. This is consistent with *Śrī* Krishna's advice to Arjuna in the *Bhagavad Gītā*:

Most of the instructions Michael received were given in the astral world. On that side of existence, his most prominent teachers were *Śrī Swāmī* Shivananda of Rishikesh, Yogiraj *Swāmī* Vishnudevananda, *Śrī Bābāji Mahasaya* - the master of the masters of *Kriyā* Yoga, *Śrīla* Yogeshwarananda of Gangotri - the master of the masters of *Rāj* Yoga (spiritual clarity), and Siddha *Swāmī* Nityananda the Brahmā Yoga authority.

The course for kundalini yoga using pranayama breath-infusion was detailed by Michael in the book *Kundalini Hatha Yoga Pradipika*. This current book was composed from meditation and breath-infusion notes which were originally shared in staple bound booklets as Yoga Journals.

Michael's preliminary books relating to this topic are *Meditation Pictorial*, *Meditation Expertise*, and *Meditation ~ Sense Faculty* (co-author). Every technique (kriya) mentioned was tested by him during pranayama breath-infusion and *samyama* deep meditation practice.

This is a result of over forty years of meditation practice with astute subtle observations intending to share the methods and experiences. The information is published freely with no intention of forming an institution or hogtying anyone as a disciple.

Publications

English Series

Bhagavad Gita English

Anu Gita English

Markandeya Samasya English

Yoga Sutras English

Hatha Yoga Pradipika English

Uddhava Gita English

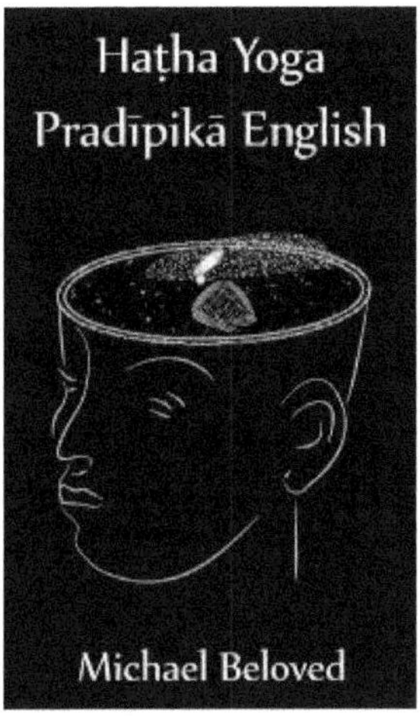

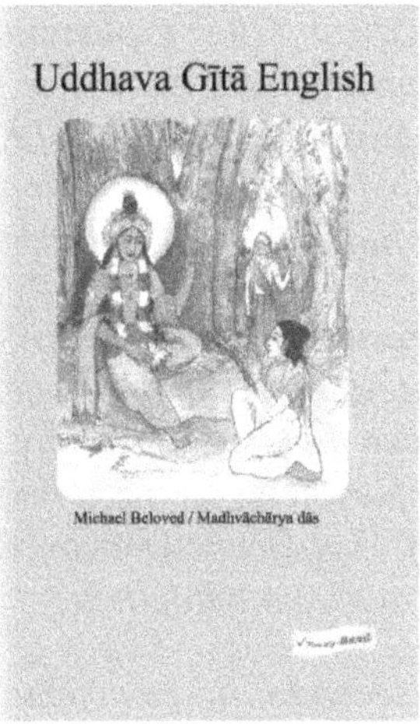

These are in 21st Century English, very precise and exacting. Many Sanskrit words which were considered untranslatable into a Western language are rendered in precise, expressive and modern English.

Three of these books are instructions from Krishna. ***In Bhagavad Gita English*** *and* ***Anu Gita English****, the instructions were for Arjuna. In the* ***Uddhava Gita English,*** *it was for Uddhava. Bhagavad Gita and Anu Gita are extracted from the Mahabharata. Uddhava Gita was extracted from the 11th Canto of the Srimad Bhagavatam (Bhagavata Purana). One of these books, the* ***Markandeya Samasya English*** *is about Krishna, as described by Yogi Markandeya, who survived the cosmic collapse and reached a divine child in whose transcendental body, the collapsed world was existing.*

Two of this series are the syllabus about yoga practice. The Yoga Sutras of Patañjali is elaboration about ashtanga yoga. Hatha Yoga Pradipika English, is the detailed information about asana postures, pranayama breath- infusion, energy compression, naad sound resonance and advanced meditation. The Sanskrit author is Swatmarama Mahayogin.

My suggestion is that you read ***Bhagavad Gita English****, the* ***Anu Gita English, the Markandeya Samasya English,*** *the* ***Yoga Sutras English,*** *the* ***Hatha Yoga Pradipika*** *and lastly the* ***Uddhava Gita English****, which is complicated and detailed.*

For each of these books we have at least one commentary, which is published separately. Thus one's particular interest can be researched further in the commentaries.

The smallest of these commentaries and perhaps the simplest is the one for the Anu Gita. We published its commentary as the Anu Gita Explained. The

Bhagavad Gita explanations were published in three distinct targeted commentaries. The first is Bhagavad Gita Explained, which sheds lights on how people in the time of Krishna and Arjuna regarded the information and applied it. Bhagavad Gita is an exposition of the application of yoga practice to cultural activities, which is known in the Sanskrit language as karma yoga.

Interestingly, Bhagavad Gita was spoken on a battlefield just before one of the greatest battles in the ancient world. A warrior, Arjuna, lost his wits and had no idea that he could apply his training in yoga to political dealings. Krishna, his charioteer, lectured on the spur of the moment to give Arjuna the skill of using yoga proficiency in cultural dealings including how to deal with corrupt officials on a battlefield.

The second Gita commentary is the Kriya Yoga Bhagavad Gita. This clears the air about Krishna's information on the science of kriya yoga, showing that its techniques are clearly described for anyone who takes the time to read Bhagavad Gita. Kriya yoga concerns the battlefield which is the psyche of the living being. The internal war and the mental and emotional forces which are hostile to self-realization are dealt with in the kriya yoga practice.

The third commentary is the Brahma Yoga Bhagavad Gita. This shows what Krishna had to say outright and what he hinted about which concerns the brahma yoga practice, a mystic process for those who mastered kriya yoga.

There is one commentary for the ***Markandeya Samasya English****. The title of that publication is Krishna Cosmic Body.*

There are two commentaries to the Yoga Sutras. One is the Yoga Sutras of Patañjali and the other is the Meditation Expertise. These give detailed explanations of ashtanga Yoga.

The commentary of Hatha Yoga Pradipika is titled Kundalini Hatha Yoga Pradipika.

For the Uddhava Gita, we published the Uddhava Gita Explained. This is a large book and requires concentration and study for integration of the information. Of the books which deal with transcendental topics, my opinion is that the discourse between Krishna and Uddhava has the complete information about the realities in existence. This book is the one which removes massive existential ignorance.

Meditation Series

Meditation Pictorial

Meditation Expertise

CoreSelf Discovery

Meditation Sense Faculty

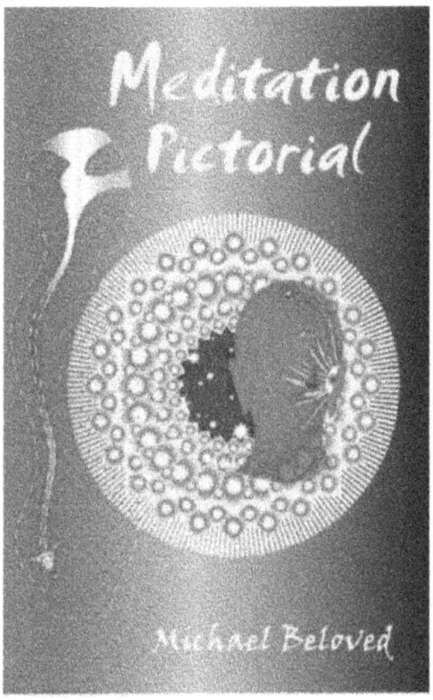

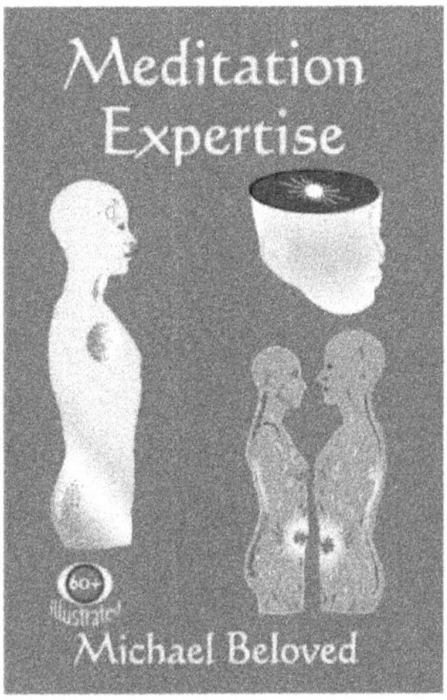

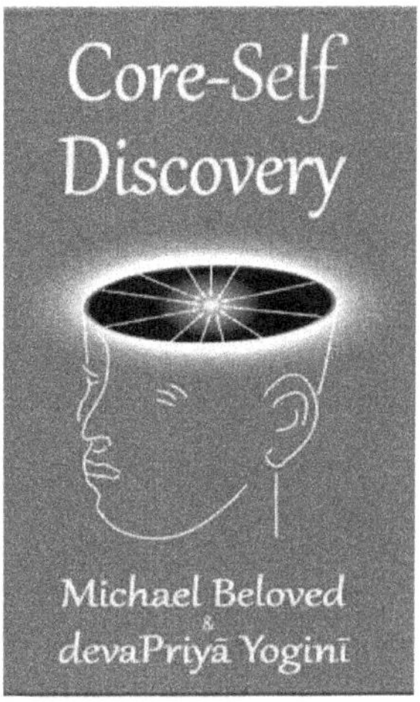

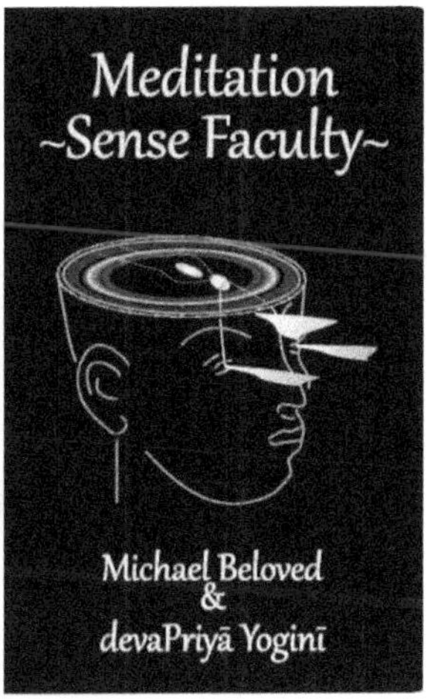

The specialty of these books is the mind diagrams which profusely illustrate what is written. This shows exactly what one has to do mentally to develop and then sustain a meditation practice.

In the **Meditation Pictorial**, *one is shown how to develop psychic insight, a feature without which meditation is imagination and visualization, without any mystic experience per se.*

In the **Meditation Expertise**, *one is shown how to corral one's practice to bring it in line with the classic syllabus of yoga which Patañjali lays out as the ashtanga yoga eight-staged practice.*

In **CoreSelf Discovery**, *(co-authored with* devaPriya Yogini*) one is taken though the course of pratyahar sensual energy withdrawal which is the 5th stage of yoga in the Patañjali ashtanga eight-process complete system of yoga practice. These events lead to the discovery of a coreSelf which is surrounded by psychic organs in the head of the subtle body. This product has a DVD component.*

Meditation ~ Sense Faculty *(co-authored with* devaPriya Yogini*) is a detailed tutorial with profuse diagrams showing what actions to take in the subtle body to investigate the senses faculties. The meditator must first establish the location and function of the observing self. That self must be screened from the thoughts and ideas which usually hypnotize it.*

These books are profusely illustrated with mind diagrams showing the components of psychic consciousness and the inner design of the subtle body.

Explained Series

Bhagavad Gita Explained

Uddhava Gita Explained

Anu Gita Explained

The specialty of these books is that they are free of missionary intentions, cult tactics and philosophical distortion. Instead of using these books to add credence to a philosophy, meditation process, belief or plea for followers, I spread the information out so that a reader can look through this literature and freely take or leave anything as desired.

When Krishna stressed himself as God, I stated that. When Krishna laid no claims for supremacy, I showed that. The reader is left to form an independent opinion about the validity of the information and the credibility of Krishna.

There is a difference in the discourse with Arjuna in the Bhagavad Gita and the one with Uddhava in the Uddhava Gita. In fact these two books may appear to contradict each other. In the Bhagavad Gita, Krishna pressured Arjuna to complete social duties. In the Uddhava Gita, Krishna insisted that Uddhava should abandon the same.

The Anu Gita is not as popular as the Bhagavad Gita but it is the conclusion of that text. Anu means what is to follow, what proceeds. In this discourse, an anxious Arjuna request that Krishna should repeat the Bhagavad Gita and again show His supernatural and divine forms.

However Krishna refuses to do so and chastises Arjuna for being a disappointment in forgetting what was revealed. Krishna then cited a celestial yogi, a near-perfected being, who explained the process of transmigration in vivid detail.

Commentaries

Yoga Sutras of Patañjali

Meditation Expertise

Krishna Cosmic Body

Anu Gita Explained

Bhagavad Gita Explained

Kriya Yoga Bhagavad Gita

Brahma Yoga Bhagavad Gita

Uddhava Gita Explained

Kundalini Hatha Yoga Pradipika

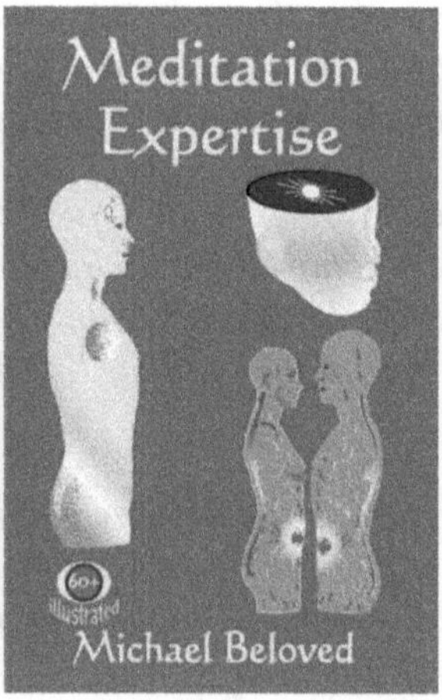

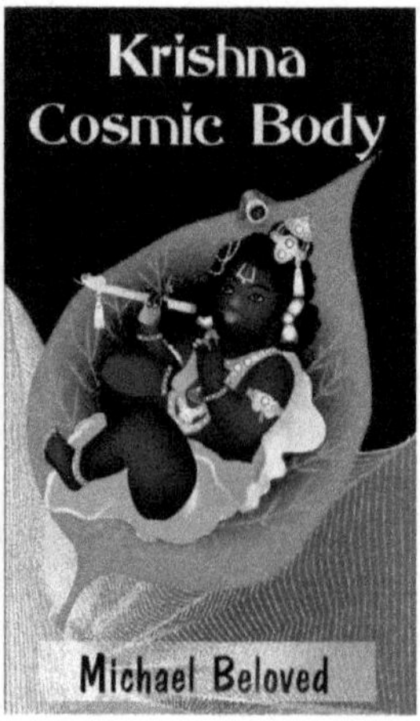

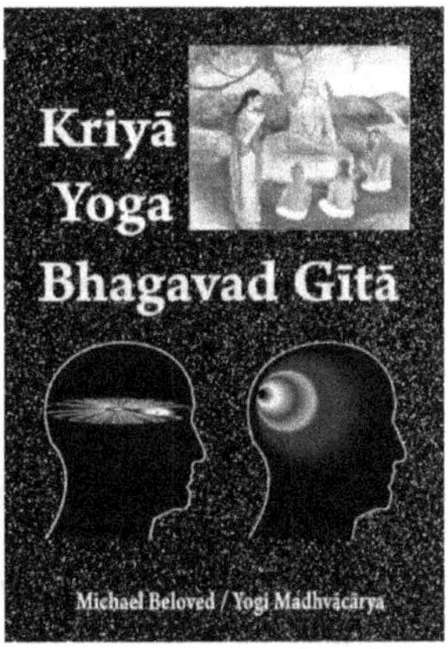

Yoga Sutras of Patañjali *is the globally acclaimed text book of yoga. This has detailed expositions of yoga techniques. Many kriya techniques are vividly described in the commentary.*

Meditation Expertise *is an analysis and application of the Yoga Sutras. This book is loaded with illustrations and has detailed explanations of secretive advanced meditation techniques which are called kriyas in the Sanskrit language.*

Krishna Cosmic Body *is a narrative commentary on the Markandeya Samasya portion of the Aranyaka Parva of the Mahabharata. This is the detailed description of the dissolution of the world, as experienced by the great yogin Markandeya who transcended the cosmic deity, Brahma, and reached Brahma's source who is the divine infant, Krishna.*

Anu Gita Explained *is a detailed explanation of how we endure many material bodies in the course of transmigrating through various life-forms. This is a discourse between Krishna and Arjuna. Arjuna requested of Krishna a display* *of the Universal Form and a repeat narration of the Bhagavad Gita but Krishna declined and explained what a siddha perfected being told the Yadu family about the sequence of existences one endures and the systematic flow of those lives at the convenience of material nature.*

Bhagavad Gita Explained *shows what was said in the Gita without religious overtones and sectarian biases.*

Kriya Yoga Bhagavad Gita *shows the instructions for those who are doing kriya yoga.*

Brahma Yoga Bhagavad Gita *shows the instructions for those who are doing brahma yoga.*

Uddhava Gita Explained *shows the instructions to Uddhava which are more advanced than the ones given to Arjuna.*

Bhagavad Gita is an instruction for applying the expertise of yoga in the cultural field. This is why the process taught to Arjuna is called karma yoga which means karma + yoga or cultural activities done with yogic insight.

Uddhava Gita is an instruction for apply the expertise of yoga to attaining spiritual status. This is why it is explains jnana yoga and bhakti yoga in detail. Jnana yoga is using mystic skill for knowing the spiritual part of existence. Bhakti yoga is for developing affectionate relationships with divine beings.

Karma yoga is for negotiating the social concerns in the material world. It is inferior to bhakti yoga which concerns negotiating the social concerns in the spiritual world.

This world has a social environment. The spiritual world has one too.

Currently, Uddhava Gita is the most advanced and informative spiritual book on the planet. There is nothing anywhere which is superior to it or which goes into so much detail as it. It verified that historically Krishna is the most advanced human being to ever have left literary instructions on this planet. Even Patañjali Yoga Sutras which I translated and gave an application for in my book, ***Meditation Expertise****, does not go as far as the Uddhava Gita.*

Some of the information of these two books is identical but while the Yoga Sutras are concerned with the personal spiritual emancipation (kaivalyam) of the individual spirits, the Uddhava Gita explains that and also explains the situations in the spiritual universes.

Bhagavad Gita is from the Mahabharata which is the history of the Pandavas. Arjuna, the student of the Gita, is one of the Pandavas brothers. He was in a social hassle and did not know how to apply yoga expertise to solve it. On the battlefield, Krishna gave him a crash-course on yogic social interactions.

Uddhava Gita is from the Srimad Bhagavatam (Bhagavata Purana), *which is a history of the incarnations of Krishna. Uddhava was a relative of Krishna. He was concerned about the situation of the deaths of many of his relatives but Krishna diverted Uddhava's attention to the practice of yoga for the purpose of successfully migrating to the spiritual environment.*

***Kundalini Hatha Yoga Pradipika** is the commentary for the Hatha Yoga Pradipika of Swatmarama Mahayogin. This is the detailed process about asana posture, pranayama breath-infusion, complex compressions of energy, naad sound resonance intonement and advanced meditation practice.*

This is the singular book with all the techniques of how to reform and redesign the subtle body so that it does not have the tendency for physical life forms and for it to attain the status of a siddha.

These books are based on the author's experiences in meditation, yoga practice and participation in spiritual groups:

Specialty

Spiritual Master

sex you!

Sleep Paralysis

Astral Projection

Masturbation Psychic Details

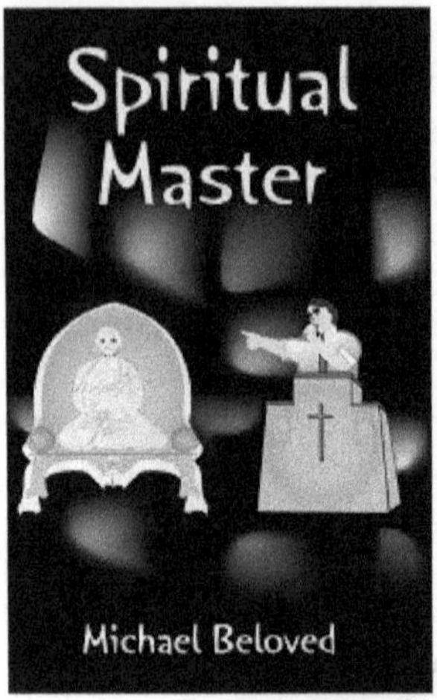

*In **Spiritual Master**, Michael draws from experience with gurus or with their senior students. His contact with astral gurus is rated. He walks you through the avenue of gurus showing what you should do and what you should not do, so as to gain proficiency in whatever area of spirituality the guru has proficiency.*

***sex you!** is a masterpiece about the adventures of an individual spirit's passage through the parents' psyches. The conversion of a departed soul into a sexual urge is described. The transit from the afterlife to residency in the emotions of the parents is detailed. This is about sex and you. Learn about how much of you comprises the romantic energy of one's would-be parents!*

***Sleep Paralysis** clears misconceptions so that one can see what sleep paralysis is and what frightening astral experience occurs while the paralysis is being* *experienced. This disempowerment has great value in giving you confidence that you can and do exist even if one is unable to operate the physical body. The implication is that one can exist apart from and will survive the loss of the material form.*

Astral Projection *details experiences Michael had even in childhood, where he assumed incorrectly that everyone was astrally conversant. He discusses the lifeForce psychic mechanism which operates the sleep-wake cycle of the physical form, and which budgets energy into the separated astral form which determines if the individual will have dream recall or no objective awareness during the projections. Astral travel happens on every occasion when the physical body sleeps. What is missing in awareness is the observer status while the astral body is separated.*

Masturbation Psychic Details *is a surprise presentation which relates what happens on the psychic plane during a masturbation event. This does not tackle moral issues or even addictions but shows the involvement of memory and the sure but hidden subconscious mind which operates many features of the psyche irrespective of the desire or approval of the self-conscious personality.*

inVision Series

Yoga inVision 1

Yoga inVision 2

Yoga inVision 3

Yoga inVision 4

Yoga inVision 5

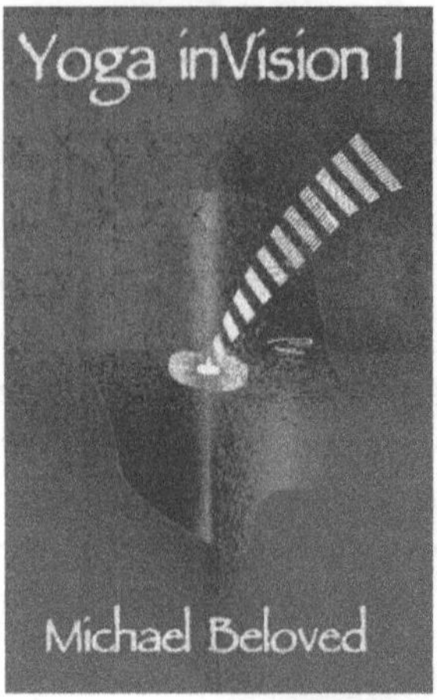

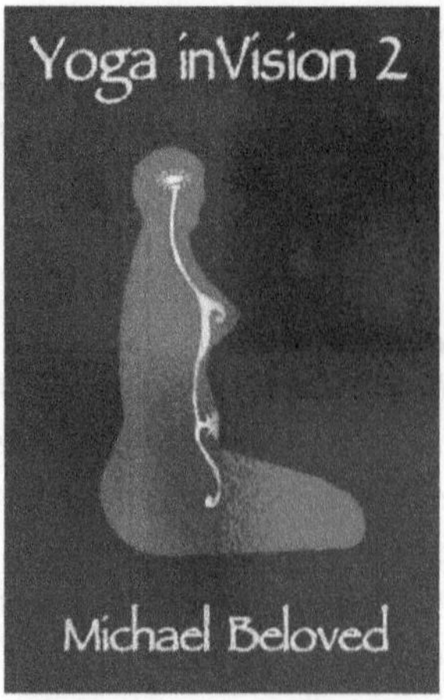

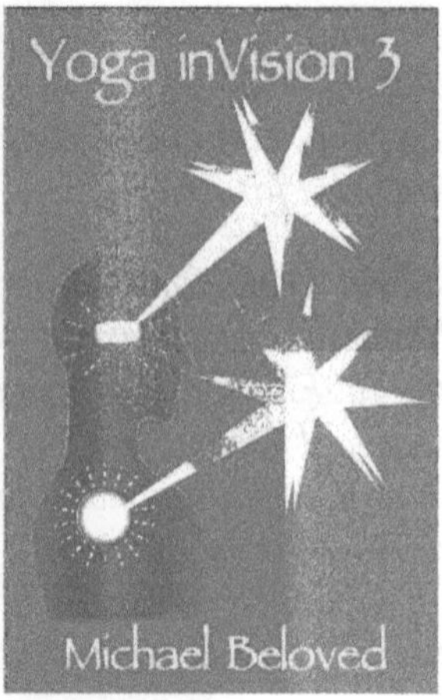

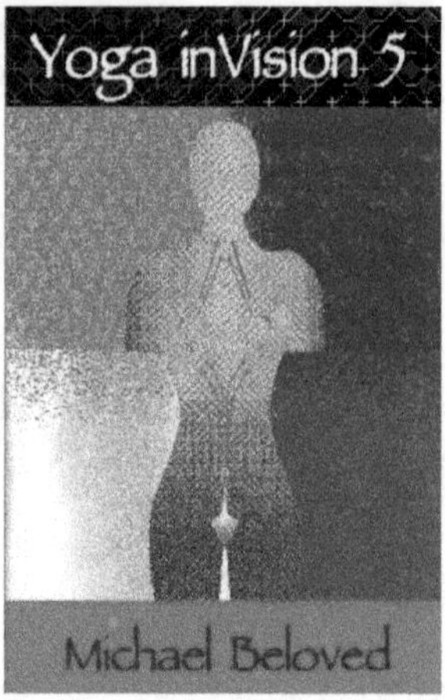

***Yoga inVision 1**, the first in this series, describes the breath-infusion and meditation practices during the years of 1998 and 1999. There are unique, once in a lifetime as well as recurring insights which are elaborated. inFocus during breath-infusion and the meditation which follows is an adventure for any yogi. This gives what happened to this particular ascetic.*

***Yoga inVision 2** reports on the author's experiences from 1999 to 2001. Each day the experience is unique, illustrating the vibrancy of practice. Many rare once-in-a-lifetime perceptions are described.*

***Yoga inVision 3** reports on the author's experiences from 2001 to 2003.*

***Yoga inVision 4** reports on the author's experiences from 2006 to 2009.*

***Yoga inVision 5** reports on the author's experiences from 2006 to 2008.*

Online Resources

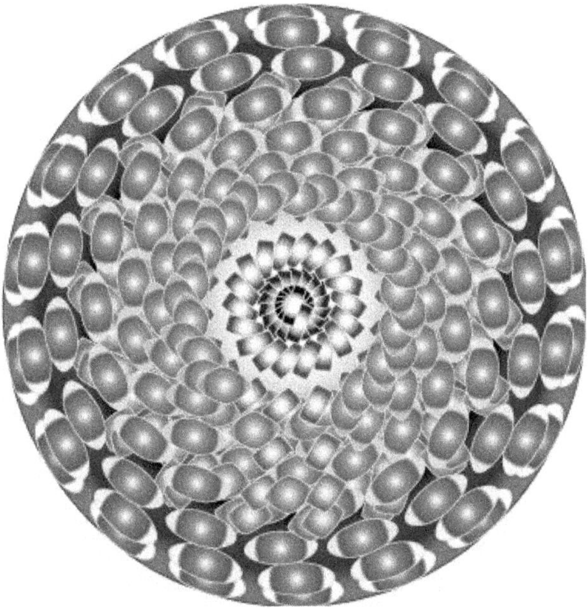

Email: michaelbelovedbooks@gmail.com
axisnexus@gmail.com

Website: michaelbeloved.com

Forum: inselfyoga.com

Posters: zazzle.com/inself